Data Leaks

FOR

DUMMIES®

by Guy Bunker and Gareth Fraser-King

WILEY

Wiley Publishing, Inc.

Data Leaks For Dummies®

Published by
Wiley Publishing, Inc.
111 River Street
Hoboken, NJ 07030-5774
www.wiley.com

Copyright © 2009 by Wiley Publishing, Inc., Indianapolis, Indiana

Published by Wiley Publishing, Inc., Indianapolis, Indiana

Published simultaneously in Canada

For general information on our other products and services, please contact our Customer Care Department within the U.S. at 800-762-2974, outside the U.S. at 317-572-3993, or fax 317-572-4002.

For technical support, please visit www.wiley.com/techsupport.

Wiley also publishes its books in a variety of electronic formats. Some content that appears in print may not be available in electronic books.

Library of Congress Control Number: 2009920902

ISBN: 978-0-470-38843-3

Manufactured in the United States of America

10 9 8 7 6 5 4 3 2 1

WILEY

About the Authors

Dr. Guy Bunker is a Distinguished Engineer at Symantec Corporation. He is responsible for technical strategy for the security and compliance management group and runs a number of research projects around security, data loss prevention, and intelligent archiving. Guy has worked for Symantec (formerly VERITAS) for twelve years in a number of product groups and roles, including as CTO of the Application and Service Management Product Group. He has been a member of a number of industry bodies driving standards in computer storage and management and is currently an active member of the Enterprise Privacy Group and the Jericho forum. Prior to Symantec he worked for Oracle and had his own consulting business.

Guy is a regular presenter at many conferences across the globe, including InfoSec, StorageExpo, the SNIA Technical Forum, Enterprise Architecture, Storage Networking World, Linux on Wall Street, and the Symantec user conference, Vision. He is regularly invited to give keynote presentations on data loss and governance, risk, and compliance. Guy is frequently in the press and media commenting on the latest security issues and scandals!

This is Guy's third book; the previous two were on Utility Computing. The second, *Delivering Utility Computing: Business-driven IT Optimization,* co-authored with Darren Thomson, is seen as a definitive text and was published by Wiley in 2006. Guy earned a PhD in Artificial Neural Networks from King's College London, holds several patents, and is a Chartered Engineer with the IET.

Gareth Fraser-King is a twenty-year-plus industry veteran, the last ten with Symantec, with extensive experience in enterprise IT, producing high level messaging, white papers, articles, presentations, and marketing deliverables, and a John Wiley & Co. author of *Data LifeCycles: Managing Data for Strategic Advantage.* He has worked extensively across EMEA in technical support, product marketing, technical authoring, business development, and quality management. Acknowledged by his customers and colleagues as a guru who understands business requirements across international markets, he has the ability to take complex product solutions and ensure that they can be understood by all — from the sales force to customers, from CEOs to IT administrators. He can capture the essence of new products and features and explain them in simple and memorable ways, tying the technology to business problems and solutions. His perceptive views of markets and technology provide a valuable input to Symantec's technical strategy and direction.

Dedication

Guy would like to dedicate this book to his very understanding wife Susanna, daughter Veryan, and his four-legged writing companions, Archie and Frank.

Gareth would like to dedicate this book to his "heavy rock drumming" wife, Elaine, four insufferable children, Alice, Ellen, Finnian, and Viola, and a small field mouse called Toby (who, most days, scuttles back and forth outside his study window).

Authors' Acknowledgments

Firstly, we would like to thank wives, children, and various friends and family for putting up with us as we wrote this.

We would also like to thank Birgit Gruber at Wiley for introducing us to our excellent project editors Tiffany Ma, Amy Fandrei, and Steve Hayes in the *For Dummies* group. We would also like to thank Barry Childs-Helton for the excellent copy editing and keeping us true to the *For Dummies* style and ideals.

Thanks also go to friends and colleagues, both inside and outside Symantec, around the globe for providing ideas, case studies, opportunities to speak and act as sounding boards for ideas. There are too many to mention and we will no doubt miss a few (sorry in advance), but here goes: Darren Thomson, Mike Spink, Dominic Cook, Abigail Lovell, Nathalie Van Krimpen, Richard Archdeacon, Sue Daley, Dominique Comerford, Michelle Bates, Kate Lewis, Stewart Room, Theresa Pa, Brendan Kelly.

Thanks also to various CIOs, legal eagles, and customers for their experiences and pointing out where improvements could be made to improve best practice.

Finally, thanks to our bosses: Ken Schneider and Kevin Bailey for being understanding when *the book* overlapped, on occasion, into *the day job*.

Publisher's Acknowledgments

We're proud of this book; please send us your comments through our online registration form located at www.dummies.com/register/.

Some of the people who helped bring this book to market include the following:

Acquisitions, Editorial, and Media Development

Project Editor: Pat O'Brien

Acquisitions Editor: Kyle Looper

Copy Editor: Barry Childs-Helton

Technical Reviewer: Peter Schwacker

Editorial Manager: Kevin Kirschner

Editorial Assistant: Amanda Foxworth

Sr. Editorial Assistant: Cherie Case

Cartoons: Rich Tennant
   (www.the5thwave.com)

Composition Services

Project Coordinator: Katherine Key

Layout and Graphics: Stacie Brooks, Reuben W. Davis, Cheryl Grubbs, Christine Williams

Proofreaders: Amanda Graham, Bonnie Mikkelson

Indexer: Broccoli Information Management

Publishing and Editorial for Technology Dummies

   Richard Swadley, Vice President and Executive Group Publisher

   Andy Cummings, Vice President and Publisher

   Mary Bednarek, Executive Acquisitions Director

   Mary C. Corder, Editorial Director

Publishing for Consumer Dummies

   Diane Graves Steele, Vice President and Publisher

Composition Services

   Gerry Fahey, Vice President of Production Services

   Debbie Stailey, Director of Composition Services

Contents at a Glance

Table of Contents

Introduction

* *

Data Leaks For Dummies has been conceived and written on the basis of an observation: The phenomenon of data loss is a big issue to pretty much everyone worldwide. Written in plain English wherever possible, this book describes the whole issue of data loss for those people who have a nagging feeling that they're not quite *in control* of their data, and it's something that they should be

- ✔ Worrying about
- ✔ Aware of
- ✔ Doing something about
- ✔ Alerting someone else to

This book will help you to become aware of the dangers that stem from data loss or leakage, show you what you can do to prevent data leakage, and provide pointers on cleaning up the mess should something terrible occur.

You can implement as many security technologies as you like, but your data will remain at risk — as will your organization, colleagues, and any individuals with whom you share data — unless you take a holistic approach to this complex problem. That means looking at the big picture as well as the details. We've written this book with that need in mind.

Who Should Read This Book

We are repeatedly told that "Information is the lifeblood of any organization."

However, it isn't just organizations that must worry about data loss. Data loss can happen to anybody — increasingly, it *is*. So this book is for *you*.

Data Leaks For Dummies is a complete guide:

- ✔ If you're brand new to the field, the book is organized so you can read it from front to back as a comprehensive guide to the subject.

- ✔ If you have specific questions, or you just need to know about a specific security subject, use the book as you would any reference guide: Find what you want to know about in the Table of Contents or the Index, and then dip in there — or at any point that looks relevant.

Each chapter is broken down into related subject headings and contains specific nuggets that

- ✔ Outline the issue
- ✔ Outline the *bigger* issue
- ✔ Outline an approach
- ✔ Outline a solution

This book covers everything from finding the types of data at risk to managing your data so you can come through third-party information audits with flying colors.

If you need more information, plenty of other titles in Wiley Publishing's *For Dummies* series can can help out. If, for example you want to dig deeper into IT security, then you could can take a look at *Hacking For Dummies* or *Preventing Identity Theft For Dummies*. We identify more of these handy *For Dummies* resources at various places in the book.

Foolish Assumptions

We make very few assumptions about you, our reader. We take for granted that you'll read the bits that relate to you and won't read the bits that don't. Aside from that, we guess that you're likely to have a computer that's somehow attached to the Internet — and that you have, or *will* have at some point in your life, some kind of relationship with one or more organizations that holds electronic information about you — or about other people you want to protect from the damage that misused information can do.

We assume that

- ✔ You are at least on speaking terms with someone who knows someone who once owned a computer.
- ✔ You are computer literate.
- ✔ You have access to a company or personal computer and to the Internet.
- ✔ You have a basic understanding of how data and information is stored in large, medium, small, or tiny organizations.
- ✔ You are familiar with some basic security measures for a computer, a network, and the data that lives on them.

How This Book Is Organized

Inside this book you find seven sections, split into 28 chapters (themselves split into subheadings) with a bunch of tips and tricks for managing data security and overcoming data leaks — whether in your organizational or private digital life. Each chapter relates to a specific area of data loss, and each subheading treats a specific part of that area.

Part I: Building the Background

This part lays out the problem of data leaks. It defines, for everybody's benefit, how the world of data has changed over the past 40, 30, 20, 10, 5, and 2 years — and how all those changes leave us in a position to be worried about data leaks. It identifies the risks that data loss entails for us as individuals and for organizations. It outlines where you're likely to suffer data leaks, where your company's confidential customer and personal information is probably stored, where your organization's intellectual property is stored, and where all that stuff *should* be stored so it doesn't leak out into the public domain and come back to bite you.

This part also outlines the requirements and responsibilities you have — as an individual and as a member of an organization that keeps electronic data. These considerations include what laws pertain to data leakage, the consequences of data leaks, and the value of data — whether to you or to a garden-variety evil genius who does bad things with good data.

Part II: Starting with the Endpoint

Okay, so you know what it's all about — but how do you stop it? That moment when your boss turns around and tells you to "*Make it so*" — and the out-of-body scream that you realize is yours reverberates through your head — this part helps you get through that (maybe even quietly). It tells you how to begin to secure your organization against data leaks, starting with the endpoint — that is to say, the laptops, mobile phones, CD-ROMs and other things people regularly lose or have stolen, especially when they're out being road warriors.

Part III: Prevention at the Office

This part of the book is devoted to fighting data leaks at the office. It covers security and data-leak prevention technologies, as well as best practices for keeping data secure within an organization. We clue you in on how to keep the good stuff (personal information on employees, partners, suppliers, customers, and company confidential information) in — which is just as important as keeping the bad stuff (viruses, keyloggers, hackers, and data thieves) out.

We look at ways to improve how your organization handles its data: protecting and maintaining a secure data center, tracking the integrity of the information held in the data center, and making sure that the people who connect to the corporate network are exactly who you think (and they say) they are. We offer pointers on controlling and managing access to sensitive information, figuring out who needs access, complying with industry regulations, and ensuring that the security measures you impose don't disable the business.

Part IV: Applications

Part IV looks at data leaks caused or instigated through applications (and those run-of-the-mill processes that all businesses go through), always with an eye toward ensuring business continuity and disaster recovery. You get a look at the danger of data compromise that lurks in backup and Web applications and get a handle on some best practices for keeping your data from walking (or skulking) out your organization's door.

We also look at some of the unlikeliest places your data is likely to turn up, why it turns up there anyway, and how you can protect these data sources.

We show how to spot (and counteract) a cavalier attitude that many organizations take toward security when they see it as a simplistic checklist. We outline an ongoing process on how to keep your data-leak prevention policies up-to-date, and describe how you can utilize your personnel to help you identify broken processes and secure your data.

Part V: Additional Preventive Measures

This part deals with a bevy of additional measures you can take to prevent data loss. It deals with the dangers of social-engineering attacks (including the impersonation of employees, contractors, partners, and suppliers). We look at the processes and procedures that organizations can use to block data loss in accordance with the best industry standards, such as these:

- ✔ ITIL (Information Technology Infrastructure Library)
- ✔ COBIT (Control Objectives for Information and related Technology)
- ✔ ISO/IEC 27702 (International Organization for Standardization/ International Electrotechnical Commission)

✔ SSE-CMM / CMMI (Systems Security Engineering-Capability Maturity Model/ Capability Maturity Model Integration

✔ PCI DSS (Payment Card Industry Data Security Standard)

Which should you use — and are they worth their salt or are they a bunch of mumbo jumbo? We get you started toward an effective choice.

We also lay some groundwork for a long-term defense against data loss, describing how to create a data-loss crisis team and develop a strong information-protection policy.

Part VI: Dealing with the Inevitable

Eventually it *will* happen to you — some of your data will get lost, leaked, or breached. Unfortunately, the most likely scenario is that someone in your organization will let data slip out by being stupid or human or both. Sure, all someone wanted to do was to keep doing a job. But what if the company's intellectual property winds up in a personal e-mail account, accidentally sent to someone's friend, or put on a USB stick and left in the back of the taxi on the way to the airport? Somewhere, somebody will mess up big-time and expose you or your company to a data leak. Then what?

We describe ways to manage your business processes so they're prepared to handle that data-leak event. We cover ways to mitigate against the potential risk caused by the loss of data, limit the damage while you get back up on your feet, and prepare for the future.

Part VII: The Part of Tens

This part contains tips, tricks, and sound bites to help ensure that you're successful in your data-leak prevention endeavors. You find out how to make quick wins against data threats, and get handy lists of best practices for medium- and longer-term data-security goals — what to do and what to avoid. These top-ten tips serve as both a starting point and a review to ensure that you've covered all your bases.

Icons Used in This Book

Throughout this book, some nice little iconic drawings appear in the margins, drawing your attention to some handy things to know:

This indicates that there is some technical detail that the authors (sadly) feel is necessary — but really isn't. (You can read them if you're sad too, but it isn't essential.)

This icon suggests that the information about to be disclosed is pretty good to commit to memory.

Stop: You're about to do something silly. This icon is used when most people are about to make a costly mistake.

This icon will either highlight and clarify a point or (more important) offer a particularly juicy tidbit of information that could serve as a shortcut that will pay off.

Remember that most organizations have served as examples of data loss at one time or another. When you see this icon, then we're about to show you how a particular organization handled a data crisis — or didn't.

Where to Go from Here

The more you know about data leaks, how your data is stored, where it's stored, who has access to it, who has access to your network, how your organization uses its data, who is likely to attack your organization, what your data is worth to a bad person, how many personal records you have, what kind of intellectual property your organization has, the better you can deal with the dangers of data leakage.

The better you are versed in the general threat landscape, the better you'll be equipped for preventing data leaks. But it's more than just the IT aspect of data security. Your understanding of the business will give you the edge in protecting the data that belongs to (and with) you and your organization.

The high-level concepts we outline here won't change much over time — not nearly as much as the threat landscape will. The lengths to which careless insiders, malicious insiders, and downright nasty outsiders will go to circumvent your well-laid plans will evolve rapidly; you'll have to stay on top of them to protect the personal information, sensitive information, and intellectual property that dwells within your organization (and, for that matter, within your home). It's a challenge to stay ahead of the bad guys. But after you've read this book, you'll have a starting point. From there, you can maintain an edge on this virtual arms race by keeping up with the latest news, practices, and technologies designed to keep your data safe.

Part I

Building the Background

The 5th Wave   By Rich Tennant

"Yes, I know how to query information from the program, but what if I just want to leak it instead?"

In this part . . .

It didn't used to be a crime to lose data — let's face it
no one cared what happened to lost laptops and CD
ROMs, or the odd e-mail that ended up in the wrong place.
The world has changed and before you can look at creating an effective solution to the problem you need to
understand what the problem is.

This first part of the book examines the risks, including
what governance and compliance mean to you, and then
looks at the consequences. It also provides valuable
insight into the value of your data, especially the value of
your data to others: the cyber criminal or the malicious
insider.

Chapter 1

Defining Data Loss

*W*hy worry about losing data — there's always more where it came from, right? Well, that's part of the problem. Like other kinds of stuff, data accumulates. By 2010, we'll have a vast pile of that electronic stuff, more than if we had a Ph.D. in Having Lots of Stuff: the most extreme an estimate up to *988 billion gigabytes* of information. Where will we put it all?

In addition, how we *handle* all that stuff is speeding up. How are we to keep up? A recent educational estimate from a North American teacher illustrates this change: For students starting studies in technology at the university level in September, over half of what they learn in their first year will be out of date by the time they get to their third year — and *all* of it will be out of date by the time they start work. The Department of Trade and Industry in the U.S. estimates that in 2010, the top ten technical jobs that will be in demand won't even have existed in 2004.

Meanwhile, computer circuitry has crept into nearly everything you use — and many of those things now gather information *from* you and *about* you. If your kids know how to program every electrical device in the house, and you gave up on that about 15 years ago, it's an indicator of what's happening. If you've been shopping for cell phones recently ("mobile phones" if you're in Europe), you've probably seen a sales pitch that points out all the "features" of the phone — especially the ways it can send, receive, and juggle information in various forms. If you're tempted to interrupt with a practical question ("But can I make and receive *telephone calls* with this thing?"), consider asking one more: "How does this thing keep my data safe?" Don't be surprised if you get a blank look.

In effect, we're sending our children to school to prepare them for jobs that don't yet exist, using technologies that haven't yet been invented, to solve problems that we don't yet know are problems. All we know for sure is that this future will be hip-deep in copious quantities of data. Which must be stored somewhere — and (more important) *protected*. Because along with all these cool new capabilities come new ways to poach, pilfer, and nab our sensitive personal and corporate data. Too often, we're too busy trying to get a handle on the technology to be aware of the threat.

How the World of Data Has Changed

Today we're almost entirely reliant on Information Technology — IT — departments at work. Organizations across the world depend on enterprise-wide applications, used by everyone from employees and customers to suppliers and partners. Numerous applications support key business processes such as e-commerce and business intelligence, but they also create a mountain of information that must be successfully harnessed, securely stored, and continually accessible to the right people at the right time. Otherwise it wanders into the wrong hands — of which there are a lot more these days.

Economic growth — a barrage of gadgets

With huge economic growth in emerging countries — India, China, Russia, Brazil, and bits of Eastern Europe (watch Hungary and Romania grow) — the growth of digital information is accelerating to humongous proportions — the primary drivers will be rich media, user-generated content, and in excess of 1.6 billion Internet users — and a boatload of photo phones. An estimated minimum of 50-million-plus laptops and an estimated 2 billion picture phones will be shipped *every year* for the foreseeable future.

One problem with all those portable devices is that they're easy to lose. For example, did you know that in 2004 — in London alone 1— 20,000 cellular (mobile) phones, 11,000 PDAs, and 10,000 laptops were left behind in taxis? It turns out that you're 12 times more likely to lose your phone than your laptop. So, if a typical organization can expect to lose up to 5 percent of its laptops per year, that means about 2,350,000 laptops — and 51,700,000 phones — will go missing this year. Along with *everything that's on them.*

And what's stored on these devices? Information — much of it (unfortunately) *very useful* to people who shouldn't have it. Most folks have multiple copies of their information, stored here and there on various devices. They don't keep track of it, and in fact they don't know where most of it is. It's easy pickings for *cyber-criminals* (bad guys who use computers and the Internet

to commit their crimes). So the more data you have, the bigger the security risk — and these days all that data requires vast amounts of storage.
Unfortunately, IT is losing control of the storage — and control of the data.
When desktop external storage drives reach terabyte (thousand-gigabyte)
capacity and are as easy to use as a little USB storage device, the walls of
the data center might as well come tumbling down. Data isn't always stored
in the data center. It wanders away to external drives, USB keys, iPods, and
cell phones. All the data in your phone's contact list, for example, is *personal
identifiable information* — sometimes referred to (irritatingly) as PII. As such
it should be protected; in fact, there are laws about protecting information,
and most people are either unaware of them or just ignore them.

The messaging boom throws data everywhere

Data is everywhere, e-mail has become the language of business, okay, so
we still use the phone, but it's e-mail that transfers data. E-mail, in fact, has
become the *business record* — essential documentation for compliance with
the laws that affect your industry. E-mail, which is so easy to send to the
wrong person — a data leak right there! Of course, e-mail is now seen as *too
slow.* So people are supplementing it with instant messaging and texting on
mobile phones. We're all going digital in our contact with other people —
compulsively sending data off to who-knows-where, usually unaware of unin-
tended side effects like these:

- ✔ The number of text messages sent daily is bigger than the population of
  the planet. (Even if your teenager seems to be sending half of those, it's
  still a huge amount of stuff floating around in the ether.)

- ✔ The average distance you have to be from a colleague before you resort
  to e-mail is (apparently) a mere 6 feet. (More usage means more data
  wandering around until someone grabs it.)

- ✔ One out of eight couples who married in 2006 in the U.S. met online.
  (Imagine the sheer amount of personal data the sweethearts must have
  exchanged without bothering to encrypt it.)

- ✔ MySpace has over 300 million registered users; if it were a country, it
  would be the fourth largest in the world, between Indonesia and the
  U.S. The average MySpace page gets over 30 visits per day. (Are *some* of
  those visitors sneakily checking social-networking sites for unauthorized
  data? You bet they are.)

- ✔ In 2007, the U.K. saw 160,000 cases at hospital A&E (Accident and
  Emergency) rooms that were related to people not looking where they
  were going while texting. That's the equivalent of 160,000 people walking
  carelessly into lampposts while staring at their phones.

> Okay, that might be understandable if you're distracted by a real, live, good-looking member of the opposite sex. One of your authors (we won't say which one) did that once, and then apologized to the lamp-post. But at least he *wasn't* generating personal data the whole time.

> ✔ The development of the Internet has seen a rapid increase in its use for everyday purposes — and a lot of that use is careless, which makes it a great target. Security is poor (because we haven't had to worry about it before), the data is valuable, and too many users are unaware of its value.

Technology gone wild; data gone missing

Not only do we have to deal with a Brave New World of mutating technology, but a much smaller one too; business is always going on *somewhere*, and people worldwide take advantage of it. Old-fashioned bankers' hours don't slow it down a bit when so many people bank online. From Beijing to Bournemouth, a startling array of banks lines up from every country to vie for market share. This shrinking world also has more people in it — close to 7 billion — most with personal information that can be used to help or harm them. This vital resource often resides in *multiple databases around the globe*. If you have a credit card and a bank account, shop a little online, and pay taxes, then your data is held in an *average* of 700 databases! Do you ever wonder whether it's *safe* there?

Sure, all the new forms of e-commerce benefit businesses. You can do business around the world at a click of a mouse; companies can be faster in getting to market, responding to requests, dealing with customers, and making contact with partners and suppliers. Result: huge opportunities to play big even if your company is small. But if you play big, you can also wind up taking big risks.

Organizations and individuals have something in common here: Leaving their data unprotected data puts them under threat from short- and long-term *data loss* — the straying of sensitive information into unauthorized hands.

Irresponsibly (or criminally) used, lost data can easily cost you revenue, reputation, customer loyalty, share value, brand equity, and market share. For openers.

Today's turbulent, networked world presents many risks to corporate information: security breaches, leaks, and losses, infestations of malware, and deliberate attacks on PCs and computer infrastructures can devastate businesses. The risks range from careless to malevolent.

Although user and operator errors account for more than 32 percent of permanent data loss, cyber-crime and computer-virus attacks are the fastest-growing cause of business disruption.

Organizations put challenging demands on their information — not only integrity, but rapid, secure, and continual availability. Although server and storage hardware continue to improve, those goals are harder to achieve as IT infrastructures grow more complex — and add new points of potential failure and vulnerability.

Watertight data-protection and security strategies are critical for every organization. Nonstop, 24-hour operations require some heavy-duty capabilities:

- Robust, scalable storage management
- Secure backup and disaster recovery
- Protection of data from desktop to data center
- Effective management of a wide range of environments from a single location

No wonder the cost of management, for both security and storage, is escalating. The IT infrastructure not only has to store more information than ever before, but also to secure, log, and discover where the most sensitive electronic information is hiding — in an environment that often isn't equipped to handle those tasks.

Gone are the days when data lived peaceably in the data center and everyone who had access worked in the same building. These days, the data — and the risks — can be found all over the map (Figure 1-1 shows what a typical organization has to deal with). Every stage of the business, any business, has the potential for data loss, data leaks, and data breaches.

As corporations expand their business operations globally, into different geography and various time zones, continuous availability of e-commerce services is expected. E-commerce is a blessing and a curse to business:

- It makes communication to customers easy to open up new avenues for sales and marketing
- It puts pressure on IT to minimize the risks associated with managing the exchange and storage of data.

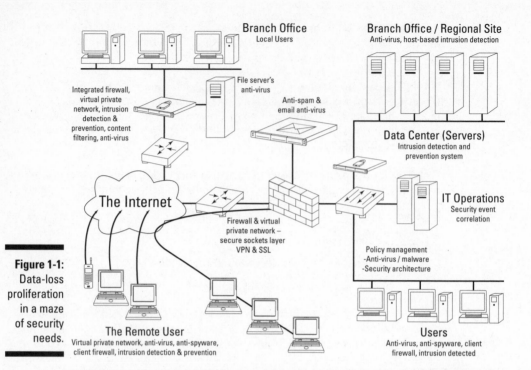

Figure 1-1:
Data-loss
proliferation
in a maze
of security
needs.

A few quick numbers illustrate why this is a growing problem. IDC estimates that in 2008 alone, human beings created more data than in the previous 5,000 years combined. That gives the digital universe an approximate size of over 250 exabytes (billion gigabytes). And IDC projects a hefty growth in the amount of information generated between 2006 and 2010 — to the tune of 600 percent per year. In addition, in 2010 around 70 percent of the digital universe will be *generated by individuals*. Guess who'll be looking after it . . . you guessed it: In 2010, *business organizations will have responsibility* for the security, privacy, reliability, storage, and legal compliance of at least 85 percent of that information.

Where will we put it all?

Managing a universe, even a digital one, will be a huge challenge for organizations. Consider: On average, the annual demand rate for digital storage was only 35 to 40 percent from 2006-2008, and the average level of disk allocation for storage (on Unix/Linux systems, anyway) was only 30 to 45 percent.

Kiss those days goodbye.

The amount of information created, captured, or replicated in 2007 exceeded available storage for the first time. Suppose that currently the amount of new technical information is doubling every year. If all things remain equal (and they won't), those growth numbers tell us that by the end of 2010, the amount of information will be doubling every 72 hours. Which is amazing or ridiculous, depending on your perspective.

If, in 2006, we created 161 exabytes of digital information — three million times the information in all the books ever written (and currently we are publishing around 3,000 books worldwide — daily), here's what that would look like if we literally piled it up: a stack of books from outside your back door to the sun and back — six times. That's 93×12 or 1,116 million miles of books. In one year. That's a cosmically awful amount of stuff we've got to store and protect — all of it with major implications for individuals, businesses, and society in general.

 ✔ The great mass of information will put a considerable strain on the IT infrastructures that organizations have in place today. (Got it in one, Sherlock!)

 ✔ This huge growth will change how organizations and IT professionals do their jobs, and how we consumers use information. (Of course it will! We must be geniuses!)

Who are we kidding? The numbers just scream at you: over 2.7 billion Google searches performed every month (by the way, to whom did we refer these searches B.G. [Before Google]?) Every year we cumulatively wait 32 billion hours for Internet pages to load. We simply can't survive without this stuff. Even if IT bursts at the seams, we've got to have our information. But if IT succumbs, we *won't* have our information. So . . .

Where will it all end?

Somebody's got to get smart about this — we must take steps, as an industry and as individuals, to make sure that we create infrastructures that make information secure, reliable, scalable, and highly available. The name of that game is *information management,* and it won't get easier. Organizations will have to use more sophisticated techniques to manage, store, secure, and protect their information if they expect to survive. To handle the increased amounts of information that we'll have to protect, store, and manage in the future, we have to start now — by getting control of the information we already have.

Information and Communication: Risky Business

Information is our most valuable asset, and yet is coming under continual, increasingly sophisticated attack from cyber-criminals who target it for financial gain. The situation has been exacerbated recently with in widespread investment in new, more efficient communication technologies. Communication is essential to business; no argument here. But if you define *communication* as "the sharing of information," you get several developments immediately:

- The more easily information is available, the more it tends to be shared.
- The more widely information is shared, the more ways it can be abused.
- If your business depends on information (what business doesn't?) but can't control its communication technology, you're in trouble.

Web 2.0 and the dark side of progress

Presently, the rapid emergence of constantly changing forms of communication is the norm. One of the most visible of these developments is *Web 2.0* — a set of economic, social, and technology trends that collectively form the basis for the next generation of the Internet. The goal: a more mature, distinctive medium, characterized by user participation, openness, and networked capabilities. One consequence: The scope of what cyber-criminals can do has opened up and left no boundaries. *Ack. We're all doomed!*

Okay, panic aside (for now, anyway), here are just two examples of why Web 2.0 is an open challenge (so to speak) to effective data security:

- **Unsecured, multiple-user technologies abound.** Examples are *wikis* (collaborative information projects) and *blogs* (online diaries), along with *services* like Flickr (sharing pictures) and YouTube (sharing videos) are prime examples of how the Web has evolved to bring about increased community participation. What these services really do is bring about freedom of speech to the masses? Unfortunately, though the masses include *the good*, they must inevitably also include *the bad* and *the ugly*.

- **Web 2.0 technologies rely heavily upon Web services.** Web services are designed to support interoperability between hosts over a network. But in the rush to develop Web services, the underlying Web applications that use them aren't receiving as much security auditing as traditional client-based applications and services. Furthermore, the policies and procedures for using these new services haven't kept up with the technology and the working practices that go along with it. As a result, threats to confidential information are on the rise.

But even before Web 2.0 is fully implemented, the IT risks that go along with it are entrenched. The next few sections take a closer look at these risks.

The business of cyber-crime

With more people going online all the time, the latest security-threat reports from the IT industry show a worrisome shift in attackers' behavior, motivation, and execution over the past five years. Malicious hacking isn't just an obnoxious prank anymore. Today's security-threat environment is characterized by an increase in data theft and data leakage, and in the creation of malicious code that targets specific organizations for information that the attacker can use *for financial gain*. Attackers are becoming more "professional" — even commercial — in the development, distribution, and use of malicious code and services. Figure 1-2 shows how the same processes used to develop commercial products are now used by cyber-criminal gangs to bring new "products" efficiently to market.

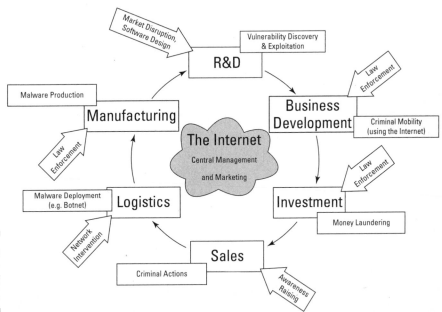

Figure 1-2: Industrialization of e-crime.

There is an *underground economy* where servers are used by criminals to sell stolen information, usually for later use in identity theft. This data can include government-issued identity numbers, Social Security Numbers, national insurance numbers, credit cards, bank cards, personal identification numbers (PINs), user accounts, and e-mail address lists. And the bad guys are selling it all, at bargain-basement prices, to other bad guys.

Target: your information

Security vendors report a rise in threats to confidential information. Of the top 50 samples of malicious code, two thirds threaten confidential data in some way. So attackers are continually refining their attacks, or enhancing their number or quality, to get what they're after: personal information, which means money. If you were a cyber-criminal, who would you target? If you zero in on individuals, you might get lucky and get one person's information. If you set your sights on a business — where you can potentially get *millions* of people's information, or even governments — where the haul can be information belonging to tens or hundreds of millions of individuals — which target is more tempting? One guess.

Spam continues to rise as a percentage of e-mail traffic, extending a long-observed trend. But it's more than just a tacky nuisance these days. Increasingly, spam is part of coordinated attacks that also use malicious code and online fraud, including data theft. A prominent example is *phishing*, a type of *social engineering* (essentially lying in order to steal) that uses a plausible pretext to lure e-mail recipients into sending valuable personal information to cyber-criminals. The information might be PIN numbers for bank accounts (guess who's making the next withdrawal), your mother's maiden name, or your date of birth.

 It only takes a name, address, and date of birth to fake a passport application, open a bank account, or obtain a driver's license in your name — opening a new floodgate of identity fraud.

As enterprises increasingly adapt to the changing threat environment by implementing better security practices and creating in-depth strategies for defense, attackers respond by changing their techniques — sometimes reviving old approaches, sometimes inventing new ones:

 ✔ **More application-targeted malicious code:** Increasingly, these attacks are aimed at client-side applications, such as Web browsers, e-mail clients, word processors, and spreadsheets — any of which can open untrustworthy content downloaded by a network client.

✔ **More social engineering:** This is an older, non-technical means of compromising security; it shifts the attack activity away from computer networks and operating systems and toward the end-user as the weak link in the security chain.

✔ **Smishing and/or SMS (text) phishing:** In this new variant of phishing, the phisher uses SMS (Short Message Service — that is, texting) messages to tell victims they're being charged for services they didn't actually sign up for. They're asked to go to a Web site to correct the situation — a process that requires the victim to enter credentials that are useful to the bad guy.

✔ **Vishing and/or voice phishing:** This approach uses traditional e-mail phishing to ask the victim to call a phone number owned by the attacker who can then fake an interactive voice-response tree — including hold music — that extracts information while lulling the victim into a false sense of security. Cyber-criminals love voice-over-IP (making telephone calls over the Internet, also called VoIP) because it makes the attacks so economical — the calls are free or cost a few cents.

More connections, more risk

The more people work online, the more opportunity exists — for doing business *and* for committing cyber-crimes. Data leakage and identity theft have grown to epidemic proportions worldwide over the last two years. They affect everybody, and they're hard to detect it until it's probably too late. Such fraud may account for as much as 25 percent of all credit-card fraud losses each year. For the criminals, identity theft is a relatively low-risk, high-reward endeavor. Issuers of credit cards often don't prosecute thieves who are apprehended; they figure it isn't cost-efficient. They can afford to write off a certain amount of fraud as a cost of doing business.

Most victims, whether individual or corporate, don't even know how the perpetrators got their identities or other sensitive information — *or how they managed to lose the data in the first place*. (Hint: There's a leak somewhere.) Companies that have lost data often have difficulty answering some basic inquiries:

✔ Describe in detail the categories of information compromised from a lost company laptop (for example, name, address, phone number, date of birth, driver's license number, or other personal information).

✔ Describe all steps that your company has taken to track down and retrieve the personally identifying information.

✔ Identify all steps taken to contact and warn consumers that their information may have been compromised.

✔ Provide an outline of the plan that will prevent the recurrence of such a data breach — and your timeline for implementing it.

The extent to which they can't provide these answers is a clue to how much control they've lost over their data.

How IT Risk Affects Business Risk

Without electronic information, business would cease to function — which is why *data loss is the biggest risk that businesses face in the twenty-first century*. Reducing that risk means meeting a daunting challenge: protecting electronic information. The risk is more intense now, because of two technological developments:

✔ More advanced and pervasive communication devices (as described in the preceding section).

✔ A massive reduction in the size of portable storage.

Both of these have business advantages — but they also make it easier to get away with more!

As these technologies continue to develop, IT organizations are faced with the requirement that critical information must be readily available for exchange to, from, and about customers, partners, and employees. Security measures have not kept pace; no wonder data leakage is rapidly becoming a major concern for businesses and consumers alike. The sad story of a data leak has become a familiar news item — complete with its embarrassing loss of customer information, potential monetary loss, and (worse) loss of faith in organizations and their ability to protect critical information.

Fortunately, the loss of sensitive information — whether by inadvertent or malicious means — can be controlled. Although information leakage is difficult to plug completely without impeding business processes, it has to be done to reduce the risk of malicious data breaches.

IT risk — buckets of it

All organizations run according to risk. Traditionally this has been limited to financial and operational risks; the operational side of the house didn't normally consider IT as a major component of risk. But the world has changed since then. Businesses can't run without IT — and IT is under attack, so the risk needs to be broken out and examined carefully. Figure 1-3 shows how IT risk is a component part of the overall risk to the business.

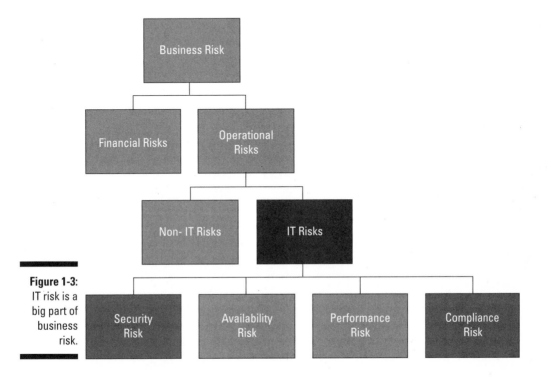

Figure 1-3:
IT risk is a
big part of
business
risk.

Note that within IT risk, there are four main *buckets*:

- ✔ **Security:** What are the security risks to the systems — hackers and the like — besides data loss?

- ✔ **Availability:** Will the systems be around when you need them?

- ✔ **Performance:** Will the systems work as quickly and efficiently as you require?

- ✔ **Compliance:** Increasingly, rules and regulations set by industries and governments shape how businesses actually *do* business. Getting it wrong can put you out of business. And guess what — data loss is one big way to get it wrong.

Of the four types of IT risk, two are directly related to data loss.

All organizations could benefit from a greater appreciation of the mounting risks to IT — a firmer, more practical understanding of the risks we're likely to be subjected to. Three areas of consideration stand out:

✔ How risk manifests itself to information technology and users (including employees, partners, and suppliers).

✔ How organizations should assess and address their level of exposure to risk.

✔ How an environment full of communication technologies, sensitive intellectual property, and personal customer information aggravates risk.

The issue is much more complicated than initially thought.

Until recently, organizations always assumed that they must somehow to be protected from *outside* threats. *After all,* they reasoned, *our employees are all good, right?* That's as may be — but these days, the whole concept of an organizational boundary is old hat — in effect, no longer valid — in even the most limited of organizations. This makes any kind of risk assessment tricky. Although IT risk management is becoming increasingly important to all organizations, creating a full-fledged, ongoing program takes time. But it isn't a bad idea to kick off this process yourself — and we're here to help:

✔ To be successful, you need senior management on your side so the effort gets decent support.

✔ IT department heads must talk with business people and vice versa.

Excruciating? Yes, we can appreciate that — but both the functional managers and the IT administrators must be able to review business operations, workflow, and the technology that affects data loss. And not just once. You'll have to keep this dialog going . . . .

✔ Periodically you have to carry out thorough security reviews to analyze changes to manage new and unseen threats and vulnerabilities created by changes in business processes, and to determine the effectiveness of existing controls.

Departments whose units handle or manage information assets or electronic resources should conduct regular, formal risk assessments. A risk assessment must

✔ Determine what information resources exist

✔ Identify what information resources require protection

✔ Help IT and the business to understand and document potential risks from electronic or physical security failures

✔ Identify issues that may cause loss of information confidentiality, integrity, or availability

✔ Provide management with appropriate strategies and controls for the management of information assets.

Although getting this juggernaut underway looks like a daunting process, it isn't rocket science. You can start with simple procedures — say, to start reining in the security of end-user laptops and desktops — or researching and listing best practices for protecting restricted data, or perhaps working out what your organization considers *restricted data*. The problem, in a hectic, 24/7 world, is that you have to make time for all this — and if you're in IT, senior management may be struggling to understand why you exist at all if you aren't directly generating income.

Actually you're *protecting* income. Here are some reasons why:

✔ Although IT professionals agree with consumers about the severity of data-leakage incidents, they may underestimate their frequency.

✔ IT professionals expect IT incidents to occur about once a month; if the preceding point is correct, then these events probably happen *more* than once a month.

✔ Work-process issues cause 53 percent of IT incidents — most often because no process is in place to manage the incident.

✔ IT risk management is more than a defensive exercise — it identifies trade-offs among risks, costs, and controls for confident, risk-aware pursuit of opportunities. (Hint: Opportunities generate income.)

From a career-enhancement perspective, all this is great news. You have no doubt heard of the CIO (Chief Information Officer), but new roles are being created, such as the CISO (Chief Information Security Officer) and CIRO (Chief Information Risk Officer). These roles are becoming prevalent in large companies; before long, they'll make it into smaller ones. If you're the person who understands the problem *and can fix it,* then it may be time to recommend that your company needs a CISO or CIRO — and you know just the right person for the job: You. Just do your homework first. (But you knew that.)

Electronic records — incoming!

There's an information tsunami on the horizon. CIOs in 2009 are under increased pressure to deliver business growth, but complexity and tight budgets are still the enemy. But if one of your basic assets is at risk, it makes just as much sense to focus on data storage and data security — you've got to get a handle on data loss, leakage, breaches, all the places data is wandering away into the wrong hands. It's out of control and growing, but hard to put in front of a CIO who's looking to trim costs, migrate to Linux (or to Windows) or not, drag the company into virtualization, develop new services or applications, reconsider managed services versus in-house operations, and the rest of the standard IT brouhaha. And now here comes this "little" data issue — that's about to get a whole lot bigger.

There's already a bunch of sensitive stuff bouncing around the ether. It's estimated that 1 in 50 documents contain confidential and/or sensitive information, given that we do everything by e-mail then: If we send a minimum 50 e-mails per day, an organization of some 20,000 strong will create over 10 million sensitive e-mails a year, just waiting to be stolen. And there are between 35 and 60 billion e-mails sent worldwide — *each day!* That's 700 million that are sensitive *every day* (best-case scenario) — that's 255 billion potential targets per year for a skilled criminal (still best-case scenario). However you look at it, this is a massive problem — and one that needs to be resolved. Meanwhile, as individual users become an ever-larger source of information, here come some more scary statistics . . . .

- ✔ Percentage of companies citing employees as the most likely source of hacking: 77 percent.

- ✔ Annual growth rate of e-mail spam message traffic: about 350 percent (estimated 2006).

- ✔ Average number of spam e-mails delivered every 30 days: 3.65 billion (estimated 2006).

- ✔ Average size of an e-mail message in 2007 (estimated): 650 KB

- ✔ Percentage of all e-mail traffic that is unwanted: about 84 percent (estimated 2006).

Even if 70 percent of the digital universe is generated by individuals, most of this stuff will be handled along the way by an enterprise, businesses, public services, governments and associations: could be on a laptop, USB key, CD, phone, PDA, iPod via a network, stored in a data center, or a hosting site, across wireless or IP network, or Internet switch, on some storage or even more likely in a backup system. This means that organizations must take responsibility for security, privacy, reliability, storage and compliance for an estimated 85 percent of all the information. Or to convert to numbers, a mere 840 billion gigabytes of information.

Getting the Whole Picture

So how do you get the *holistic* (big-picture, everything-accounted-for) per-spective you need if you're going to bring your data under control? You could get hold of a risk-assessment tool to identify your assets (as well as the risks to those assets), to estimate the likelihood of security failures, and to identify appropriate controls for protecting your assets and resources. The problem with these tools is that they often have an inclination toward the technology that the particular tool vendor is touting. Worse than that, most of the tools are aimed at the world as it was yesterday — back when it wasn't front-page news to lose a laptop or have a CD-ROM vanish in the mail. Too often, the tools miss one of today's unpleasant realities: Losing a laptop can do more damage to the reputation of a company than losing a whole data center.

Knowing and controlling what you have

The toughest part of protecting the data is *finding* it. If you don't know where it is, how can you protect it? Subsequent chapters in this book help you achieve this — and much more. If you want to jump-start the process, then you're probably better off trying to find some kind of discovery tech-nology. SRM (Storage Resource Management), for example, may be a bit old-fashioned but it can still discover the file types you have in storage. A more recent technology, DLP (Data Loss Prevention), analyzes the data it finds — and can identify and protect confidential information on file servers, databases, collaboration sites, e-mail systems, Web servers, and other data repositories — such as (yes) laptops. This kind of technology can discover and create an inventory of confidential data stored on laptops and desktops, as well as help prioritize the high-risk areas of data storage.

When an organization knows what it has and where, it can then monitor (or prevent) downloading or copying as needed — both internally and externally. Data being copied (for example) to those handy keychain-size USB devices, burned to CDs or DVDs, downloaded to local drives, sent via Web mail, instant messaging, or peer-to-peer networks and generic TCP — can all be monitored and controlled.

A one-size solution does not fit all

It isn't good enough just to motor down the technological route in search of instant data-leak prevention solutions. Too often, it's thought that technology will solve all problems — to which we can only say, *Dream on*. Often technol-ogy, especially when it's applied badly, makes the situation worse — unless you've considered all the options. A much wider approach is needed, taking into account such vital data-management activities as these:

- ✔ Creating data-protection policies
- ✔ Classifying your data
- ✔ Organizing data storage into tiers
- ✔ Archiving your data
- ✔ Encrypting your data
- ✔ Digital rights management
- ✔ Discovery of confidential data
- ✔ Applying data policies consistently

Technology by itself can prevent small-scale stuff — say, keep an engineer from copying confidential CAD diagrams to a USB stick, or prevent a call-center representative from inappropriately copying the customer database to a CD-ROM or DVD. Technology can even manage offline machines and remote office systems. And it can give on-screen warnings and notifications to employees who attempt to violate a company's data-leak prevention (DLP) policies. What it *can't* do is manage the growth and development of the cyber-criminal's arsenal, or catch and correct the inconsistent practices of the end-user.

Much of what we do that's called "user error" happens simply because we don't know what we're doing wrong. One more thing technology can't do: Write the policies and procedures in the first place.

A mind map of data loss

The subject of data leaks is huge. You might think it impossible to put on a single page — but we have: Figure 1-4 shows a mind map that provides a bird's-eye view of data loss. In essence, this diagram shows all the major components that make up the data-loss problem. Each area is then subdivided further. It's an example of a holistic view — a Big Picture.

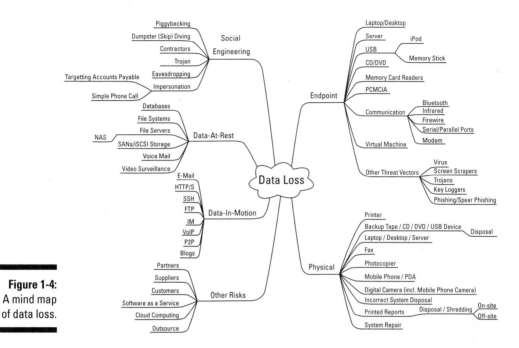

Figure 1-4:
A mind map
of data loss.

A specific data-loss solution can be helpful in multiple areas, so when you start looking at the problem, look at *your* Big Picture — and at how you maximize your investment while minimizing the risk.

Chapter 2

Examining Your Data Environment

· ·

In This Chapter

▶ Discovering the types of data at risk

▶ Listing the most common types of data

▶ Ferreting out where your at-risk data lives

▶ Finding out who we're protecting our data from

▶ Understanding that this is more like an arms race than you might have thought

· ·

*M*any companies (and people) don't know what data they have in their environment! Part of the security process is simply identifying all the valuable information that you need to protect. This chapter covers the different types of data you need to protect — and how to identify them within your organization.

If you know exactly what data you have, you can skip to Chapter 3.

Discovering the Types of Data at Risk

The types of data are many and varied. To find a way through the maze, you can start looking at the *context* surrounding a body of data — what it's used for, who uses it, why it was collected, what's at stake, that sort of thing. This is an effective way to start thinking like a cyber-criminal and work out whether (as a bad guy) you could use the data — within its context.

CASE STUDY

Driven to a solution

There was a well-known case of a third-party data-processing company that lost some records — basically the names, street addresses, and e-mail addresses of people who were in the middle of taking their driving tests. The government official said that this particular incident wasn't an issue because anyone could find names and addresses in a telephone book.

Wrong. Remember, it's all about *context* and what a cyber-criminal could do with the information, given the context. In this case, known information lends an air of authenticity; such details make a fairly realistic phishing e-mail easy to craft. The figure shows a sinister example that says, in effect, "Here's a nice letter — now give me your bank-account details."

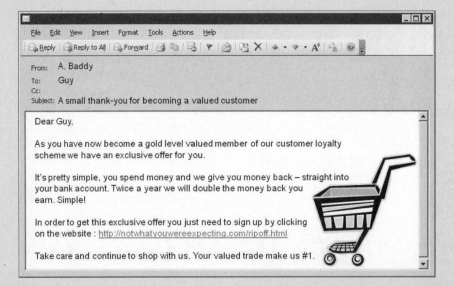

Context is everything; cyber-criminals are experts in social engineering (fooling the vulnerable) when crafting their phishing e-mails!

In this case, the vulnerable target audience consists of hormonally-charged teenagers

who can't wait to drive. They don't have a large disposable income, so an offer to receive some *free money* would probably seem too good to refuse. Of course, after the criminals have reeled in the bank-account details, the money will be coming *out* of the account, not going in!

Don't try to find all the at-risk information in your organization alone. The lone-wolf approach has some built-in downsides:

- ✔ You'll probably miss some of that information.
- ✔ It will take forever to collect it all.
- ✔ You'll miss being able to tell people what you're up to and why — and alert them to the threat.

Data at rest

Information *at rest* resides in application databases or files on the network, waiting to be used.

Talk to a few individuals from each business unit — not necessarily managers, but the workers, the ones who input information or send it out. When you have your list of people, call a meeting. The goal of the meeting is simple (though ambitious):

> *Discover the sensitive data you have in your organization.*

What do you have that could be misused? At this point all data is equal; you need to know about customer-loyalty card information as much as you do about credit-card details — or know about computer source code as much as you do about business-development documents.

Data in motion

Data *in motion* is moving from person to person, or system to system, doing its work. It can follow any of various routes:

- ✔ **E-mail:** This is, perhaps, the most important business tool in common use. Data flows around the organization via e-mail, as well as coming in and going out.

    Your security plan should both include your organization's own mail system and *Web based e-mail.* These technologies have crept into the organization and become part of business process, often without the IT department even realizing the potential risk.

- ✔ **Instant Messenger:** Employees can transfer files quickly and easily. That's an easy source of data leaks; employees can be tempted to bypass corporate systems for the speed of instant messages!

- ✔ **Backup tapes:** Yes, the backup tapes (or any portable backup medium) — especially if they go offsite or are transferred by third party or courier. Ten years ago the backup tape was the simplest way for criminals to engage in industrial espionage; if you aren't encrypting your backups (even if they're not on tape), that's still true. An unencrypted backup puts all your important data in a single place — and with no security protection. Whoever can get hold of it has the equivalent of your crown jewels!

- ✔ **CD-ROMs, DVDs:** Even with today's increased bandwidth and access to the Internet, users still copy and send information by CD and DVD! It's quick, easy and cheap — and makes the news on a regular basis because the discs are often lost en route.

- ✔ **USB sticks, iPods, and other USB memory devices:** Companies use these devices instead of CDs and DVDs, storage on them is easy to create, and you don't need specialized drives — just a USB port. These devices also have much greater capacity — a 1TB external USB disk is only a few hundred dollars!

Every day more data is created, new business systems come online and different *gadgets* are used by employees during their working day — so this list isn't static and should be revisited regularly.

The most common at-risk data types

There are lots of different types of data that you don't want leaking out, and we probably won't manage to list all the different types you have in your organization, but here are some to get you started.

This information can probably be found in multiple places and in multiple different forms.

Customer information

The most familiar forms of customer information make up what might as well be an identity-thief's shopping list:

- ✔ Names, addresses

- ✔ Credit cards, bank accounts

- ✔ Social Security Numbers

✔ Health records

✔ Financial records

✔ Loyalty card

✔ Orders

Company information

What the company records for its own use is potentially an illicit goldmine for competitors:

✔ Financial statements

✔ Business plans

✔ Product designs

✔ Customer lists

✔ Price lists

✔ Human-resource records

✔ Partner and supplier information

✔ Source code

✔ Intellectual property, including patent information

Where to Find Data at Risk

The discovery that you have more types of data that you need to protect than you originally thought may come as a scary revelation. While we're at it, here's another: You can find it in so many places!

Finding all the places where your different types of data may hide is a task best done as a group. If you try to go it alone, you'll run into some familiar problems:

✔ You'll miss some of the places the data has migrated to.

✔ It will take forever to find all the nooks and crannies on your own.

✔ The sooner users realize that there is a real threat from data loss — and it can happen anywhere — the better!

You need a plan so you can do this methodically, keep a record, and continue to update your findings later. As with the data types themselves, this plan isn't a one-off; it has to be constantly revisited and updated.

Discovering where your data hangs out

In the good old days (about five years ago) the important customer data was held in databases — in *just a few* databases. Now sensitive data is *everywhere*. So you need to leave no stone unturned — and even then you probably won't get it all.

Start with the obvious

Get the easy stuff out of the way first and you'll find it sends up some new leads as to where to go next.

- **Databases:** What are the applications that use databases and what is the information that is in them? Data is stored on servers and on storage devices.

- **E-mail:** Can your customers communicate with you by e-mail? Do you have other electronic forms of communication, perhaps Instant Messenger or other Web-based means? E-mail systems in large organizations are often distributed, with multiple servers and storage holding the information. Copies of e-mail are also held on client systems (laptops, PCs, and mobile devices).

When you send e-mail, it always involves at least two people — the sender and the recipient. Of course, there might be thousands of recipients, especially if a company-wide distribution list is involved. Each recipient may well have a copy of the e-mail stored locally; the places you might find that information go well beyond just the sender and an archive. If you're getting a sense that tracking e-mail isn't as simple as you first thought, you're on the right track.

Of course, e-mail is also a great way to send *files* as well . . . .

- **Unstructured data files:** What do you mean *unstructured*? Well, that's basically all the usual files out there, word-processing documents, spreadsheets, presentations, computer-aided design (CAD) documents, you get the drift — it's all the stuff you (and your computers) create every day. The struggle here is that examples of this output are everywhere, including places like these:

    - Laptops

    - Desktops

    - Servers

    - Mobile devices (phones, PDAs and so on)

    - Network-attached storage

- USB disk drives (and other portable storage)

- CD-ROMs and DVDs

✔ **Internet-based communication:** Besides your in-house e-mail, this includes *Web-based* e-mail, instant messaging, wikis, bulletin boards, and other data-sharing sites.

You name it and there will be some (usually unstructured) data there! Worse than that — *copies* of the data files are all over the place as well — in some cases, hundreds. Different versions, extracts (good old cut and paste) and combinations (good old cut and paste — did we already say that?) that become even harder to trace or identify. Coming to grips with where all your unstructured data went is no mean feat — and as with so many things, it's an ongoing task.

Move to the derivatives

The most common derivatives are reports — and reports from databases are often overlooked. While these can be printed out, they can also be copied electronically, cut-and-pasted (yep, this has cropped up before — several times — call it a demonstration of the problems this simple action can cause) into spreadsheets and documents, and then sent by e-mail. Because databases contain considerable quantities of information, the reports do as well.

Speaking of reports, spreadsheets can create them "unofficially" by extracting data directly out of databases — so they need to be closely examined, monitored, and controlled.

While we're on the topic of discovering your data, the other place you can often find it is on old systems. Pay special attention to those about to be thrown out or taken away for recycling. Remember to remove or destroy all data residing on these before they go!

Telling the forest apart from the trees

Not all data is equally sensitive; if you try to treat it as such, then you can't protect that which needs protecting in an effective and cost-efficient manner. When you have a good working grasp of the different types of sensitive information you have — and its various locations — then you can draw up a table to summarize what data is where, and how it's accessed.

A simple spreadsheet (such as Table 2-1) is a quick way to get started toward preventing data leaks.

Table 2-1   **Examples of Matching Data Types to Locations**

Data type	Database	Internal e-mail	External e-mail	Files	Reports	Unencrypted	Backup tape
Names and addresses	Yes	Risky	Bad	Risky	Yes	Bad	Yes
Credit card details	Yes	Very bad	Very bad			Very bad	Yes
Bank account details	Yes						Yes
Health records	Yes		Bad			Very bad	Yes
Financial records	Yes			Risky			Yes
Loyalty card details	Yes	Yes				Bad	Yes
Orders	Yes		Yes		Yes		Yes
Financial statements		Yes	Bad	Yes			Yes
Business plans		Yes	Bad	Yes		Risky	Yes
Product designs		Yes	Bad	Yes			Yes
Customer lists						Risky	Yes
Price lists	Yes	Yes		Yes	Yes		Yes
Human Resources records	Yes	Risky				Bad	Yes
Partner/supplier information	Yes	Yes		Yes			Yes
Source code	Yes		Very bad			Very bad	Yes
Intellectual property and patents	Yes	Yes	Risky	Yes	Yes		Yes

Make a list of the different data types in your organization and where you found them during your investigations. You can also indicate where they are *usually* found as well as where you *actually* found them. For example, credit-card details should only be found in a database — but you might have found them in an e-mail or a file as well — bad news if you want to prevent data leaks.

Who Are We Protecting Against?

When it comes down to it, there are three groups of people who are affected by data leakage:

- ✔ **Bad people:** Hackers, thieves, cyber-criminals, phishers — all the usual suspects. For them, data leaks are a free ride.

- ✔ **Good people:** That's the likes of you and me — that's right; we can be responsible for data leaks, even if we don't realize it. For us, data leaks are a real (if often hidden) risk.

- ✔ **Malicious insiders:** These are people inside the organization who are determined to steal your data and use it for their own nefarious purposes. They are the really tricky ones.

Bad things happening because of bad people

This is the obvious category — hackers, spies, thieves, and even organized crime. In fact, the mob is now where one of the biggest threats lies — cyber-crime is no longer a matter of individual bragging rights among hackers.

For organized crime, this isn't about glory, or infamy; it's all about *money* — and the perpetrators have a number of tricks up their sleeves.

If criminals can extract your data, they can use it in a number of ways:

- ✔ **Sell it on the black market or in the underground economy.** This is where those credit-card details or bank details end up. It's pretty much a fixed price and so the trick here, if you are a criminal, is to have a lot of them. Customer databases are the target — millions of pieces of information all in one place!

✔ **Sell it to the competition.** Sometimes (and to be honest, this isn't as big an issue as it used to be) the bad guys can sell the information to other companies. Imagine if you obtained the recipe for a particular cola — other cola manufacturers could well be interested in that information. Nowadays, most companies would report someone selling black-market competitive information to the authorities.

✔ **Sell it back to you (as a company).** This is the easiest ploy. The criminal has hacked the network, or at least found a way to extract the information. In selling it back to the company, they get the money; the company gets its information back — and is alerted to a security breach. Not really win-win for both sides, but it could be worse.

✔ **Sell it back to you (as an individual).** Suppose you went to a dodgy Web site and downloaded (by accident) some malware — which stole some information off your system and sent it back to the criminal. Now the criminal is targeting you — *so that you won't get into trouble . . . just pay me $$$*. Of course, it could just be that they have a confidential document with your name on it from another source — the possibilities are endless. Best thing to do: Tell your manager or the legal department; those folks can then decide on the best course of action and help you out.

✔ **Use it for blackmail.** This is where they have found some information, usually about an individual, but sometimes it can be about a company and they then blackmail you with it. Perhaps there were some awkward pictures from the latest holiday party which show you in incriminating circumstances — another good reason not to store such items at work!

✔ **Use it for fraud.** If the data contains enough information, then it can be used in counterfeiting or other fraudulent activities.

As with most fraud and blackmail, if you are subject to it, whether as an individual or as a company, the best thing is to let others know. Where appropriate, let the relevant authorities know as well — they are there to help.

Criminal gangs are now recruiting individuals in companies so that they can get access to sensitive information. The people with the lowest pay grades have access to sensitive information. Does your CEO have access to your bank account? No. Does the Human Resources or Payroll department have access? Yes! When you go into a bank, can the bank teller access the details on your account? Yes! When you call support personnel for a service, can they get access to your personal information? Yes! So who do you think a cyber-criminal would recruit for maximum data access?

Bad things happening because of good people

But I'm a good person. I don't lose data. Of course you don't, at least not on purpose. The reality is that *when* you lose it, you probably don't even realize it. There are three basic types of data loss: systemic, negligent, and unlucky.

Systemic data loss

A business process can go wrong even if it's done exactly the same way as it has been for years. If the rules of the game (industry practices, technology, market conditions, and such) change, then the consequences of a wrench in the works can change as well. If a business process doesn't evolve to keep up with current conditions, it's gone wrong.

Suppose, for example, you're accustomed to sending data to a branch office on a CD-ROM through the mail. On a Friday, say, you burn a disc and send it to its usual destination. (No big deal, right? Always worked before.) But now you get a phone call on Monday that the disc hasn't arrived, and could you send another? Quick investigation (after all, we're now an information-centric society) reveals that the data on the disc you sent wasn't encrypted . . . so now it could be anywhere, where just anyone can see it. Alarms go off inside your people's heads and panic ensues: A data leak has occurred.

Negligent data loss

The restrictions of a business process can be annoying, but failure to follow the process properly can result in data loss and is incompetence. Pure and simple. Panic over a lost data disc (which unfortunately seems to show up almost weekly in the press), can be averted if you make one change in the process: Encrypt the data *before* sending it. Yes, that would be one more stage in the process of preparing data for sending — and if it isn't easy to do, it might be skipped — and we're back to the data-leak-and-panic scenario. The same thing happens if a working system unexpectedly goes on the blink.

Suppose, for example, a company takes credit-card orders over the phone, and enters those orders directly into a secure computer system. So far, so good. One day the system isn't working as it should — so during the downtime, incoming orders get written down instead of being entered directly into the system. Hey, they can be entered later, right? Customer happy. Company happy. Then the paper on which the credit-card numbers were written gets carelessly thrown in the garbage. Oops. What a great find for someone — name, address, number, expiration date, and security-verification number. Customer . . . *not* so happy.

What should have been done? Easy: The paperwork should have been shredded, not just thrown away. Is this negligence (they should have known better) or systemic (the process should have allowed for the system not working and *specified* shredding the paper), or was it plain unlucky?

Unlucky data loss

This is really a combination of the other two categories, but it is generally taken as unlucky. You don't plan to have a laptop stolen, especially if it is in your house — but it has happened. You don't intend to have the datacenter ransacked and servers taken — but it has happened. You don't intend for someone to rummage through your garbage to steal your information — but it has happened.

Unfortunately, *unlucky* isn't a good excuse — not with your customers anyway!

The malicious insider

Finally, there is one further category — the malicious insider. These are the people who work for you and *go bad*. Apparently, at any one time, 8 percent of employees are disgruntled and looking for a new job. That said, not all employees in this category are malicious — thank goodness.

Disaffected insiders are big potential trouble:

- They have access to information — it's part of their jobs.
- They are trusted with copious quantities of information.
- They know the good information from the bad.
- They know the valuable information from the less valuable.
- They have access to systems that may be chock-full of sensitive information — even if those systems aren't part of their day-to-day jobs.
- They have physical access to systems — some of which they may not have *logical* access to (such as passwords or network permissions).
- They have physical access to the network.
- They are trusted implicitly.

Unfortunately, because of human nature, insiders can go bad, be bribed (or even be planted) by criminals, become spiteful because of an incident, or discover they aren't being paid as much as their colleagues and decide they need more money. Or they could decide that taking some information with them to a new job will give them an advantage over others there — maybe a shot at looking like the "best" new team member!

The big problem here is implicit trust — you give someone the authorization to look at or do things with your precious information, and you trust that person will *do the right thing*. If that trust has been broken, you need to consider doing something about it — and prevent the break from happening again.

The only way to combat a hostile insider is to have some essentials in place:

- ✔ **Rules, policies and procedures:** Let users know what the information protection policy is and how it affects them.

- ✔ **Overt system auditing and control:** If users know that the systems are being monitored (or at least if they think the systems are being monitored) then this will deter them from doing something wrong.

- ✔ **Covert monitoring:** There are applications that watch applications for anomalous behavior. This will detect someone running a report that he or she doesn't usually run — and alert you to the event. You can then check up on it — it may well be entirely innocent. But it's best not to assume that.

- ✔ **Regular physical and logical audits:** For example, check for the correct access-control rights on systems and applications — and check wireless access points regularly.

- ✔ **Monitoring employee behavior:** Look for strange behavior, especially when they hand in that two weeks' notice — are they spending longer at their machines than they used to? Are they copying data that they shouldn't be?

The Arms Race Continues

In times gone by, it wasn't a *crime* to lose a laptop or a CD — but now it is — or at least it might as well be! Judging from the way legislation is moving, it will become a crime unless you can prove that you have done absolutely *everything* in your power to prevent it from happening.

Cyber-criminals initially targeted individuals; they were the easiest target that would get them the most bang for the buck. Networks of computers could be rented (or hijacked with malware) to send spam e-mail — and there were enough gullible respondents to make it worthwhile for the criminals. However, anti-spam and other anti-malware technologies got better over time, so the criminals needed to try a different tack. Attacking corporate information is the next-lowest-hanging fruit.

These attacks often have a similar objective — except instead of getting one individual's personal information they can end up with *hundreds of thousands* or *millions* of people's sensitive data. Furthermore, the perpetrators are no longer interested only in bank-account details or other *instant-access* information; they are now after *any* information they can get hold of — and as long as they have some context as well, they can then target individuals with much greater efficiency.

Complacency is what the bad guys count on; there will always be a next generation of attacks, using the next set of information. Just when you think you're covered, there's always some new vulnerability that someone will find useful. Staying ahead of the game means keeping track of your data, its different types, the different devices it's stored on, and the different ways it moves around. That's as close as anybody gets to winning the arms race.

Chapter 3

Governance, Risk, and Compliance

In This Chapter
▶ Protecting information to comply with the rules
▶ Getting to know the regulations
▶ Proving compliance to yourself
▶ Proving compliance to an auditor

*O*tto von Bismarck, the nineteenth-century German chancellor, is famous for purportedly saying:

> *Laws are like sausages. The less you know about how they are made, the more respect you have for them.*

Well, sometimes you need to know more than you might want to. This chapter is where the beef hits the band saw.

Protecting Your Data — or Else

Organizations of all shapes and sizes must be mindful of a plethora of government laws and industry regulations — which tend to bring on new breach-notification laws.

Besides laws such as HIPAA, GLBA, and Sarbanes-Oxley in the U.S., the majority of digital-aware countries in the world have similar — and numerous — data-protection laws. Not least of these are the *Data Protection Directive 1995 — E.U.* and the *Data Protection Act 1998 — U.K.* These are good news for the likes of you and me; they require companies to look after our data. Of course, as we all know (especially from recurrent news articles on this theme), this protection doesn't always go as planned. Anyway, back to regulations.

Article 17 of the Data Protection Directive 1995 — E.U. states:

Member States shall provide that the controller must implement appropriate technical and organizational measures to protect personal data against accidental or unlawful destruction or accidental loss, alteration, unauthorized disclosure or access, in particular where the processing involves the transmission of data over a network, and against all other unlawful forms of processing.

Having regard to the state of the art and the cost of their implementation, such measures shall ensure a level of security appropriate to the risks represented by the processing and the nature of the data to be protected.

Which means what, exactly? Well, basically . . . .

✔ You must prove that you have taken steps to protect the data in your care; whether that is intellectual property (IP), M&A (merger and acquisition) plans, and other assets in both stages where such sensitive data are being transferred or stored.

✔ You must have a process to protect any personally identifiable information wherever it's collected and stored in digital form (or, for that matter, in any other form).

✔ Even many non-regulated companies also must secure sensitive data records such as

- Healthcare records
- Criminal justice investigations and proceedings
- Financial institutions and transactions
- Biological traits, such as genetic material
- Residence and geographic records
- Ethnicity

These are all considered *personally identifiable information* or PII. Most security in the past has focused on preventing outsiders from hacking into the organization instead of keeping the good stuff in. Unfortunately, the majority of all leaks are the result of unintentional information loss from the internal organization and its extended partner family.

Some sensitive types of data are especially risky for any individual to leave lying around — these, for example:

✔ **Religion:** The suppression and persecution of various religions over the years litters the history books. Unfortunately, we haven't grown up much over the last 2,000 years or so. Religious bias is as strong today as in past centuries. In some cases, physical violence and exclusion are as common now as they were in Hadrian's time (AD 76–138).

✔ **Sexual orientation:** Other people knowing your sexual orientation can be a social or professional liability in some circumstances.

✔ **Political affiliations:** These have been a concern for millennia. The secret ballot is nearly universal in modern democracy, and is considered to be a basic human right. Sometimes, even where other rights of privacy don't exist, this type of privacy often does.

✔ **Personal activities that might be revealed:** If you're like most of us, even if you're Hadrian (and even *he* had a few tricky moments), a full disclosure of *everything* you've been up to can lead to stigma and embarrassment (even if you thrive on publicity).

Some activities, though perfectly legal, may have been kept from public scrutiny to avoid discrimination, personal embarrassment, or damage to one's professional reputation.

✔ **Financial privacy:** Information about a person's financial transactions, including the amount of assets, positions held in stocks or funds, outstanding debts, and purchases *can be sensitive*. (Okay, that may seem dumb and obvious — nobody wants anyone else to know about such steps along the money trail as account or credit-card numbers, history of purchases, places visited, and products used.)

✔ **Internet privacy:** The capacity to manage what information one reveals about oneself over the Internet, and to control who can access that information, is more than a growing concern. Although some data-protection laws are in place, there are still concerns about whether e-mail should be read by third parties (Internet service providers and the like) or whether organizations should track the Web sites someone has visited, or even whether anyone should share personally identifiable information with third parties.

✔ **Medical privacy:** Medical records can be sensitive; some conditions and treatments, if made public, might affect insurance coverage or employment, bias others negatively (for example, some medical or psychological conditions or treatment), or provide inappropriate knowledge about someone's personal life (such as about sexual activity).

The legal protection of the right to privacy in general, and of data privacy in particular, varies greatly around the world.

> *No one shall be subjected to arbitrary interference with his privacy, family, home or correspondence, nor to attacks upon his honor and reputation. Everyone has the right to the protection of the law against such interference or attacks.*
>
> —Universal Declaration of Human Rights, Article 12

All organizations attempt to exploit the information they hold *to better serve customers* (yeah, yeah, yeah . . .). Okay, all organizations strive to exploit anything they can lay their hands on. But they've also figured out by now that it's probably a good idea to make a stab at protecting the data they hold. The snag is that this task is only easy *if* you have a static IT environment and a lazy workforce. It's a little trickier when you have a business or organization striving for competitive advantage in an environment full of new, disruptive technologies.

Every new business system tends to mean adopting a new IT service — which complicates how information is exchanged between customers, partners, and employees. And every time we entrust a piece of data to any of those folks (or to a new system), there is a new opportunity for information to leak.

Data breaches are of significant concern to industry bodies, governments, and consumer organizations — all are vulnerable to the dangers of that data falling into the wrong hands. Over the years, organizations have spent large amounts of resources to protect information. But IT now has a brand-new headache: regulatory compliance. Regulations usually have big teeth: financial penalties imposed if you don't comply.

Most organizations are subject to multiple regulatory or industry bodies that mandate controls over almost all the information they handle. Standards and laws such as SOX and EuroSOX, HIPAA, Basel II, BS17799, and PSI all have one requirement in common: An A-word person (auditor) must do an A-word task (audit) of an organization's controls and due-care processes to ensure that its data has full integrity and an utter lack-of-stolen-ness.

Just so you know: A-word people are a nasty, aggressive species — I was one — so there! Grrr! [GFK]. And so was I — but hopefully not such a nasty one! [GB]

One good thing about being an auditor is that you look at the problem in a different light — and if you've been audited as well, then you can see both sides of the story. Don't be surprised if auditing starts off being a real pain in the backside but ends up improving the processes and product. In this instance, the auditing should result in *better data security* and reduce the possibility of data losses, leaks, and breaches.

Data breaches, audits, and full disclosure

Some regulations require a regular, strict audit of information technology. Failing an IT audit can have a profound financial impact on the business. IT has to integrate all of its systems to ensure compliance, which can be especially challenging for ERM or ERP systems. But the motivation is clear: to avoid a heavy financial slap.

The plethora of publicity surrounding data loss, leaks, or breaches has meant that some consumers, press, analysts, and governments are calling for full disclosure. This has already happened in most of the U.S.A.; it's gaining momentum in the European Union.

Full disclosure basically means that if you have had data stolen, you must admit it. The spirit of the full-disclosure laws basically emphasizes the *right-to-know* principle; the assumption is that publicity and public awareness of data-loss crime will stamp it out. If nothing else, this approach highlights an organization's poor security controls — which helps create an incentive for all businesses. Supporters of full disclosure believe that the laws will force organizations to internalize more of the cost of a breach through a number of actions, including these:

- ✔ **Notification letters:** Tell the customers what happened.
- ✔ **Customer-support call centers:** Let the customers speak to someone about what happened.
- ✔ **Mitigating actions such as marketing campaigns:** Tell the world what happened, and what you've done to prevent the debacle from happening again.
- ✔ **Free credit monitoring:** Just to keep the customers happy that they're not being defrauded.

All of these are fine as long it's not a government that's done the losing — and then it's the beleaguered citizen who gets to foot the bill!

Consumers feel that they have the right to be informed when organizations use or abuse personal information about them. Presumably, having being notified of a breach that puts their personal information at risk, consumers could then make informed decisions and take appropriate actions to prevent identity theft. For example, they might alert their banks and credit-card companies, close bank accounts, change account numbers, or place a freeze on specific transactions. Full disclosure can also enable police, researchers, security or data-management vendors, and governments to better understand which organizations and sectors are best — or worst — at protecting consumer and employee data.

The downside of full disclosure is that it highlights a breach where (perhaps) no cyber-criminal was aware of vulnerable data lying around — but is now.

The U.K. government's HMRC (Her Majesty's Revenue and Customs) incident is an embarrassing example: Two CDs, containing 25 million records, were purportedly mailed to the Audit Office and didn't turn up. There are four major possibilities:

- ✔ The CDs were stolen by a really bad person who knew the time that the CDs were to be put in the mail, when the mail was to be picked up, how the mail was being transported (and via which route) and in the midst of this fairly complicated procedure, managed to steal the CDs without anyone noticing. (Okay, that's not really very likely.)
- ✔ The CDs were put in the mail, lost, and probably dumped in a bin somewhere. (This seems the most probable scenario.)

> ✔ The CDs were lifted by a mail thief who had absolutely no idea what they were — and, as often happens with a snatch theft, probably dumped them in a bin somewhere. (See preceding item.)
>
> ✔ The whole thing never happened. The person(s) responsible for burning the records onto the two CDs forgot to do it — and when asked whether they had done that particular job, swore they had — like any red-blooded employee trying to hang onto a job in precarious times. (Unlikely scenario, but possible!)

We're especially interested in the second and third scenarios because of what happened next: After disclosure had taken place, masses of people began hunting high and low for those CDs — and not all of them were on the side of the angels. Even worse, the second the U.K. government admitted the loss, pranksters and hoaxers had a field day — a pair of "government CDs" even turned up on an auction site (which just proves you shouldn't trust everything you find on the Web).

What can you really do about stolen data?

If legislation that requires the public exposure of data breaches isn't always helpful, what else does it aim to achieve? Those who argue for full-disclosure laws rally behind the belief that they help more or less automatically, and cite a string of high-publicity data-loss incidents. *Let people know,* they cry, *what data has been lost and by whom . . . .*

So they can do what, exactly?

If an organization has lost a bunch of your personal data and lets you know about it, what do you do next? You can't change your age, race, number of children, health records, fingerprints, or other biometrics. Changing address may be possible, of course, but changing your name or your gender to escape the threat of identity fraud seems excessive.

Starting with passwords

If you want to do something useful in the wake of a data breach, change your passwords. Throw out any that are names or words in the dictionary (they're easily guessable), and change them to random numbers and letters. "Oh, but I have so many, and I can't remember them all." That's no excuse. Try using a limited number of different passwords for specific purposes:

> ✔ **A simple password:** Use this for multiple sites that need a password but *don't* keep much data that's of (personal) value (such as addresses and credit-card details). This will probably hold true for about 80 percent of the sites you use that require a password — for example, news Web sites.

Even your simple password should be a mix of letters and numbers.

✔ **A more complex password:** Used for social-networking sites, personal e-mail, shopping sites, and credit-card management (if it isn't with your bank). There will probably be around 10 sites with this password.

✔ **The strongest password:** Just for bank accounts. You may have no more than one or two sites that require this password.

What else can I do?

If a company loses your data, presumably you could try to sue the company immediately for . . . for . . . what? Hmm, good question. On what grounds? What's the damage? Can material loss or emotional damage be proven if yet nothing's happened so far? And even if someone *has* made a grab for your identity, how can you prove it was the result of that particular breach?

The argument that 25 million people have lost their identities to some person who might as well be called Thief in Robberyville won't have much clout in court unless you can prove something has actually happened to you because of the lost data. If the information isn't personally identifiable but simply sensitive personal data, then who but a blackmailer is likely to use it? Any reputable company can't use the information — so a claim of material loss or emotional damage wouldn't be aimed at them. There is some legitimacy in the argument that individuals should be able to trust the organizations they do business with or share data with. However, we also deal with some organizations because we have no choice — the Internal Revenue Service, for example. Swaths of junk mail that notify us of who lost what from organizations we never trusted in the first place won't help much!

The Symantec MORI omnibus survey of 1000 people in the U.K. shows that

> 94 percent of respondents would want to be notified should a government department or private-sector company lose personal details about them.

> 85 percent of respondents would most want to know about the loss of their bank-account details over any other types of personal data loss.

> 46 percent of respondents would want to hear about data loss by letter.

> 70 percent of respondents are worried about the amount of personal details held about them.

Moral of the story: People care about data loss — and they aren't just worried about bank-account details — but they don't know what to do about it. Correctly or not, they figure that full-disclosure laws make *somebody* do something about it. What organizations do is comply.

What not to do with a password or username

At a recent exhibition, we mentioned to a fellow exhibitor that we'd come across a Web site that listed more than a thousand usernames and passwords lifted from social-networking Web sites. We remarked, "You wouldn't believe the stupid things some people do." "Why?" asked our acquaintance. "Well," we replied, "there was at least one username or password that was the same as the one used for the person's bank account — which used to have $27,000 in it, but no longer." There was a small pause, followed by a rushed question: "Where's the nearest Internet access?"

Regulations You Need to Know About

Today every government worth its salt is on the disclosure bandwagon, following in the wake of the U.S.A. The European Parliament recently voted on the amendment of ePrivacy Directive (2002/58/EC). The key issues within this vote were the inclusion of a mandatory breach-notification requirement, compelling all providers of electronic communication network and services to notify users of security breaches and data leakages (breach notice). This measure is now catching up with existing regulations on data breaches in the U.S.A.:

- ✔ Breaches defined as serious require that users be notified.
- ✔ The holder of the data must have appropriate security measures in place.
- ✔ If the data is lost but protected, then the data holder need not notify.

    In essence, if the data is encrypted, you don't have to tell anyone you lost it!

- ✔ The data holder must have in place appropriate backup and recovery and/or availability technologies.

Existing full-disclosure legislation

As laws proliferate that require the disclosure of data breaches, we figured that a look at a representative sampling of existing laws would give you a good working idea of what to expect.

We're not attorneys, so we make the following recommendation: If you're not sure whether your organization is in compliance with applicable disclosure laws, get professional legal help and find out.

HIPAA

The Health Insurance Portability and Accountability Act (HIPAA) requires the establishment of national standards for electronic healthcare transactions, as well as national identifiers for providers, health insurance plans, and employers. It helps to improve the efficiency and effectiveness of the U.S.A.'s widespread use of electronic data exchange. HIPAA defines numerous offenses for healthcare and sets civil and criminal penalties for them. It has several programs to control fraud and abuse within the healthcare system; the aim is to increase that system's efficiency by creating standards for the use and dissemination of healthcare information. It regulates the use and disclosure of Protected Health Information — any information about health status, provision of healthcare, *or payment for healthcare* that can be linked to an individual. Specific rules include

✔ **The Privacy Rule:** Organizations affected by the law must take reasonable steps to ensure the confidentiality of communications with individuals, that individuals are notified about the use of Protected Health Information (sometimes known as PHIs), that organizations covered do keep track of disclosures of Protected Health Information and document privacy policies and procedures together with the appointment of a privacy officer responsible for receiving complaints. (This is a good idea for any organization. After all, everyone has customer data to protect.)

✔ **The Security Standards Rule:** This one complements the Privacy Rule and deals specifically with Electronic Protected Health Information (EPHI). It outlines three types of security safeguards required for compliance. For each of these security types, the Rule identifies various security standards (and for each standard, required implementations):

- *Administrative:* Policies and procedures designed to demonstrate how the organization will comply by adopting a documented written set of privacy procedures with a privacy officer for developing, documenting and implementing all required policies and procedures. The procedures must identify employees or classes of employees who will have access to Electronic Protected Health Information; access is restricted to only those who need it. Contingency plans — including those for backup, disaster recovery, or business continuity, are also required.

- *Physical:* This standard mandates controlling physical access to protect against inappropriate access to protected data. Such controls usually relate to IT specifically; they include applications, hardware and software inventory, lifecycle management, equipment access, hardware and software control, facility security plans, maintenance records, and workstation use.

- *Technical:* This standard requires the control of access to computer systems, as well as the protection of communications, databases, information systems, and networks. This section also includes traditional IT security (which can include encryption, but is primarily about the protection of data).

Gramm-Leach-Bliley

The Gramm-Leach-Bliley Act is a U.S. Financial Services Act that allowed commercial and investment banks to consolidate. It opened up competition among banks, securities companies, and insurance companies, allowing financial organizations to put more money in investments when economy was good, and to put money in savings accounts when it turned bad. But this law also has some data-privacy restrictions because of the open business architecture it establishes.

This Act's main rule is the Financial Privacy Rule, which controls the collection and disclosure of customers' personal financial information. It applies to all companies — *regardless of whether they are financial institutions* — that receive personal financial information. The rule requires organizations to design, implement, and maintain safeguards to protect customer information from foreseeable threats in security and data integrity. Of primary importance in Gramm-Leach-Bliley are these specific rules:

- **Financial Privacy Rule:** Organizations must provide a privacy notice explaining the information collected about the consumer, how it is to be used, and how it is protected. This rule functions as a contract between the company with the consumer, detailing the protection of personal information. It also gives the consumer the right to opt out of sharing information with the organization's partners, and to refuse marketing of products or services.

- **Safeguards Rule:** Organizations must develop a written information-security plan that specifies procedures to protect customers' personal financial or other non-public information. These measures must include

  - One employee as security officer

  - A risk-management program for all departments (with tests)

  - Sufficient safeguards to protect the collection, storing, and use of the information

- **Pretexting Protection:** This rule refers to social engineering — in particular, when someone tries to gain access to personal, nonpublic information without proper authority to do so, whether by phone, mail, e-mail, or phishing — as when someone impersonates the account holder, the organization, or the customer. Any safeguards should also include training employees to recognize any form of fraud.

Basel II Accord

The Basel II Accord is the latest Swiss recommendation on banking laws and regulations from the Basel Committee on Banking Supervision in Switzerland. The original purpose of the Basel Accords was to ensure that financial institutions had sufficient capital put aside to guard against financial and operational risks. The idea was to help protect financial systems if a major bank

(or a series of banks) collapsed. The regulation sets up rigorous requirements for risk and capital management; the goal is to ensure that a bank
holds capital reserves that are appropriate to the risk the bank has under-
taken through its lending and investment practices.

So far, so good. But here's where data security enters the picture: These obli-
gations force banks to gather data they haven't necessarily collected historically. It involves accessing a wide range of disparate systems, and identifies
three main processes for controlling credit and operational risk:

- Gathering data for reporting and analysis of credit and market risk.

- Developing data capture and reporting systems for operational risk.

- Implementing automated and standardized business processes to mitigate the risks highlighted by the reporting.

Greater data categorization is required to manage the increased amount
of data that must be made available. The expanded scale of gathered data
means expanding the bank's storage facilities, increasing the use of disk
media for retrieval purposes, and (inevitably) increasing security to protect
the information obtained. It's difficult to overemphasize how important effective data-processing and data-retention procedures are for financial services.
Financial data is likely to be especially sensitive; loss of reputation is potentially substantial, as is the risk associated with a breach of data security. The
legal risks are no less serious; they can impose criminal liabilities on financial
institutions — and on their directors for failure to comply with money-laun-
dering legislation. Hence these organizations must

- Ensure the security and confidentiality of customer records and information.

- Protect against any anticipated threats or hazards to the security or
  integrity of such records.

- Protect against unauthorized access to or use of such records or information which could result in substantial harm or inconvenience to any
  customer.

Payment Card Industry Data Security Standard

The Payment Card Industry Data Security Standard (PCI DSS) is many things,
including a royal pain in the IT. Developed to help organizations that process
card payments prevent credit-card fraud, it has tied companies up in auditing
knots. Any company that processes, stores, or transmits credit-card payment
data must be PCI DSS-compliant or be heavily fined — or even lose the right
to process credit-card payments. The validation is conducted by PCI DSS
Qualified Security Assessors. The current version of the standard requires
organizations to undertake some major tasks:

✔ **Build and maintain a secure network.** Here you start with the basics:

- Install and maintain a firewall configuration to protect cardholder data. These must be updated on a regular (always-on) basis.

- Don't use vendor-supplied defaults for system passwords and other security parameters.

Consistent and thorough password policies are usually the best way to ensure that you don't fall into this trap.

✔ **Protect cardholder data.** Encryption is a major factor here:

- The protection of stored cardholder data can include encryption but certainly encompasses as much of the security arsenal as is reasonably possible.

- Encrypt any transmission of cardholder data across open, public networks. This requirement speaks (clearly) for itself.

✔ **Maintain a vulnerability-management program.** Managing your vulnerabilities must be an ongoing activity:

- Use and regularly update anti-virus software. Probably this also entails managing endpoints with security in mind.

- Develop and maintain secure systems and applications. This also means managing the security systems and applications used.

A centralized Information Manager can be the best role to create for meeting this requirement.

✔ **Implement strong access-control measures.** Controlling access to your network *and* your applications is applicable to all points here:

- Restrict access to cardholder data to only those businesses that need to know it.

- Assign a unique ID to each person who has computer access.

Network Access Control securely controls access to corporate networks and enforces endpoint security policies by unique ID, regardless of how endpoints connect to the network.

✔ **Restrict physical access to cardholder data.** NAC has three functions that are relevant here:

- Control the discovery of information on the network.

- Evaluate the compliance status of endpoints.

- Provide appropriate network access.

✔ **Regularly monitor and test networks.** This requirement may seem obvious but it's rarely met; make sure that you can meet it:

- Track and monitor all access to network resources and cardholder data.

  Various Network Access Control systems can perform this function while also reporting on access.

- Regularly test security systems and processes.

✔ **Maintain an information-security policy.** This is a major key to a consistency.

- You must have a document that spells out what employees are expected to do to safeguard the information held by the organization.

- *Maintaining* your information-security policy usually means reviewing and updating it periodically as needs change, which they do frequently..

Sound like a lot of stuff to do? It is. And if you don't comply? Well, you can be fined — which is not so good — or (worse) you can lose your legal permission to process credit and debit cards. For many organizations, that would be the end of the business.

Regulations in Europe and North America

Although develped on opposite sides of the Atlantic, some regulations are providing occasions for international cooperation in protecting data privacy.

Canada

In Canada, the Personal Information Protection and Electronic Documents Act (PIPEDA) went into effect on January 1, 2001. By January 1, 2004, it included all organizations. It is designed to protect personal information that is collected, used, or disclosed through electronic means. The aim is to support and promote electronic commerce by

✔ Ensuring accountability

✔ Identifying the purpose for collecting personal information, limiting use and collection of data

✔ Obtaining consent

✔ Ensuring disclosure, retention and accuracy of information mined

The act seeks to ensure organisations have sufficient security and appropriate access. The act also gives individuals the right to information about themselves and the ability to challenge an organization's compliance with the act.

Europe

In Europe, the right to data privacy is heavily regulated and strictly enforced. The European Convention on Human Rights provides a right to respect for private and family life. The E.U. Court of Human Rights has given this article a very broad interpretation in its jurisprudence. For example, various government activities are considered to raise data-privacy issues:

- ✔ Collecting information for an official census
- ✔ Police taking photographs and fingerprints
- ✔ Collecting medical information or details of personal expenditures
- ✔ Implementing a system of personal identification

United States

In the U.S., data privacy isn't nearly so highly legislated or regulated. Access to private data is acceptable for employment or housing purposes, although partial regulations exist in specific laws (such as HIPAA, described earlier).

There is also a wish to minimize the power of the U.S. government so as to protect personal information. The First Amendment to the U.S. Constitution protects free speech — and in many instances, privacy conflicts with this amendment. Very few states recognize an individual's right to data privacy, with the exception of California (SB1386) — although increasing numbers of states have passed data-privacy laws or require organizations to notify consumers when their information may have been exposed.

The Safe Harbor program was developed by the U.S. to give U.S. companies a means of demonstrating compliance with European Commission directives and simplify business relations between the U.S. and Europe. The Safe Harbor certification program has an impact on the exchange of Passenger Name Record information between the E.U. and the U.S. The European Commission declares in Chapter IV Article 25 that personal data may only be transferred from the countries in the European Economic Area (EEA) to countries that provide adequate privacy protection. Establishing adequacy requires the creation of national laws broadly equivalent to those implemented by the EU Directive. As a result, Article 25 created a legal risk to organizations that transfer personal data from Europe to the U.S.A. However, the Safe Harbor program encourages those organizations to have a number of standards that are deemed adequate for the purposes of Article 25; therefore E.U. organizations can guarantee that the U.S. company will comply with the data-protection rules.

European Union

All European Union member states have enacted their own data-protection legislation.

Common restrictions on processing data

By and large, these laws have some features in common; in Europe, data may be processed only under the following circumstances:

- ✔ **When the data subject has given consent:** Personal data can only be processed for specified clear and genuine purposes and may not be stored or processed if outside these parameters.

- ✔ **When the processing is necessary for a contract:** Examples of when such processing is necessary include (a) the performance of a task carried out in the public interest, (b) in the exercise of official authority vested in the controller, or (c) by a third party to whom the data has been disclosed.

- ✔ **When processing is necessary for compliance with a legal obligation:** In this case, processing would have to be essential for the purposes of the lawful interests of an organization to whom the data is disclosed — except where fundamental rights and freedoms of the individual override those interests.

- ✔ **When processing is necessary to protect the vital interests of the data subject:** Individuals concerned have the right to access all data processed about them. They have the right to demand the adjustment, deletion, or blocking of data that is incomplete, inaccurate, or not processed in compliance with the data-protection rules.

Implications of the restrictions

In practical terms, here's what the E.U. restrictions require organizations to do about processing and protecting personal data:

- ✔ Personal data may be processed only insofar as it's adequate, relevant, and not excessive for the purposes that governed its collection and/or further processing.

- ✔ Personal data must be accurate and, where necessary, kept up to date. Every reasonable step must be taken to ensure that inaccurate or incomplete data is deleted or amended.

- ✔ Personal data shouldn't be kept in a form that permits the identification of the people it's about.

- ✔ Personal data should not be kept — nor further processed — for longer than is necessary to satisfy the purposes for which it was collected.

- ✔ When sensitive personal data (which can be religious beliefs, political opinions, health, sexual orientation, race, or membership of past organizations) is being processed, extra restrictions apply.

- ✔ The individual may object at any time to the processing of personal data for the purpose of direct marketing.

The U.K. has no explicit data-breach notification law. Although various bodies have been calling out for one, opponents of the idea hold that there's little point in passing one. They contend that the U.K. already has a requirement that covers data breaches: Under the Data Protection Act (1998), organizations that lose unencrypted personal data are obliged to notify the data subject as a part of "good security practices."

The European Commission lines up its data-protection regulations with the E.U. Directive on the Protection of Personal Data. These rules are based on some key principles that make good sense if you have any information that *could be construed as being sensitive* — and nearly anyone *can* have such information. These rules state that data must be

- Fairly and lawfully processed
- Processed for specific limited purposes
- Adequate, relevant, and not excessive
- Accurate
- Not kept longer than necessary, and deleted as required
- Processed in accordance with the data subject's rights
- Secure
- Not transferred to countries without adequate protection

Bottom line: Compliance with data-protection laws and regulations is a big job unto itself. But it's not all doom and gloom . . . .

How Good Governance Helps Compliance

When it's done consistently, compliance protects not only the business but also its investors, customers, and employees — and plays an important role in a business's organizational processes. All of which makes good business sense. By getting compliant now, organizations can get ahead of the competition by using compliance standards, regulations, and policies as essential tools for staying in business. Compliance isn't just about e-mail; it's about *all* data. It's about being ready to deliver corporate data resources when required by law or regulation. (Of course, wouldn't it make sense to do this anyway, just for the sake of the business?)

That said, regulations can have a negative impact on IT budgets — not just from a data-management or security point of view, but also simply because organizations have to store, secure, and manage *more* data for longer periods of time. But that requirement also holds a hidden opportunity for making storage more efficient. Read on . . . .

Data classification to the rescue

By failing to classify data correctly, organizations can end up storing data on inappropriate storage devices. Most organizations don't have a well-defined data classification scheme, nor are they aware of all the ways data can move inside and outside their organizations. Written policies don't hold up against real-world day-to-day business practices, and data classification, such as it is, can evaporate as soon as information is copied into a spreadsheet, typed into an e-mail, or shoehorned into an instant message.

If you're going to protect your data, you have four tasks that are relevant to classification:

- ✔ **Discovery:** Develop an accurate picture of what data you have and just how sensitive or critical it is.

- ✔ **Classification:** Categorize your data according to how vital it is to immediate business processes,

- ✔ **Appropriate storage:** Storing your data on the media best suited to either (a) fast retrieval or (b) high-capacity long-term storage.

- ✔ **Policy-driven data protection:** Make sure that you have a clear, consistent policy in place, available to all employees who handle data, that regulates what can come in and what can go out.

For a closer look at how data classification fits into an overall data-protection strategy, see Chapter 13.

The right technology for record retention and retrieval

After you've solved the problem of which data goes where (and why), you have to make sure that your organization has the necessary technology not only to store all that well-classified data, but also to retrieve it when it's called for (as in an audit). Here's a checklist of the capabilities you need:

- ✔ Backup and recovery of all critical data types

- ✔ Tracking and support for disk, tape, and optical media — including unalterable types

- ✔ Archiving capability for all file types, including e-mail

- ✔ Automated, policy-driven retention and deletion

- ✔ High-speed content search and indexing

- ✔ Affinity grouping of business data (for example, by product line)

✔ Access control for specific business lines

✔ Consistent management of storage practices and policies

✔ Consistent management of security policies

Using data-loss prevention solutions

Knowing what data to protect and how to define it is tough enough, but organizations also typically fail to identify (or even imagine) the myriad ways users can let sensitive information escape into the world. This is where *data-loss prevention* (DLP) tools can help with a couple of vital tasks:

✔ Detecting data leakage

✔ Identifying lax business processes

The idea is to help the organization tighten up its act through a combination of data consolidation, stronger controls, and policy reinforcement.

To protect data effectively and achieve compliance, IT needs a simple, centralized way to manage all the differing business requirements across the organization. An important part of this approach is the capability to set, measure, and report on clearly defined levels of data management — and (equally important) to track data movement across the *entire* environment.

The idea behind using DLP to monitor network activity is to give organizations insight into broken business processes that would otherwise be impossible to see clearly. For example, you might find employees with authorized access to financial performance information who can *also* forward it out of the organization via e-mail, or communication that goes out to partners unencrypted.

By grouping like data types, IT can improve data tracking. Automated, centrally managed policies can deliver consistent operations, reducing the risk of legal noncompliance and end-user error.

Balancing privacy and data protection

When information comes into or leaves your organization, you have to pay attention to not only to the sensitivity of the information, but also to which information is transferred — and how. For example, is an IP address personally identifiable information? The debates on this subject are complex and problematic. It's a political minefield that can be hard to traverse — either toward more privacy or away from it.

When you interconnect information systems that follow differing privacy rules — and information is shared — you have data-leak potential unless you have both a data-protection policy and the means to enforce it. *Policy-based appliances* are required to reconcile, enforce, and monitor the growing maze of privacy-policy rules and laws. Here's a look at some concepts and standards that can help you get through the maze:

- **The Platform for Privacy Preferences:** P3P is a standard for communicating privacy practices and comparing them to the preferences of individuals.

- **XACML:** The Extensible Access Control Markup Language together with its Privacy Profile is a standard for expressing privacy policies in a machine-readable language which a software system can use to enforce the policy in enterprise IT systems.

- **EPAL:** The Enterprise Privacy Authorization Language is similar to XACML, but isn't a standard.

- **WS-Privacy:** Web Service Privacy will be a specification for communicating privacy policy in Web services. For example, it may specify how privacy policy information can be embedded in the SOAP envelope of a Web service message.

Creating Auditable Processes

Helping your organization become complaint with laws and regulations means managing the actual process of complying. How does an organization create an auditable process? Well, the quick answer is to use document and policy *templates* (these are standard with many compliance-enabling software packages and process software packages, such as backup and clustering software) so you can document and publish operation logs for internal review and external audit — all with relative ease.

Retrieving data in its original form, however, is useless if the application must modify the data in order to make it available. IT must therefore be able to

- Retrieve the data.

- Access the data, using the appropriate application (in the appropriate version).

- Establish different levels of access and control for different classes of user.

That's why we've included a handy "compliance technology" shopping list for your IT department . . . .

Compliance technology requirements

To attain (and maintain) compliance with the laws and regulations that govern the use of data in your industry, you need these capabilities:

- Documenting and publishing policies
- Automated logging and journaling of events and activities
- Role-based administration
- Independent oversight of policies and practices
- Tracking of user access
- Support for existing access and security
- Alignment of resources with business goals and priorities
- Organization of IT resources by logical groupings (business views)
- Creating and publishing documents as a network service
- A clear window into how resources are consumed
- Capability for users to request standard network services

Making your organization as strong its data

A worldwide flood of legislation now insists that organizations take responsibility for not only their own business data, but also for the personal data of their customers and employees, as well as for data shared with partners and suppliers. In effect, organizations must be ready to do a continuous, all-inclusive self-audit as a means of self-preservation.

Self-auditing provides an organization with several benefits:

- Protects against many kinds of data loss.
- Prevents the fines that result from noncompliance with certain regulations.
- Provides a solid framework of good practice that can help streamline procedures.

Fortunately, these best practices are fairly straightforward:

- **Identify the data you have.** Establish and maintain an inventory of all data, including data coming from outside sources.

✔ **Identify what applications you have.** You'd be amazed that there are thousands of applications out there being driven by IT systems across the world with no one accessing them. Silly but true. It's a good idea to create an application audit.

✔ **Identify who is accessing which parts of your network.** You'd *also* be amazed (at least we hope so) at who still has access rights after they leave the company.

✔ **Analyze the data.** When you know what you have, where you're storing it, and who's accessing it on which applications (got all that?), you can then determine the likely vulnerabilities and liabilities relative to all that data. It's really important to audit the data from a target's point of view: How would bad guys use this? How would they obtain it? Take it from there.

Strictly speaking, any audit must be complete or it fails. What we mean by that is that any policies should include (for openers)

✔ Unstructured as well as structured data

✔ All application data

✔ E-mail and instant messaging

✔ Transaction log files

✔ Portable devices such as USB keys

✔ SQL statements and other ways of imposing control from without

✔ Excel and other application downloads

✔ Any way that information can be passed around the organization.

The audit must show an entire record: who accesses data when, through what application, on which machine, where the contextual changes take place, and where files are saved or moved to. It should record all database design changes, all schema changes, and all changes to access permissions. Again, that's for openers. Your complexities may vary.

Self-audit — the pain that's good for you

Some legislation may bring business benefits; in fact, most of them do, although they're rarely seen in this light. For example, complying with Basel II is beneficial for financial-services organizations: Banks that can demonstrate an advanced level of risk management can reduce their capital and long-term costs by being a better credit risk.

Organizations that pursue compliance aggressively and consistently will inevitably be more efficient simply because they have a better understanding of what their business is doing. Typical benefits include these:

✔ It's easier and safer to work with organizations that comply with legislation than those that don't.

✔ Companies are more willing to partner with businesses they know to be secure.

✔ In disaster recovery, an audit trail comes in especially handy. It shows the details of all structural changes, as well as transactions and their consequences, makes recovering from disaster much easier than it would be if you had to figure out what has changed and had no clear idea of where to start.

So, even though compliance and auditing can be a pain in the IT, these processes can greatly enhance the operational integrity of a company.

Automating the audit for fun (?) and profit (!)

Automating an audit is ultimately much more effective and efficient than always struggling through it by hand. Even so, an audit is never simply a put-a-tick-in-the-box process; it must adapt to reflect changes in the organization. Here are some guiding principles:

✔ Automating an audit process saves money. It isn't very difficult. It just takes time and common sense. As the costs of annual audits rise, automation is more effective and efficient.

✔ A fully automated audit is much less prone to human error, much more scalable and manageable, and much less susceptible to compromise.

✔ Controlling operational procedures from a single point reduces costs and simplifies both the audit process and any analysis required.

✔ The auditing process must accommodate growth and the addition of new feeds; by keeping its operation transparent.

✔ The audit should be scalable so it remains cost-effective as the organization changes size and complexity.

✔ Your data-audit system must be independent of other IT systems.

✔ Audit information must be restricted to a WORM (Write-Once-Read-Many) format; no one should be able to alter an audit trail.

✔ The security of the audit must also be guaranteed.

Although every area of IT is more sophisticated these days (and getting even more so), it's amazing that there is no one way to provide a watertight, bulletproof audit. To do so, all usage would have to be closely controlled and audited, maintaining a complete record of who accessed information in any way. (Good luck with that.)

Making an organization completely accountable for all of its data seems a mammoth task. Very few companies have implemented any kind of audit trail for data movement; of those, most use database triggers or modify their applications, which can increase risk instead of reducing it.

Which Regulations Are Relevant?

Where to begin? This is a long chapter, with reason. Compliance is a minefield of conflicting rules and regulations. Unfortunately, it isn't a simple matter to map the regulations to your specific case. Getting it wrong prejudices the company's chances.

However, understanding that there are multiple regulations out there means you can ask the right questions — which will drive you to find the *relevant* regulations. So here are some useful questions to start with:

- **Are we in a regulated industry?** Many industries are regulated, including healthcare and finance. Which are relevant to your industry?

- **Do we accept credit cards or debit cards as a means of payment?** If we do, then the Payment Card Industry standard (PCI DSS) will apply.

- **Do we have data we might lose?** You will need to know about disclosure laws, encryption technologies, or both!

- **Do we trade in different countries?** If the answer is yes, then you'd better be sure you understand the different regulations about moving data from one country to another.

 Armed with the answers to a these questions, you can also ask your colleagues for advice on which regulations they think must be considered. Most people have worked in other companies and have come across regulations there as well. They may not have been directly involved with auditors or auditing (yet), but they'll have a valuable opinion or two!

Chapter 4

Data Loss and You

*P*retty much every week we hear about this company and that organization mislaying customer records or employee personal records, or perhaps millions of credit-card details. Many of these incidents come back to haunt everybody who has a credit card, in one way or another, in the ensuing weeks or months (or perhaps *years*).

Risks and Consequences of Data Loss

Technology can't help understanding the risk and specific associated with a data loss incident. The implications fall into two categories:

▶ **Direct losses:** These are easily measured.

▶ **Indirect losses:** These are tough to measure, but carry the most consequence.

Direct losses

The direct losses associated with a data loss can be measured. Here's a basic list of these costly consequences:

▶ **Fines and settlements:** For TJX Companies, Inc., the fines and settlements are ongoing. Just one of the settlements was for $40.9 million, and involved having some financial institutions help with the ongoing costs.

But because it was credit-card information that had been lost, credit-card companies were — and are — still at risk from potential fraud; compensation had to be paid, in part to help fund additional investigation into requests for new credit cards.

✔ **Litigation:** Class-action lawsuits are often brought against companies that lose personal customer information. These suits take many years to resolve and can have a long-term damaging effect on the business while waiting for resolution.

✔ **Theft of money:** When bank or credit-card details are compromised, there is a strong risk that money will be either siphoned off from accounts or the card fraudulently used.

✔ **Customer compensation:** If data has been lost, then compensation will be paid for inconvenience caused; perhaps this also means offering ongoing credit checks.

✔ **Cost of response:** When a data-loss incident occurs, business as usual stops. Time will be taken up with additional support calls, senior management will be involved in resolving issues and new processes will need to be put in place to prevent further data loss.

✔ **Loss of future sales:** If data has been lost then there will be a knock-on effect for future sales. Sales are usually forecast and monitored, so a drop in sales due to the data loss can be estimated.

✔ **Remedial action:** Processes and procedures will need to be changed to ensure that the same thing doesn't happen again. Often a technology solution is brought in to protect the data at risk, this could be as simple as encryption on laptop computers, or it could be a complete data loss prevention suite of products.

✔ **Credit monitoring:** All information has a value to someone, and it usually has a value because it can be used for financial gain. When a data loss occurs often the first line of defense for the individual is to ensure that their credit rating isn't impacted. Credit-monitoring services exist for individuals to keep a close check on their credit rating, and in the event of a data loss the organization responsible will often pay for such a service for one to three years.

✔ **Investigation fees:** These are the additional costs associated with discovering the cause of the data loss incident.

✔ **Audit fees:** After an incident has occurred, the fees for auditors often increase as more detail is required.

Indirect losses

In addition to the relatively obvious direct costs, data loss can impose indirect loss to your business. Such losses are not only harder to control and forecast but also (potentially) more expensive. Here's a sinister sampling:

✔ **Share-price hit:** The old saying that "there is no such thing as bad publicity" goes out the window in the event of a data loss. Often the organization ends up as front-page news, in a humiliating light; one result is a drop in the share price. While this may not have an immediate impact on the business, it can have a long-term effect.

A report by attrition.org states that this loss averages 8 percent of share price for publicly-traded firms.

✔ **Customer churn:** When data loss occurs — especially if it involves financial information such as credit cards — customers lose confidence. Result: customer churn (turnover), which in turn results in lost business.

The Ponemon Institute report on the cost of data breaches looked closely at this effect, and found that the average increase in customer churn is 2.5 percent; the highest was 7 percent.

✔ **Brand and reputation damage:** If the data loss incident makes it to the front pages of the newspaper then there is a strong likelihood that the company's reputation will be damaged.

Weber Shandwick studied this problem discovered that it takes an average of three and a half years to recover from a damaged reputation (see Figure 4-1).

There are cases where either the company has gone out of business (for example, the Ratner jewelry chain in the U.K.) or the company ends up being sold at a drastic discount.

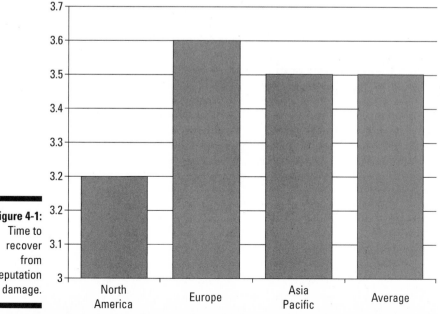

Figure 4-1: Time to recover from reputation damage.

The total cost of data doss

Calculating an organization's total financial loss due to data loss isn't just simple arithmetic. Data loss generates many tangible and intangible effects that must be factored into the equation. A simple calculation only touches lightly on the real costs to the organization.

As organizations become more interdependent across business units, take on partners, extend supply chains, expand networks, and gather more customers worldwide, the impact of data loss can escalate rapidly. Simply, the whole business can be affected. To truly assess the financial impact of any data leak an organization must consider all the aspects that are in use at any time within that business.

Recent studies by the Ponemon Institute, in both the U.S. and the U.K. in 2007 and 2008, analyzed the cost of data loss. Figure 4-2 shows a breakdown of costs in the U.S., and Figure 4-3 shows a comparable picture for the U.K.

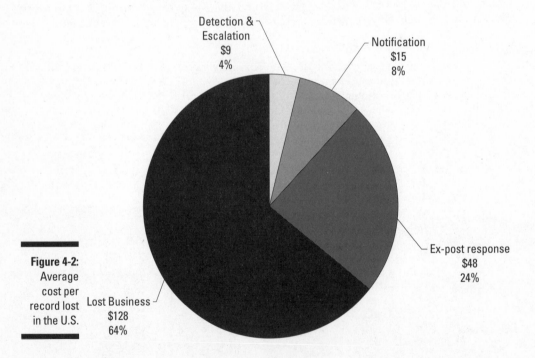

Figure 4-2: Average cost per record lost in the U.S.

Detection & Escalation $9 4%

Notification $15 8%

Ex-post response $48 24%

Lost Business $128 64%

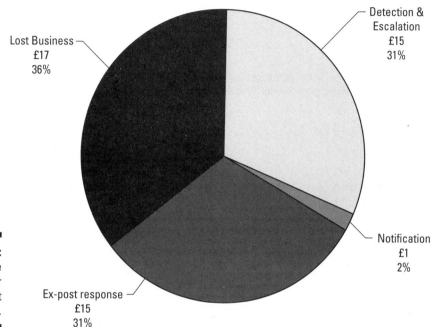

Figure 4-3:
Average
cost per
record lost
in the U.K.

In the U.S. in 2007 the total cost of data loss averaged $6.3 million per breach; in the U.K., in 2008, the average total cost was £1.4 million per breach.

One of the numbers that deserves a closer look is the cost associated with notification when a breach occurs. The U.S. has disclosure laws in the majority of the states — but there are no similar laws in the U.K. This results in a significantly higher cost of notification in the U.S. than in the U.K. (where notification is, essentially, a letter to the affected party).

In both cases, however, there *is* a cost associated with lost business.

Data loss is real and needs to be taken seriously; the cost to a company is tangible. It should be considered a disaster, not only in terms of the potential loss of money, but also in terms of damaged reputation.

Disclosure Laws and Cyber-Crime

Lobbyists spend their time banging the drum for security-breach disclosure laws (which are aimed at *letting citizens know* if their personal information is lost or put at risk) and the creation of agencies to address special types of cyber-crime (also known as *e-crime*).

To trigger the U.S. security-breach disclosure law (SB 1386) , certain types of information must have been exposed — specifically, customer names, accompanied by any of the following data:

- ✔ Social Security Number (SSN)
- ✔ Driver's license number
- ✔ Credit-card information
- ✔ Bank-account details
- ✔ Medical and health insurance information (as amended by AB 1298)

Security-breach disclosure laws are rapidly evolving. Good places to find out the latest information are government websites, or just type "security disclosure law" and the name of your country into your favorite search engine.

But when organizations around the world suffer data loss, whether globally or locally, the consequences, reactions, and loss of records pile up. Business gets disrupted, sometimes severely, and the creation of a well-resourced operation to address computer-assisted crime takes on great urgency as the theft of information from data and call centers increases.

Of course, a lost laptop might be just that — a *lost* laptop. Alternatively, it can be a source of income for enterprising cyber-criminals if they can exploit the details found on it.

The threat of data loss has become an established business risk that must be planned for. Those plans must include the reality that criminals use the Internet to automate old crimes and invent new ones.

New (cyber-) crime versus old habits

Data loss didn't just suddenly pop up in the press; it's been going on for years. It's just that it hadn't really caught on yet as a big-money crime; bad people hadn't figured out how to turn electronic data into ill-gotten gain. But now they have. So they're constantly trying to get the rest of us to disclose data that they can use.

We actually help them do that because old habits die hard. We've been giving away our names, our bank-account details, even our signatures (the forgers must love it) for years — every time we wrote a check, every time we handed over a credit or debit card. But it's only recently that such data became a serious target for criminals.

The new crime is cyber-crime. A proliferation of professional criminals are looking to exploit organizations and individuals electronically, in increasingly sophisticated ways. To survive, organizations must arm themselves against exposure. In essence, that is what this book is about:

- ✔ Creating an information-protection policy, backed up with processes and products to support it.
- ✔ Creating a plan for when something goes wrong.

The fact that remains that worldwide there need to be new police cybercrime units on the same scale similar to cyber-crime operations in the U.S., with additional funding and resources coming from other government departments and industry, not just from existing police budgets.

In today's world, where there's data, there's money — and where there's money, there's crime. So it's worth starting with the realization that *all data is of value to someone* — including information on who falls victim to cyber-crime attacks, and when.

Where there's data, there's money

"Time is money," says the old adage. Well, so is data. A bad guy who steals your personal data can do any number of bad things with it and make a profit. The most obvious, of course, is when he pretends to be you and then uses your information to extract financial resources. But a whole bunch of traditional criminal activities are now exploiting the ease with which data can be manipulated, including

- ✔ Applications for new bank accounts and credit cards.
- ✔ Applications for unsecured loans.
- ✔ Applications for mortgages and secured loans.
- ✔ Trade on other people's good reputation on auction sites.
- ✔ Impersonate people by hijacking social-networking sites.

The big difference today is that now all of these can be done on line. So, if you happen to have thousands of peoples' details and a computer you can make lots of applications. Some will be successful.

With the average cost of a single internal data breach estimated in the millions, companies are forced to look beyond simply protecting network perimeters from external threats. In days gone by, it was pretty simple to put in a firewall, chuck everyone behind it and call the job done. No longer. Now that firewall is constantly in danger of being breached.

The breach can come from a lot of different sources. Here are some seemingly innocent and common examples:

- ✔ You're given a presentation from a colleague, partner, or occasional passerby (trust us, it happens) via a USB memory key.
- ✔ You allow your children to use your company laptop to do their homework.
- ✔ You work on e-mail on corporate servers via a handheld device.
- ✔ You utilize the free Wi-Fi at the hotel you're staying in.
- ✔ You provide a partner with a guest access to the corporate network to download materials for marketing.

Companies are being forced to implement solutions that guard against the insider threat, as well as employee carelessness, by delivering unified protection of data wherever it's stored or used.

Here are some scary statistics:

1 in 400 e-mails contains confidential information.

1 in 50 network files contains confidential data.

4 out of 5 companies have lost confidential data when a laptop was lost.

Half of the USB drives out there contain confidential information.

The average cost of a single data breach is $14 million.

Companies that incur a data breach experience a significant increase in customer turnover — as much as 11 percent.

Laws in over 35 states, in addition to several federal mandates, require organizations to protect confidential information.

(These come to us courtesy of the Ponemon Institute, and are copyrighted 2008 by Symantec Corporation. All rights reserved.)

To make matters worse, attackers are no longer as fond of large, general-purpose attacks against traditional security devices. Long gone are the days when hackers launched threats as raucous "practical jokes" (mainly to say, "Look at the virus I've written!"). Exploits used to be indiscriminate — making lots of people suffer for no particular apparent reason — randomly disruptive, and sometimes difficult to overcome.

These days, hackers focus more on regional targets, looking to steal corporate, personal, financial, or confidential information to exploit or sell. Threats to network security are becoming more sophisticated and damaging. Today's threats are the work of cyber-criminals, and they are silent, precisely targeted, motivated by profit, and underground.

Recently a 19-year-old and some accomplices wreaked havoc in Florida by using counterfeit credit cards to buy stacks of gift cards from a certain well-known store. They cashed in the gift cards to buy TVs, PCs, and jewelry. The scam's goal was easy money: With credit cards, the team of counterfeiters bought gift cards in $400 increments — just below the $500 limit that requires a manager's approval. The team then went on extravagant shopping sprees, purchasing an estimated total of $1 million in goods. The well-known store took a $17 million hit in its last two fiscal quarters for costs related to *this one breach.*

Where there's data, there's crime

Money is driving the growth of targeted attacks against everyone — they don't care who — individuals, small businesses, large businesses, governments, public-sector organizations. The financial damages from security breaches already run to millions, and that's likely to continue. Cyber-crime is a booming business. Viruses, malware, and online crime have moved from hacking vandalism into a major shadow economy that closely mimics the real business world, right down to its motivation: Organized cybercrime is profit-driven.

We have recently seen the development of sophisticated business models among criminals, much along the lines of "legit" business models. What began as business-to-consumer (B2C) and business-to-business (B2B) has its shadow equivalent: criminal-to-criminal (C2C) business models with "crime-ware" developers who supply hacking toolkits to other criminals, as well as step-by-step guides to infecting a system and then retrieving data for financial gain.

The more traditional criminals purchase data collected by Trojan horses, keyloggers, and other such malware, and then use the information to systematically rake in the money. The more sophisticated bad guys use the Web as a highly effective attack path for a wide range of illegitimate and malicious activities, including identity theft through spyware, financial fraud, industrial espionage, and intelligence gathering.

Comprehensive endpoint security fights back. A comprehensive endpoint security solution — on your laptop, desktop, or whatever else you work on — provides protection against attacks by combining host-based security technologies (such as anti-virus) with a desktop firewall, intrusion detection and prevention, and peripheral device control. These are essential for eliminating exposure from home computers, kiosks, and guest laptops. The product creates a virtual desktop environment, which protects network sessions. It can also detect and kill malicious code (such as keyloggers), prevent the capture of usernames and passwords, and stymie *screen scrapers* (programs that steal the screen output of other programs, essentially spying on user activity). The product deletes all session information when a session closes. For more about this comprehensive approach, see Chapter 8.

Who are the data police? Sorry, nobody yet . . .

Both businesses and political committees are urging governments to do more to tackle cyber-crime — or risk losing public confidence in the security of the Internet. Undoubtedly there is a need for an organization that businesses can talk to. There is no organization that businesses and public organizations can turn to that clearly understands what data loss means, is familiar with what cyber-crime is, and knows how to tackle it. Even so, companies that have fallen foul of cyber-crime attacks really should report any such incidents to the local police — and if necessary, help law enforcement understand exactly what (for example) a Denial of Service (DoS) or phishing attack is.

This is simple when it is a stolen laptop, or perhaps a burglary, but when it comes to more insidious attacks, such as SQL Injection (see Chapter 17), then the problem is harder. For a start, the attack might have been going on for weeks or months without anyone noticing; when it *is* finally spotted, ascertaining exactly who has been affected is difficult. The result is that everyone has to be told, or notified. The other oddity with data loss is that it is really a misnomer as almost undoubtedly there will be a copy of the data elsewhere in the IT environment, so it is really a copy that has been lost, or copied — not a loss of something unique, like a great painting.

Each geography or country needs a body of some sort to report to, one that is capable of dealing with cyber-crime and (more specifically) data loss. Currently, no such body exists, at least not one that can bring together threatened organizations and coordinate efforts to identify and resolve instances of data loss.

Cyber-crime — what can I do?

Here's a checklist of possible ways to get involved in the control of cyber-crime:

- ✔ Lobby your local government to call for the formation of a central police e-crime unit to deal with the growing threat of cybercrime.

- ✔ Petition central government on behalf of your local businesses, in favor of forming an anti-cybercrime unit.

- ✔ Join and work with corporate IT Forums to form a single reporting body for cyber-crime; without such a dedicated unit, the situation will only get worse.

- ✔ When an e-crime reporting body forms for your company or industry, join it, and develop policies that support countermeasures against data loss.

- ✔ If it happens to you, report it. Organizations must tell the police when they fall victim to cyber-crime but are often too embarrassed to do so, fearing bad publicity.

Hiding from the issue is no solution; before long, organizations will have no choice *except* to disclose a data breach if the laws change (as they have in the U.S.), to require that all data breaches be disclosed.

In the long term, the growing cyber-crime threat affects organizations as profoundly as it affects individual victims of identity theft. Failing to prevent data loss will have an increasing impact on the bottom line of these businesses as cyber-crime becomes more sophisticated. We're now in a world that relies entirely on the Internet, e-mail and computer systems to carry out both large- and small-scale commerce. Organizations around the world hold data on employees, partners, suppliers, customers, and prospective clients; each of these records is a potential target for the skilled criminal.

Commerce can't afford to allow the customer to lose confidence in the modern route to market. Any loss of data will inevitably have a major impact on customer confidence — but organizations can't afford to lose customers to their competitors.

Treating Data Loss as a Disaster

Organizations need a comprehensive approach to counteracting data leakage but many don't yet have the right skills (at the right level) to scope out how big a problem data loss is. Here's a rough idea:

✔ It spans the data center.

✔ It affects everyone, from backup administrators to end-users.

✔ It involves all departments.

✔ It has spectacularly disruptive connotations.

✔ It isn't going to go away.

✔ It's going to require a well-thought-out, comprehensive approach.

There may be no epic movies about data loss (yet), but it qualifies as a disaster. And forget fleeing to higher ground. Many organizations, especially in the public and financial sectors, are coming under increasing pressure (typically from auditors) to provide *proof of care* (evidence that they've prepared for this disaster) by demonstrating rigorous risk-management controls.

It isn't an easy problem to tackle. Many technical, environmental, and human-based factors must be considered when you're trying to discover and mitigate the risks posed by data loss. These include a range of motives and actions (whether deliberate or accidental) that put sensitive information at risk of being disclosed, lost, misappropriated, abandoned, or generally mislaid:

✔ Loss of laptop computers, PDAs, and phones.

✔ Loss of IT equipment, storage media, or hard drives, including those built into printers and fax machines.

✔ Incorrect, lax, or subversive use of e-mail, instant messaging, and Internet access.

✔ Incorrect (or just plain dumb) use of Internet sites, blogs, or social-networking sites.

✔ Incorrect disposal of confidential data and information on electronic media (often that means *non*-disposal of stuff you don't want leaked).

✔ The use of USB memory sticks and other portable hard disks such as iPods and other MP3 players.

✔ Unencrypted desktop storage devices (which continuously diminish in price, size and power requirements while growing in storage capacity).

✔ Unsecured wireless networks. (Okay, nitwits who leave their Wi-Fi enabled but unattended probably deserve to have their Outlook contacts swiped. But your company doesn't deserve the security breach.)

Data loss may have started out as a minor concern, but these days it's huge It's sparked regulations and controversies around breach notification, identify theft, and the protection of intellectual property. For openers. Clearly, organizations and individuals need to get smarter about the nature, causes, and incidence of data leakage.

Evaluating risk

An organization should start data-protection projects slowly, conducting a test first in order to understand exactly what data (or behavior) it's trying to catch. Most companies struggle with even this first step, so here's a question that might help clarify the goal: What does sensitive data *mean* in your organization? What happens when data is either exposed or gets into the wrong hands? If you can work up a worst-case scenario, it's easier to identify what most needs protection and then carry out a *risk evaluation*.

In essence, the risk evaluation looks at the information and then the potential risks that threaten it and the consequences its loss entails. For example, having unencrypted sensitive data on a laptop is a risk. Worst-case scenario: The laptop may be stolen and the company may have to notify all its customers of the potential data breach. Likewise, if you send your backup tapes to a third party, there is a potential risk that they may be lost. If the consequences of that loss are high, you may have a justification for encrypting the backup data so you won't have to notify your customers.

Understanding the damage to reputation

A single data-loss incident can cost an organization millions. The negative publicity, subsequent loss of brand reputation, potential costly litigation (real or unreal litigious threats) and compromised competitive advantage are real enough. But so is reputation; in today's globalized world, it means more than it did 20 years ago. Reputation is everything.

Today, organizations face not only a plethora of competition in the marketplace, but also a customer base under continuous attack by advertising and media. Customers are continuously berated, bombarded, and beguiled into buying this product or that service. The marketing assault made the customer both more confused and more choosy about what to buy and from whom.

Even today, however, customers are more likely to buy from someone they know than from someone they don't know. That means brands are even more important than before. Publicized data loss hits a brand where it lives — in some cases, devastatingly.

As most organizations struggle to find out where their most important or sensitive information is stored — or, for that matter, how it's being used, who has access to it and how to prevent it from being lost or compromised — the health of their brands hangs in the balance. If defenses are measly and security policies, then any incident of data loss will open your organization up to scrutiny — and even ridicule — when the defects in the its defenses are publicized.

It's harder and costlier to rebuild a damaged reputation than to preserve a good one.

Over the past five years the subject of information and data loss, data leakage and endpoint data protection has become a boardroom topic — and with good reason.

In 2006, more than 50 percent of companies admitted to having significant data loss in the last 12 months. The loss of confidential records (particularly where these records contain sensitive personal information, belonging to customers) has a severe financial and brand-related impact on organizations entrusted with this type of information. A loss of reputation equals a loss of that trust, followed by a hemorrhage of money. The cost of data loss is escalating. Recent years have seen many well-documented cases of fines and lawsuits costing astronomical sums (not to mention some very high-profile executive resignations). Why do you think they call it "damages?"

So what can damage a reputation?

✔ Pirated goods.

✔ A phishing e-mail with your company's name on it can damage your reputation.

✔ If your Web site is hacked and malware (such as a virus or a Trojan) ends up in your customers' computers, that's a hit to your reputation.

✔ If you lose customer data and your company's name is spread across the front page of the news then people won't trust you with their details and they won't buy stuff from you.

Unlike other forms of IT risk, information and data loss isn't often caused by random acts of nature, too costly to prevent. Rather, our research and experience shows that most data losses could have been prevented with the adoption of well-defined policies, best practices, and products to help you out.

Facing the prospect of fines

If your data slips out the back door, then at the very least, your organization may have to shell out. Much of the data residing on computers has become subject to provisions mandated by law — some of which carry significant financial penalties if they aren't met. These penalties will only get heavier in the future; laws will probably change to prohibit (or at least restrict) the movement of data, whether personal or otherwise sensitive, from country to country and/or business to business, perhaps even within sister companies.

International regulations as well as local laws govern the use of data — specifically personal data, but also other forms of intellectual property shared by employees, partners and supply-chain organizations. One U.S. retailer had 45 million customers' personal details stolen by wireless hackers — and now faces multiple charges and fines relating to the data breach.

Protecting the data (or doing jail time)

Laws change all the time, and the loss of personal data is taking giant strides toward becoming a criminal offense on both sides of the Atlantic. In April 2008, for example, the House of Lords in the U.K. backed a move to amend criminal-justice laws to criminalize two major aspects of data loss:

✔ The intentional or reckless loss of personal/IP information.

✔ Repeatedly and negligently allowing information to be lost or stolen.

Governments have begun to put teeth into legislation to improve the trust and confidence that the public has in the arrangements to protect personal data. Bottom line: Protect the data or risk jail time.

Protecting information technology

Most companies start down the regulatory path, but then realize that preventing data leakage from their organization can also protect their intellectual property. The Ponemon Institute agrees, and identifies not only sensitive data, but its security, as one of the "most significant" business issues. They see IT as a vital infrastructure to be protected.

Even if your organization seems like a sieve of electronic leaks, all is not lost. There is a whole discipline of how to treat sensitive data. All data is created equal — but, of course, this isn't the case. By building a storage structure to manage the differences in data categorization you can apply similar policies to protect sensitive data. For example, e-mail from the CEO is probably highly sensitive; that from a lowly engineer is usually not. Likewise, documents with the latest financial results *before they are made public* are very sensitive; announcements about the company picnic are not.

At one time, data protection deferred to customer convenience. This was enforced by legislation such as the data-protection laws, most of which were written down and then presumed to be operating; customers didn't worry much about whether the protection happened. (After all, what real difference did it make to them? None. Or so everybody assumed.) Today we're faced with a far bigger issue than convenience. Any organization that holds any information about its customers, partners, and employees can't afford to lose it. Information leaks aren't the sole worry of organizations scrambling to meet customer-data or regulatory requirements; many non-regulated companies share the need to secure sensitive data. Intellectual property (IP), merger and acquisition plans (M&A — basically, which company are you going to buy next — probably some of the most sensitive information your organization has), and other critical assets *in the form of data* are strategic to many organizations' success and competitive advantage.

Lately, for all these organizations, data must be protected against both external *and* internal leakage.

Over the years, organizations spent tremendous resources in hopes of protecting their information against malicious outsiders, foiling hackers trying to pry into the organization, educating employees, and securing data at rest. But not all leakage is the result of external attack. In fact, most data leaks result from unintentional information loss; data wanders out to employees and partners because someone didn't realize that it shouldn't. The high cost of a breach can have a profound effect on an organization's profit and loss, market presence, and competitive advantage as a result of damage to brand and reputation, and loss of customers and IP. Why? Well, the old cliché from the spy movies — "this information must not fall into the wrong hands" — is literally true these days, for quite a range of data. In addition to customer information like credit-card or bank details, other items such as patents, company operating plans, price lists, and future developments can damage the organization if they find their way into the wrong person's hands.

In spite of the media focus on data leakage, we really don't have any accurate idea of how much data has actually been lost. To get a true perspective on both the amount and the consequences of data loss, we have to get a more detailed picture of the actual problem. Then focusing on the resources required to combat it will be more effective.

We have our work cut out for us; data loss is hard to identify, to report, and to deal with. Although a fog of jargon often moves in around any problem with an "e" in front of it, cyber-crime need not be high-tech crime; it can be as basic as bribery, deception, or petty thievery, and carried out for a basic reason: money.

Starting to Rethink Data Security

Businesses are beginning to realize that they have to reconsider their attitude toward data security. All organizations are subject to the dangers of data loss if they don't put reasonable and appropriate security measures in place. Such measures aim to prevent data loss, foil unauthorized access, and maintain consistent, reasonable protection for the security, confidentiality, and integrity of personal information that the organization collects from — or about — consumers.

Looking at the basics of data security

As organizations invest millions in business systems they hope will increase the availability of information to build or maintain a competitive edge, suddenly there's a lot more confidential information flying around inside the company. Result: a slew of security-related considerations, including these:

✔ Where is the organization's confidential and sensitive data?

✔ How, where, and when is the data transmitted, and by whom?

✔ How can the data be controlled and protected?

✔ What is my organization's financial risk (from a leak)?

What you can do is to start putting your organization's house in order. A thorough policy that addresses data security must contain administrative, technical, and physical safeguards appropriate to

✔ The size and nature of the company's business.

✔ The sensitivity of the information contained in its electronic and physical systems.

It makes absolute sense not to keep information that an organization doesn't need — or at least provide access only to those who require that information for legitimate purposes.

It's not enough to create data-driven security policies and then pay lip service to the idea of privacy and protection of confidential information. If you're going to get real about it, here's what that entails:

✔ Businesses and government agencies need to have comprehensive training programs detailing the importance of protecting private data and the policies in place to do so.

✔ Compliance with policies must be automated as much as possible to stop incidents of human error and outright disregard of a company or agency's policies.

✔ Penalties for breaking policies must be rigorously enforced, each and every time.

Although the damage to reputation (and to public trust) associated with data loss can be just as devastating as the financial loss, sometimes numbers are just what you need to spur better data security. So here they come . . . .

Putting a monetary value on your data

One way to get a handle on which data is sensitive (and why) is to ask yourself a question: *Who is this data most valuable to?* You and your company, of course, but who *else?* The list may seem short — only a few names and addresses within the company, perhaps a few customers — how much value could that possibly represent?

Basically that value is equivalent to the value of your company, especially if you consider that IT represents the arteries of a company and data is the lifeblood to be kept flowing. You don't want it all to bleed out through wounds such as

✔ Loss of brand integrity

✔ Loss of actual money to theft, fraud, fines, and litigation

✔ Loss of customers

Before working out whether a solution is viable from a financial perspective, it's worth doing a few quick calculations, starting with the hourly rate.

Figuring out the hourly rate

This is the simplest calculation, which you can do whether you are a multinational or a corner shop. Take the gross turnover and divide it by the number of hours worked in a year. If you are only open from 9:00 to 5:00, then the total hours will be less than if you trade on the Internet, where your business is open 24/7, all day every day. The goal here is to get a feel for the numbers, not an exact value (which would be out of date by the time you calculate it). So if you assume that your organization is 24/7 and Internet-driven, the hours stack up like this:

Hourly Rate = Turnover / {Hours Worked}

Where Hours Worked = $(8 \times 5 \times 52) = 2080$ (working 9-to-5 every day)

Or:

Hours Worked = $(24 \times 7 \times 52) = 8736$ (working 24/7)

Now you know what is at stake for every hour that business is disrupted. Of course it is more than this, customers who can't but today may well go elsewhere and never come back to you — but at least you have an idea.

Figuring costs by customer

En route to working out the overall costs that data loss entails — so you know how much you'll have to pay out, even though there might not be as much coming in — you could calculate how much each customer is worth to you. This number can be a little tough to figure out, as you have to take into account the number of active customers (those who have bought something in the last 12 months), not just those who are on the list.

Figuring the loss in terms of employee time

The next step is to further divide hours worked by the number of employees you have. Okay, so all employees aren't the same, some get paid more than others, some do more important jobs, but the calculation gives you a good average:

Individual Hourly Rate = Hourly Rate / {Number of Employees}

If you have a data-loss incident that results in the Web site closing down, and you are an Internet business, then you'll be losing money at the hourly rate calculated. (Scary thought, isn't it?)

If half your staff are involved in resolving a data-loss incident, then once more you have a ballpark figure for the losses you are incurring.

Considering your options

All these numbers help push the decisions that need to be made faster. Nothing focuses the mind like money! So if our organization is headed for data-loss trouble, our options are

- **Fix it ourselves.** We have the skills and the time to sort this mess out.

- **Get someone else to come and fix it.** If no appropriate skills or sufficient staff time are available in-house, get some experts in.

- **Employ a third party to help out with support.** Ongoing support of our customers is critical — but we don't have the personnel to support them in the way we'd like to.

- **Fix the business processes so the problem won't happen again.** Something has gone wrong, we need to sort it out — can we do it internally, or would some consultants help us.

- **Acquire and deploy new technology to help provide a data-loss solution.** We know there is technology that can help — but which system will help our particular situation, and how much will it cost?

These numbers can also be used to help justify implementing a data-loss solution *before* a crisis occurs! (What a concept.)

Keeping an eye on the why

Organizations have not only had to face hefty fines, but have also had to go through a comprehensive information-security program. The U. S. Federal Trade Commission, as well as other regulatory bodies in countries around the world, make the message perfectly clear: Companies that collect personal or sensitive information have a responsibility to ensure that the information is kept safe.

Data losses usually hurt third parties — you and me. After all, most of the press surrounding data loss focuses on personal data — information about individuals — instead of intellectual property. If you hold personal information about a customer, you have a moral (and legal) responsibility for that information. Losing that information can have a huge impact on that individual and his or her family — followed by a swift and negative impact on your own business.

Most people agree that personal data loss must not be tolerated. Organizations might become casual, even flippant about data breaches — to them it's only some data (if only they knew) — but to the individual, it can be catastrophic. This means that data management, data storage, data backup, and data movement *must* be policy-driven — and automated as much as possible to limit the effects of human error.

In a recent data-loss debacle in the U.K., employees at all levels of seniority neglected security policies and procedures, copied database information to disks, and sent data unencrypted in the mail. In fact, there was an article at the time that pointed out an interesting lapse: The security policy was graded so lower-grade employees could not view it. Let's see — a security policy that's so security-self-conscious that no one is allowed to see it? So how can they follow it? That's one good way to make your organization look really . . . well . . . stupid.

We do have government regulations that require companies and agencies to protect private data, as well as corporate security policies that address the same issue. Sadly, confidential data isn't being handled in accordance with these privacy regulations. Far too often, companies and government agencies establish good data-security policies — and then everyone signs off on those policies but does exactly what they want. That needs to change — preferably *before* more of our personal data is lost or stolen.

Don't expect change to happen unless you educate people *why* the changes are needed.

Chapter 5

Calculating the Value of Your Data

. . . .

. . . .

*B*efore developing a strategy to prevent data loss, you need to know the value of the data you hold. Its value to you — expressed in monetary terms — is also related to its value to a data thief. Chapter 2 shows how to examine your data environment, find the different types of data you hold, and figure out where you'll find it. Chapter 4 offers some preliminary steps in the direction of evaluating your data and rethinking data security. This chapter takes all this information one step farther: putting a realistic, quantitative, monetary value on your data assets. The goal is to help you put together a cost-effective solution to protect those assets.

There are many solutions and their costs vary widely. Matching the solution to the value of your data is important; you want to avoid both underspending and overspending.

Modeling Information

The value of your data to your organization is something that only the people who create and/or use the data can decide accurately.

One increasingly popular way to view it is the "CIA" model (illustrated in Figure 5-1):

> ✓ **Confidentiality (C):** How private must the data be kept?
>
> ✓ **Integrity (I):** How important is it that the data and the systems have not been tampered with?

  ▮ ✔ **Availability (A):** How available must the data and the systems be?

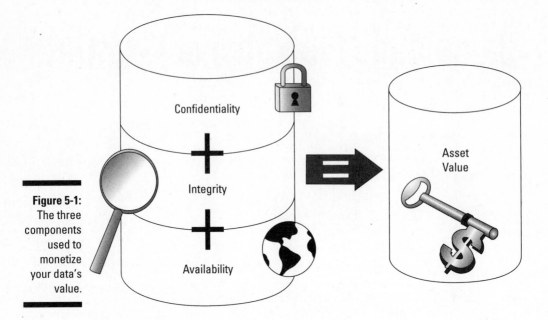

These three components need to be applied to all the information in your business.

$C*x + I*y + A*z = Value$

The multipliers x, y, and z are arbitrary constants to make the numbers fit into a good range. More often than not the whole process is carried out on a spreadsheet. As data is identified it's added to the spreadsheet and scored according to what else is already there: Is this data more or less confidential, more or less available? Many organizations don't have any concept of *integrity* when it comes to information. The assumption is that it won't change—an unfortunate fallacy where data loss is concerned.

For example, if we're referring to the customer database and the addresses were corrupted, then this loss could be catastrophic to the business: Orders couldn't be delivered; your contact with customers would be severely disrupted.

Clearly, the higher the CIA scores, the more valuable the data. The more valuable the data, the better it needs to be protected — and the place to begin, when preventing data loss, is at the top of the list.

You may well have already looked at some of this information in a disaster-recovery or business-continuity plan. When you're looking at systems, the *cost of downtime* might have already been calculated, which gives you another vital detail in the total picture of your data's value.

For example, if you're an online trader, then your Web interface *is* your business. Without the Web server, you can't trade, so its availability must be very practically constant. To calculate the cost of downtime, in this case, you'd multiply the average hourly revenue by the hours needed to bring the system back online.

If the system has been compromised and data stolen, then how long will it take to bring the system back online? Well, that depends on three factors:

- You have to take the system down to apply security measures.

- The application that runs your business may have to be altered to remove its vulnerabilities before it can be brought back up.

- The data may need to be inspected and scrubbed before it can be used.

Adding risk and consequences into the equation

To get an accurate value assigned to your data, you have to figure in the risks and consequences associated with data loss. Traditionally this is a subjective evaluation, arrived at by looking at incidents that have already occurred and working through the implications from there. Here are some examples:

- **What if a laptop is lost or stolen?**

  The answer is . . . it depends! If the laptop held no sensitive information, then it wouldn't matter.

- **What if a stolen laptop contains customer names and other details?**

  The answer is . . . it depends! If the data was encrypted and the laptop was password-protected, then it wouldn't matter. (Remember: In the eyes of the law, if a laptop is encrypted and subsequently lost, then the loss doesn't have to be disclosed!)

- **What if your database is hacked?**

  First, how would you know? If this was found by chance then how long has it been occurring? What if it had been *recurring* for months — or even years?

A growing number of scenarios should be examined:

- What if your Web application were compromised?
- What if an employee sent out your price list to your competitor?
- What if your intellectual-property database was exposed to the world?
- What if your financial results were leaked to the press before the announcement was made?
- What difference would it make if a lost laptop belonged to (say) your CEO (or to a salesperson, which would be bad enough)?
- What information can be found on a portable phone?
- What information do you allow on removable media or USB sticks?
- What would happen if you lost a backup tape?
- What would be the consequence of having the third-party paper shredders lose your printed reports *before* they were shredded?
- What happens to data when old systems are decommissioned?
- What happens to hard drives (and the data they contain) when systems are repaired?

For most commercial organizations, customer data is the most valuable data. You don't want to be front-page news for the wrong reasons.

Obviously, it's really easy to lose a laptop or a cell phone; you have to factor in how "losable" a particular device is.

Different perspectives for different devices

Data can be held, and lost, from multiple different places in the network and the IT environment. The risks to the organization are also different in these different places. If you're working at your desk, behind a corporate firewall and on a computer that is attached to the corporate network, then the risk of an intruder hacking in and getting access to your machine is significantly lower than when you're in a coffee shop connected to the Internet through an unprotected wireless connection.

These days the mobile phone or PDA is just as powerful as a laptop and gives access to e-mail and other corporate applications. So it's worth noting that you're 22 times more likely to lose a mobile phone than a laptop, which makes the data-loss risk greater. This is an example of the factors you have to take into account when you're determining the value of your data. The policies that govern holding sensitive or confidential data on a mobile device should probably be different from those governing data in a desktop unit.

Different perspectives for different markets

Just as you have to take different devices into account, you also have to consider the value of your data in different markets or industries. If you work in the oil and gas industry, for example, survey data is of critical importance — but if you work in the surveying industry, cost estimates are more vital.

One particular CIO told us that while the execs in his company were very concerned about the customer data that the company held, they were most concerned about the company's business plan — specifically, the operating model. They're in the business of delivering stuff, and on some services, they make money; on others, they don't. The CIO said, *"If our competitors get our model, they can change their model — and put us out of business overnight."*

Identifying Sensitive Data

Sometimes it can be hard to figure out what data *is* sensitive. Employees who deal with data don't often think of it as information that has an impact on individuals. Employees need to be educated about which data is sensitive and why; then they can help you get a much clearer picture of both the data and the processes that involve it.

Sometimes you have to "stay the courier"

A health authority has provided their employees with mobile phones on which they can receive e-mail. However, due to the confidential nature of some information they can receive, the organization created a new policy (and new technology) to restrict e-mail on the mobile device. In essence, they use content-classification software to decide whether a particular e-mail message can be sent to a mobile device. If the e-mail contains sensitive personal information (such as patient records), then it isn't sent — and the employee doesn't see the e-mail until he or she gets back to the office. Enabling mobile e-mail for the workforce has increased productivity — and because the policymakers were aware of the need to protect sensitive information, the consequences of a lost device have been minimized.

Credit cards and bank details

As you might expect, credit-card and bank-account details top the list of sensitive data. The dangers of losing these are obvious: If a cyber-criminal has access to them, then the bad guy *also* has access to someone else's cash and credit. Result: data loss, followed by a spending spree (usually somewhere far away).

You might imagine that a company would have only *one* copy of a customer's credit-card data or bank-account details; unfortunately, that isn't the case. Even if you've found one copy, don't assume it's the only one. You need to keep looking until you've exhausted all possibilities.

Start with the obvious place to look: databases. Don't be surprised if you find multiple applications that use multiple databases behind the scenes. When customers order something over the Web, the data usually ends up in a database. Unfortunately, these databases usually aren't consolidated. So each time a new service is offered, a new application is developed and a new database implemented — resulting in multiple records for a single customer, and multiple copies of credit-card information.

A well-known airline looked for all the applications that held credit-card numbers — and they found 19. When asked how this sensitive information wound up in all those places, they were just as mystified as anyone else in the room; then the answer came: marketing. The marketing department was an innovative group; each time they came up with a new program it would spawn a new application and database. Often the program would reach the end of its life, but the application and the database would remain *"just in case."* After they had found all the instances, the airline started to consolidate the databases. This wasn't about reducing the number of programs that marketing could run — in fact, it had the opposite effect; new programs became easier to put together — but it did mean the information was consolidated. The company managed to reduce the number of instances to three. Then they only had to protect 3 databases, not the 19 they had started with — saving both time and money.

Customer-loyalty cards

Nearly everyone has multiple *loyalty cards*. The idea behind a loyalty card (the name gives it away) is to keep the customer loyally buying more things from you. To do this bit of magic, the organization sends letters or e-mail containing vouchers that will entice people into the shop. Usually, at least one voucher is for something the customer has bought before.

The customer-loyalty database contains everything that would interest a cyber-criminal looking to start a phishing scam: names, addresses, loyalty-card numbers — and sometimes other information, such as when and where the customers last shopped.

E-mail addresses

E-mail is a wonderful business tool; companies can communicate with their customers for virtually nothing. You can send money-off vouchers for the customer to print out and bring to the store, or to redeem online. The possibilities are almost endless. Unfortunately, the same is true for cyber-criminals. All they need is a customer's e-mail address and some stolen context to make their messages seem legitimate. In this case, they know the context: the organization that they stole the information from!

It's really easy to construct a simple and convincing e-mail, complete with corporate logos, and to send it out. How do they get logos? Well, one simple way is to pretend to be a customer and sign up for a newsletter or a loyalty-card. Then the bad guys receive all the official communiqués they need to rehash for their own nefarious purposes. They can also get the logo from the real Web site or by taking a photograph and editing it into an electronic copy.

Often cyber-criminals are patient about developing a scam. They might not ask for anything specific in the first communication, and just send a "welcome to our new service" e-mail. The next message can set the bait and talk about special offers that will be coming next month. Finally there is the "sign up now" e-mail offering money back, or vouchers so you can order at a discount . . . if only you put in your credit-card details . . . or perhaps your bank-account details so they can siphon off the money directly.

To find all the places that you have e-mail addresses, start with loyalty cards and databases and then look to marketing. These days, most marketing initiatives require customers to sign up for something over the Web — and the first requested information is the e-mail address.

E-mail and other communication from customers

You can find e-mail addresses in support systems or e-mail systems that customers use to communicate with your organization. Of course, customers can communicate electronically in other ways as well — such as Instant

Messaging, a Web cast, Web-based discussion boards, blogs, Web feedback forms, and even Voice over IP (VoIP). All these systems store information that cyber-criminals can use; all should be protected accordingly.

Health and welfare information

Health and welfare information is personal — and can be exploited in a number of ways to extort money. Even if it's just lost, the information can cause embarrassment to the individual concerned. A number of regulations protect health information, but that doesn't mean that losses don't happen.

Sensitive corporate data

Because you'll end up on the front page of the newspaper — or having to send out an apologetic letter to all your customers — if you lose sensitive personal information, the emphasis has been on locating that type of information. But that isn't the whole story. Lots of other information is sensitive to the business. Here are some major categories:

- Corporate data, such as

  - *Financials:* The latest set of information on how the quarter or the year has gone.

  - *Merger and acquisition plans:* Which companies are being targeted and how much they're worth to you.

  - *Human resource and employee data:* Names, addresses, bank-account details — you hold it all for your employees!

- Intellectual property, such as

  - *Product-design documents:* The next generation — which will attempt to put the competition out of business.

  - *Source code:* You don't want to lose the cool algorithm that gives you the competitive edge.

  - *Pricing information:* Just how much discount *do* you give for bulk orders?

Other sources of sensitive data

Sensitive information may already be posted on the Web. Use your favorite search engine to find out what's out there:

- ✔ Look for your price lists or patents; see whether you can find orders, especially from other suppliers.

- ✔ Look on the Web. Employees can inadvertently post sensitive information on the Web, perhaps on a blog or discussion forum, but more likely on a social-networking site (for a typical horror story that actually turned out well, see the accompanying sidebar).

Develop a policy that spells out what your employees can and can't do:

- • Can they post their work locations and their job title?

- • Can they post pictures?

  When posting pictures from work, ensure that there's nothing useful to the cyber-criminal (or, for that matter, to the competition) in the background. A quick search for images of people at work reveals a whole host of people sitting at their desks, surrounded by yellow-sticky notes full of useful information!

Which information are cyber-criminals after?

There is a lot of information in your organization and so it depends which perspective you view it from as to whether it's useful to a cyber-criminal:

- ✔ **Customer details** are of most general value. Names, addresses, and credit-card details are always easy to sell on the underground markets.

- ✔ **Corporate secrets** are tougher to unload. The disgruntled insider who makes off with a customer list when changing jobs is unlikely to compromise the data by giving it to cyber-criminals. On the other hand, a hacker who gets into the network and steals plans for the next product may sell that information to the competition — or (more likely) sell it back to the original company, with the threat that otherwise it will go to the competition or get posted on the Internet.

Sometimes the information on its own isn't useful; to *become* useful, it needs to be combined with other information. And that brings us to . . .

The fine art of zippering

A bad guy doesn't have to get all the sensitive information in one haul, from one place at one time. Instead, he can assemble multiple pieces of information — maybe from multiple sources or gathered over a period of time — and then make nefarious use of the collection. Bringing together multiple pieces of information is called *zippering* (see Figure 5-2).

Here's how zippering works. Imagine that you (as an imaginary bad guy) could obtain someone's name — okay, that isn't hard — and then look up the person to find a home address. That's *two* juicy tidbits of information. Many countries have other records online as well — births, marriages, and deaths, for openers — and from this you can find the mother's maiden name, the spouse's name, the children's names. Seems innocent enough, but . . . if you had a bank-account number, you could probably take a pretty good guess at what the password might be; if you were phoning the bank, you may well have enough information to succeed in impersonating the victim.

Bottom line: Even "everyday" items of information can add up to an at-risk asset.

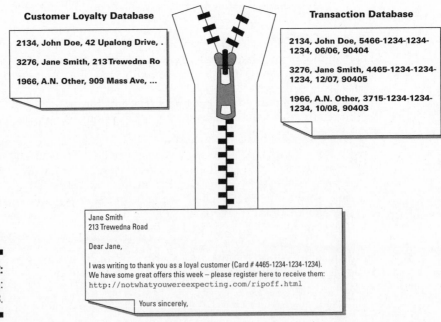

Figure 5-2: Zippering: when 1+1=3.

Ten-hut!

An army found that pictures of sensitive military installations were posted on a social-networking site. The people who posted the images were actually posting pictures of themselves at work. It just so happened that they worked at sensitive sites. ("And this is me wiping up the coffee I spilled on the captured UFO. Another boring day at Area 51." Something about that bad.)

A policy was developed (and rapidly rolled out) that allowed individuals to post pictures of themselves so long as it didn't include sensitive information in the background.

The other knee-jerk reaction would have been to ban the use of social-networking sites — a reaction that not only wouldn't have worked, it would probably have promoted more (and sneakier) use, as well as disillusionment. In this case, the solution lay in thinking it through, educating the employees as to where the risks were, laying out what the consequences might be (a risk to national security) and coming up with a solution that all agreed with. Cooperation averted disaster.

The Elusive Total Cost

There are some additional intangible costs that you should take into consideration. Unfortunately, no formula exists that can magically calculate the total impact on the losing company, the individual, the individual's bank, and so on. Even business mavens and sages (such as Guy and Gareth — Guy says he's a maven, so Gareth must be a sage) spend their time writing about how difficult this total impact is to write about (which it is). Frankly, we haven't yet come up with the one set of rules that captures and describes the complete impact of data loss. Calculating an organization's total financial loss is tricky, and by no means simple; so many tangible and intangible impacts must be factored into the equation.

That said, the simple equation is easy; most of us can do it in our heads. Say cyber-criminals make off with 25 million business records on two CDs with access to 8 million customers over the age of 18. Using the identities on those discs, they could potentially fleece around $2,000 from each back account before all those General Public Joes spotted the discrepancies and figured out that someone has lifted cash from their accounts. The haul is about 8 million $\times$ 2,000 = $16 *billion* . . . not bad for a day's work! But that's a relatively superficial formula — and probably wildly inaccurate (as in, too *low* an estimate of the total cost). For starters, it misses all the intangible impact costs — such as these:

- Potential lost revenue
- Loss or corruption of contact data
- Legal costs, regulatory fines, and penalties
- Failed Service Level agreements
- Lost business opportunities
- Lost potential customers
- Loss of existing customer loyalty
- Reputation damage (brand damage)
- Loss of employees
- Poisoning of goodwill toward the company
- Share depreciation
- Loss of supplier faith
- Additional vendor costs to fix the hole following the breach

The bottom line is profitability — or, in some cases, survivability. Every business should ensure that it has (and that its employees have) appropriate levels of data security and management to match its unique financial, operational, competitive, and marketing situation. Investing the time and money it takes to investigate and understand those interdependent factors will help guard against the ravages of data loss.

Chapter 6

The Price of Your Data to Others

*W*e know that your data is valuable to *you*. If it isn't, then, "Note to self: Delete the stuff that isn't valuable."

Just because a particular bit of data doesn't appear useful now doesn't mean that it isn't useful. Useful information must include (for example) information about litigation, and all those project-related facts and figures that you would normally just archive. Keep that stuff, but encrypt as you go. Skip the rubbish (information on the level of "Hey John, did you catch the game last night?") if you can. If you work in the IT department, then it probably isn't your call to start deleting information or data. But that's where you need a policy and probably technology that covers discovering, monitoring, managing, encrypting, and (when appropriate) deleting data in the course of archiving it. (After all, in the middle of 2007 the world ran out of storage-disk space for a while. Deleting stuff is a must.)

If it's valuable to you, then it's also valuable to someone else (who may not mean you well):

 ✔ **Competitors:** If they could get their hands on your customer list they could market directly to them. If they have your pricelist they can price their products lower. If they have your innovations their products could become more innovative than yours.

 ✔ **Malicious insiders:** These people either sell your information or use it to their own advantage; for example, going to a new job with a list of your customers.

 ✔ **Cyber-criminals:** This is the catch-all group. If they can get individual pieces of customer information, they can sell it or use it for their own devious purposes.

How Much Is That Data Worth?

If you need a password to protect it, then the data you're protecting is valuable to someone. This is just as true at home as in the office; it's just that at the office a cyber-criminal can get away with thousands of records at a time, rather than just one.

Just because you don't think a random bit of information from your company is worth much doesn't mean that a criminal agrees.

Any piece of information can be used, especially in conjunction with other pieces of information to target an individual. People like a bargain (don't we all?). If you can offer something for a perceived value, people will go for it. "Sign up here for discounts of 50 percent — if you could just give us your credit-card details, we'll refund the difference!" (*Sure* we will.)

Information that can be immediately used to access funds, such as credit-card details or a bank account is more attractive than other types, but as we become better at protecting some types of information, other types rise in value and popularity.

The most popular data for criminals to acquire

Table 6-1 gives examples of the data for sale and the price you pay. Regular studies of the cost of black market information are made and the costs are coming down, because the quantity of information is increasing!

Table 6-1	Goods and Services for Sale on "Underground Economy" Servers			
Rank (Previous Rank)	Goods and Services	Current Percentage	Previous Percentage	Range of Prices
1 (2)	Bank accounts	22%	21%	$10-$1000
2 (1)	Credit cards	13%	22%	$0.40-$20
3 (7)	Full identity	9%	6%	$1-$15
4 (Not ranked)	Auction accounts	7%	Not applicable	$1-$8

Rank (Previous Rank)	Goods and Services	Current Percentage	Previous Percentage	Range of Prices
5 (8)	Scams	7%	6%	$2.50/week-$50/week for hosting, $25 for design
6 (4)	Mailers	6%	8%	$1-$10
7 (5)	E-mail addresses	5%	6%	$0.83/MB-$10/MB
8 (3)	E-mail passwords	5%	8%	$4-$30
9 (Not ranked)	Drop (request or offer)	5%	Not applicable	10%-50% of total drop amount
10 (6)	Proxies	5%	6%	$1.50-$30

(Source Symantec Corporation, 2007)

You can also purchase gaming accounts, social-networking accounts, and all manner of other information. You need to protect this seemingly innocent information the same way you'd protect a bank account. What could the bad guys do if they had it? That's easy: Impersonate you.

If thieves have made off with your auction account, they could fraudulently use your reputation to sell something in (say) a Web-based auction or any of many other routes to market — and then deliver either substandard goods or no goods (and there goes your reputation). If that account is compromised, then not only will your customers not get what they pay for, they'll think less of your company and take their business elsewhere. Then you may find that the auction site seeks damages — and probably bans you from selling your stuff there.

Pile 'em high, sell 'em cheap

The BOGOF (Buy One, Get One Free) sale promotion rules the world. Wherever we are, we expect discounts— especially for two or more of something. This is equally true in the murky world of the cyber-criminal.

Recent analysis of data for sale has highlighted the cyber equivalent of BOGOF: You can buy personal information in bulk. If you want to purchase 50 credit-card numbers, the cost is $40 ($0.80 each) — but if you want 500 credit-card numbers, the cost is only $200 — $0.40 each!

How cheap this information is reflects just how *available* such information is. A credit card might have been compromised a number of times (multiple places where it can be bought) and it might have been already noticed and the account stopped. Therefore, from the criminals' point of view, buying in bulk is worthwhile; all they need is to get lucky a couple of times to make a tidy profit on their investment.

Where to look for your data on the Web

There are too many places to look and (unfortunately) they appear and disappear all too quickly. You could search for your credit-card number on a search engine — of course, if it doesn't turn up, it doesn't mean it isn't out there. It just means that the search engine you happened to use hasn't indexed it. Of course, that could be a silly thing to do too. Just by putting the number out there, it might then be "harvested" (stolen). Remember, cyber-criminals aren't good people! Figure 6-1 shows a very simple scam: It plays on the fear that *someone, somewhere* has stolen your credit card. It may well be that nobody has yet. But if you respond, then that *someone* just did!

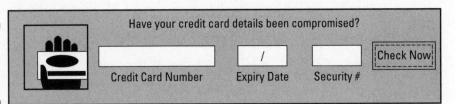

Figure 6-1: Would you use this "service"?

Internet Relay Chat (IRC) tends to be the place to both buy and sell information. A search through some of the popular Internet news groups will find an (in)appropriate chat forum where data is exchanged.

You're dealing with the criminal underworld here, not a friend:

- ✔ Don't trawl underground-economy sites looking for your data. You may end up infecting your machine with malware and losing *more* data.

- ✔ Don't believe services that offer to find your data on the Web. They can easily use the information you give them against you.

- ✔ If you think your details have been compromised, behave in the same way you would if you had lost your purse or wallet. Cancel credit cards and inform your bank.

- ✔ If you're threatened, go to the police.

As an individual, what will you do if you find something? Regularly check your credit rating. A number of subscription services can do this for you on a regular basis.

If you've lost customer information, offering your customers a free 12-month subscription to a credit check is a good idea. It reassures your customers that

- ✔ You care about them.

- ✔ You care about their financial well-being.

- ✔ You're doing what you can to help.

A number of service providers can help you and your company watch for other information about your company out there on the Web. If you suffer a data loss, employing them can really help you find answers to some disturbing questions:

- ✔ **Are your customers are being targeted with phishing e-mail?** If they are, then you can forewarn them of an actual threat, not just a potential one.

- ✔ **Are your products or services being mis-marketed or your brand abused?**

  If this is happening on a public forum, look to your legal department to help craft a message that you can post. If this can't be done, the legal department can help put together an action plan to inform the appropriate authorities to stop the problem.

- ✔ **Are your products being pirated and resold?**

  If they are, inform your legal department, which can act to stop the pirates. This won't happen quickly or easily, but it can be done.

These companies work by keeping a close eye on the Internet and specifically ferreting out where information traders ply their wares (or "warez," if you're looking for the hip spelling).

Information goes out of date; _everyone_ knows the lottery numbers 30 minutes after the draw. But if you knew them 30 minutes beforehand, it would be a whole different story!

The Value of Data Over Its Lifetime

Does data have a lifetime? Yes, of course it does — starting with when it's created. In order to protect information, you need to know the complete lifecycle of your various types of data; the idea is to protect it in the most appropriate way at the most appropriate time. Funnily enough (ahem), there is a really good book on managing data lifecycles — called *Data Lifecycles: Managing Data for Strategic Advantage* by Roger Reid, Gareth Fraser-King, and W. David Schwaderer (Wiley Publishing) — if you're interested in the details. Figure 6-2 shows an overview of the lifecycle of your data.

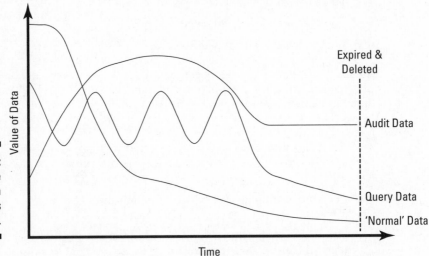

Figure 6-2: The value of data changes over time.

After you've identified the sensitive information in your organization, figure out whether that data has a lifecycle, and what the time period(s) might be. Here are some handy examples:

- **Financial statements:** These are sensitive before they're released to the public. Access before this time can be used to manipulate the share price (it's called *insider trading*). Protection needs to be high until your financial statement goes into the public domain; after that point, you can back it off.

- **Health records:** Generally health records have a lifetime of "life of the patient" plus two years. Information can be used for phishing or for blackmail and bribery. Security needs to be high at all times.

- ✔ **Credit-card details:** Most credit-card details expire two to three years after the cards are issued. They're very valuable to cyber-criminals while still in date, but should be protected even when out of date!

- ✔ **Bank-account details:** Most people don't change bank accounts often, so even ten years after the details have been lost, chances are good that they will still be valid!

- ✔ **Transaction details:** For many businesses, transactions (sales) are important until they get paid. Utility companies are interested in usage so they can bill correctly, but after payment, the details of the transaction are of little use, except in planning.

- ✔ **Intellectual property:** Patents, copyrights, and business plans all have lifecycles. Patents might be valid for 15 or 20 years, other media rights can be valid for 50 years — so all need to be suitably protected. Business plans are valuable until they're superseded and even then they often have forward-looking data that could be useful to the competition — so they need to be protected even after they've been superseded.

- ✔ **Price lists:** Old price lists aren't that valuable; even the competition won't be interested in old numbers!

- ✔ **Customer lists:** New customers are of obvious value — but over time, their value dissipates.

- ✔ **Other documents:** If a company is in a legal case, then those documents that were previously thought of as having little value suddenly become important and need more security.

Old data can be dangerous. If it can be deleted, then it won't be available to criminals or otherwise be exploited. Finding the value of the data, including the residual value, will help you decide how to best deal with it in the long term.

Customer data, employee data, partner data, product data, service data, financial data, even business procedures (which are, after all, represented by data) — can be found in a multitude of places. The more places, the more open to the risk of being compromised, both inadvertent and malicious. Compromise a business's data in any way and you compromise the business. In today's world of e-threats, regulations, laws, and industry standards — public expectations notwithstanding — organizations must go beyond simply securing their data.

Ideally, we should monitor all our information, even in the form of raw data, all the time. To get close to that goal, we need to know when it was created, who created it, where it's stored, who has access to it, who can modify it, when the modifications took place, what copies have been made, where those copies are, and who did exactly what (as well as when and how) to every layer of those copies. The stakes are high — all organizations are totally reliant on their data. It's a critical asset and needs to be treated that way.

Part II
Starting with the Endpoint

The 5th Wave   By Rich Tennant

In this part . . .

1t's a tough task to prevent data leaks, losses and breaches and you have to start somewhere. Where's the best place to start? The endpoint.

This part looks at how the threats are evolving, as well as the different technologies you need to consider to protect the most troubling of endpoints — the laptop. It also looks at other common data loss threats — CD ROMs, USB devices, mobile phones and PDAs.

Finally, it examines how geography is also related to data loss and where you are most at risk.

Chapter 7

IT Security

*T*o say IT security is only worthy of one chapter is underselling it — hugely. There are hundreds of books on the topic in all of its aspects. However we are looking at IT security from a data-leak perspective. We start by looking at the threat landscape, what's out there and coming to get you. If you know where the threats are, you can protect yourself from them. The other key to understanding IT security is to understand the people who are after your information: the data thieves and cyber-criminals. Forewarned is forearmed (there's that refrain again).

Surveying the Threat Landscape

So just what is a *threat landscape*? No place to camp out, for sure. Basically it's the big picture that encompasses a range of cyber-criminals and the threats they pose. Once that landscape was relatively flat — back in the time of the first viruses and computer attacks. While the first known spam (e-mail sent to people who didn't ask for it) cropped up back in the late 1970s, it wasn't until the mid-'80s that first viruses started becoming known. Figure 7-1 provides an overview of the constant march of computer threats.

Back in the '80s, there was no Internet as we know it today. Academic institutions and big high-tech companies used a forerunner of the Internet, but it certainly wasn't for the likes of you and me and the consumer. (Some of us had university e-mail addresses back then, but we didn't know people outside the organization who could *receive* e-mail!) Thus the early viruses were written out of curiosity and for notoriety; today they're all about crime and profit.

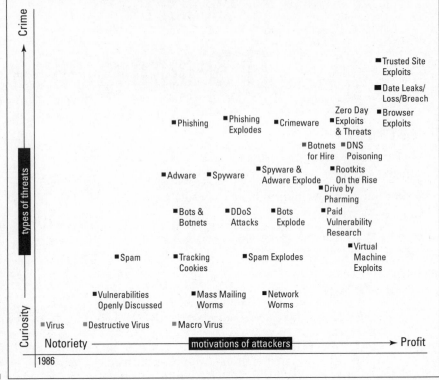

Figure 7-1: Computer threats from 1986 onward — creating an ever-more-hilly landscape.

What viruses can't do

Even modern viruses can't do some things (except in the movies). They can't.

✔ Blow up printers or monitors. Nope — despite what their messages might tell you.

✔ Melt down your processor or generally destroy hardware. No way — at least not literally.

✔ Spread through electrical cables unaided. They can't do that, either — so it's no good pretending you didn't do anything!

✔ Occur naturally. Nope. Computer viruses are human creations; someone must have programmed them.

✔ Infect the user (you). Some people are actually worried that they can catch a computer virus! Don't worry about that unless you're a cyborg.

Back then, of course, viruses spread mainly by lurking on floppy disks. As the technology improved, computers got faster, more bandwidth became available, and more computers got attached to networks, the threats grew — because the opportunities grew.

To gain a basic understanding of the ways you need to improve IT security, first you need to know what the baddies are putting out there and what they're trying to achieve:

- **Viruses:** In the early days, these infectious little programs were like high-tech pranks; they would take control of a system and pop up a message saying the equivalent of "You've been hacked!" Ha-ha.

- **Destructive viruses:** These got into a system to do something nasty — for example, wipe data off a screen or delete a few files. What can a virus do these days? Anything you can do — and then some. They have full access to files — so they can delete them, change them, or just steal the information out of them and send it off to some sinister lair in cyber-space. That's bad enough, but what people *think* they can do is worse (see the accompanying sidebar).

- **Macro viruses:** As computers get more powerful, so do the applications that run on them. When word-processing and spreadsheet applications introduced their own programming languages, for example, virus writers had *another* tool they could use for bad things.

- **Worms:** We now know that even the latest operating systems have bugs in them, but there was a time when no one talked about that. Hackers could then write applications to take advantage of the bugs (or vulner-abilities). Today the bugs *are* talked about and vendors publish fixes (patches) at regular intervals.

- **Bots and botnets:** If someone can get your computer to do something for them, then why not take it over full time? That's a *bot.* Then the criminals can rent out your computer, along with thousands of others in the network, to do bad things for anyone who is willing to pay!

- **Adware and spyware:** This is still a curse today but is the forerunner of today's data loss and data leaks. The big change here is that criminals are after your data, not just your system.

- **Phishing:** If you can't steal data directly, then maybe you can tempt people to give it to you. That's where phishing comes in.

It would be great if this was an exhaustive list, but the truth is that the goal posts are forever moving. Just when one exploit is resolved, another opens up.

Sometimes the target actually gets wiser. For example, not many people today get caught out by opening an e-mail attachment from someone they don't know, for several reasons:

✔ They know it's a bad thing to do!

✔ Technology such as anti-spam and anti-virus scanners remove it before the user gets a chance to click on it.

✔ E-mail is no longer the only way people communicate over the Internet.

However, viruses are still a problem as they infect new media. Criminals now send them through instant-message applications, deliver them through Web browsers, and tack them on when unsuspecting users visit spoofed (faked) versions of trusted Web sites. In effect, the outcome is the same: Your system can still get infected — and if that happens, your data is at risk.

The evolution of a script-kiddie to a cyber-criminal

Many hackers of yesteryear were spotty-faced geeks (although we used to call them nerds back then) — teenagers who wanted to prove they were brighter than the other kids at school, and would hack into systems to prove it. Today that still goes on. Recently a teenager broke into his school computer network to change his grades. This was only noticed when a university sent a letter asking for a reference, and one of the teachers realized that the student in question was not the "A" student that the university thought he was. The student was caught and suitably punished — but that's only a small-scale example of hacking for personal gain.

The business of cyber-crime takes place on a vaster scale — with a lot more sophistication. Budding cyber-criminals can find everything they need on the Internet:

✔ **Phishing applications:** These are for creating e-mail scams that try to trick users into offering valuable personal data to total strangers. You can buy them for $1,000 — and that includes a year of technical support! They're even offered with specialized modular components (to build such nasty tools as phishing e-mails, Trojans, keyloggers, and Web browser downloads); you can put together your own attack from off-the-shelf parts.

✔ **E-mail-database lists:** Essentially collections of stolen data. Once again, these are easy to acquire for only a few dollars per thousand names.

✔ **Botnets:** You need somewhere to run your scam from, and the botnet is the easiest — it sneaks into other people's computers and takes them over to carry out its evil tasks. It works them like a phantom spamming network; users notice only a slowdown in their computers, if anything at all. Cost: about $100 per thousand systems per hour.

✔ **Black market:** When you've gathered all the information, you can use it yourself or sell it on the black market (the underground economy).

The development of *malware* (that's what we call up-to-no-good applications such as viruses and spyware) is now a full-fledged business. It's no longer an individual with something to prove; it's a gang operating much like a big corporation, with all the usual business groups:

- ✔ **Research and development:** Looking at the latest vulnerabilities and developing applications that exploit them.

- ✔ **Marketing and sales:** People selling the malware to anyone who wants to buy it — often explaining why their *solution* is better than the competition. (That's right, there are various gangs of baddies out there, and they're competing with each other.)

- ✔ **Support:** If you've invested in this product, the criminals want you to be successful, that way you'll buy again . . . and again . . . and again. So they set up support organizations to help you out!

Inside the mind of a data thief

What drives a data thief? *Money.* That's all there is to it. However we need to delve a little deeper to combat the problem of data loss.

While money is foremost on the mind of a data thief, we can figure out some other character traits from what the bad guy does:

- ✔ **Cunning:** "How can I beat the system?"

- ✔ **Devious:** "If I send this e-mail, with this information, and make it look legit, they might send me their bank-account details."

- ✔ **Patient:** "If I send one e-mail containing this information, followed a couple of weeks later with this, then they might visit my Web site . . .

    . . . and then they might download my virus."

- ✔ **Thoughtless:** "What I do hurts you? Like I care." Someone who's out to trick you into giving away your valuable data really doesn't have your best interests at heart. But you knew that.

- ✔ **Sneaky:** "Anything goes." Whether it's a big sporting event or a large charity appeal, it looks like an opportunity to the data thief.

- ✔ **Underhanded:** "Okay, who do I get to be this time?" If they can get a name and telephone number inside a corporation, then phoning up and impersonating someone else is well within their criminal repertoire.

For the data thief, the idea is to find an idea that works, exploit it till people catch on, and then find a new way to steal data and exploit *that* one till it stops working. For companies trying to defeat the cyber-criminal, it's always a race against time (see Figure 7-2).

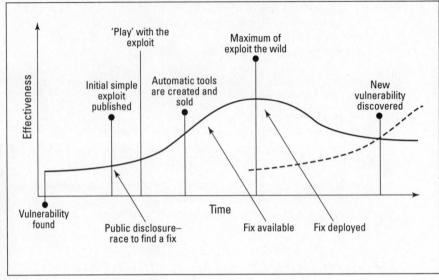

Figure 7-2:
It's all about
finding the
next exploit
before the
first one
runs dry.

The Basics of IT Security Threats

It used to be that IT security threats were handled by a few in-house special-ists. They would maintain the corporate security (basically a firewall around the company) and prevent the bad people from getting in.

Today, IT security is something we all must be aware of. While companies don't expect everyone to be an IT security expert, they do expect their employees to be aware of the threats — and (more often than not) to have policies in place (which people are supposed to read) that they believe will help secure the company. Of course, the threats evolve more quickly than the policies change (and they change much faster than people read them), so IT security isn't all it's cracked up to be.

When a new IT security threat appears, send out an e-mail. If you have an online, computer-based training scheme, create regular mandatory training courses for employees to attend.

How anti-threat technology has evolved

As the threats have evolved from the simple virus to the browser exploit, so too has the technology to prevent them. This is good news — all is not lost! As we can see from Figure 7-3, as the threats have evolved, so too has the technology to combat them.

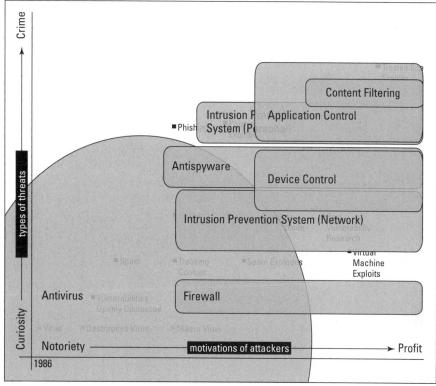

Figure 7-3:
Technology
to beat the
cyber-
criminal —
targeting
the specific
threats.

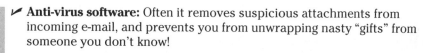

As viruses rose in prominence, so did anti-virus software. The most popular
IT security applications are

- ✔ **Anti-virus software:** Often it removes suspicious attachments from
  incoming e-mail, and prevents you from unwrapping nasty "gifts" from
  someone you don't know!

  Anti-virus software only works if you keep the definitions for viruses up
  to date.

- ✔ **Firewall applications:** This countermeasure started off as a barrier
  between the network and the Internet, designed to keep the bad guys
  out. It was (at one time) thought to be adequate for corporate IT security; all the IT equipment was on-site and therefore could be protected
  behind the corporate firewall at the gateway to the Internet.

- ✔ **Personal firewall:** Okay, so it turns out that laptops and other mobile
  devices arrived on the scene (not to mention the growth of home computing), so a personal firewall was required — still to keep the bad guys out.

- **Intrusion detection and intrusion prevention:** This can be software or hardware; basically it's the capability to scan the network for suspicious behavior. If the system sees something untoward — could be malware, could be an attack — then it shuts it out. This can be run on local machines or on servers or gateways. Pretty flexible, eh?

- **Vulnerability scanner:** Does what it says on the box: It scans your system for vulnerabilities. What it finds could be simple stuff (like not having the right patches) or it could poke around for more complex flaws (say, by testing the strength of passwords).

- **Content filtering:** Now we're talking. This is some of the coolest technology around and is designed to prevent data leaks and data loss. The idea is simple: The system looks at the content and decides whether it is sensitive or confidential and can then protect it accordingly.

  For example, if you try to send unencrypted credit-card information outside the organization, it could warn you and prevent that from happening. If you have a list of employees and their bank details on your screen, the system would spot it and prevent you from copying it onto a USB memory stick unless it was encrypted first.

- **Device control:** More cool stuff. This technology uses rules to check to see whether hardware can be attached to a computer or a network (think USB device). If a device can be used to transfer data, the rule won't allow it to be used.

- **Network Access Control:** This is one of the coolest, most sophisticated capabilities out there. Basically, it checks devices that attach to a network, and validates them if they're compliant with policy. It can then grant access to other resources. What you can access depends on who you are and what rights you've been assigned.

- **Access control:** Authentication with usernames and passwords — followed by authorization as to what you can and can't do.

Okay, so all this seems like a lot — and it is. That's why expertise in IT security takes lots of books and years of training to develop. But if you know the basics of the technologies out there (that's what you've just been reading about) and what they can offer you — coupled with some savvy about what cyber-criminals are trying to do and how — then you stand a good chance of beating the bad guys. If you're still struggling to understand it all, then ask at least you know some good words to use as starting points when you ask an expert.

Even if you think you already know everything, IT security is a moving target. It pays to continue to read about this stuff in your spare time and to stay up with the trends! The landscape changes, sometimes subtly — say, a new nuance added to a virus — and sometimes, like a volcano explosion, a whole new genre of threats appears — and a whole new technology appears to combat them.

Information is the cyber-criminal's priority

Today's cyber-criminal wants *data* — the raw material of useful information. There is a subtle difference between data and information: you can have a lot of data but only a little bit of information.

For example, if you were looking for oil, then there would be huge amounts of geographical survey data and the key information would be where exactly to pinpoint the best place to drill for oil. So terabytes (1,000,000,000,000 bytes) of data could be reduced to a simple longitude and latitude — eight bytes of *information*.

Cyber-criminals are really after information, but to get that (and to be sure they've got it), they need to get hold of a *lot* of data. Picking one person's bank-account details (for example) could be interesting if that account had a million dollars in it. On the other hand, all the cyber-criminal finds might be an overdraft and a bad credit record (no point even applying for a credit card!). Of course, if the thief steals ten *thousand* accounts, odds go up that several could prove lucrative.

To the cyber-criminal, all information is valuable. It might be easier to sell bank-account details, or a credit-card number, but even the details from customer loyalty-card schemes can be useful — you can readily use them to target individuals in a phishing attack. After all, if someone sent you an e-mail that appeared to be from your local supermarket, offering *$10 credit and cash back from every bill* if you register your bank-account details, what would you notice most about the offer?

Chapter 8

Protecting the Endpoint

*W*hen you're looking at the data-leak problem (or any problem, for that matter), there comes a time when you must make a start. Being faced with a blank sheet of paper is the toughest part for any writer; it's the same when you're looking at preventing data leaks. The task ahead seems immense, there doesn't appear to be a good place to begin, and (more to the point) there doesn't seem to be an end in sight.

With that in mind, here's the start: the endpoint.

Why the Endpoint Is a Risk

The *endpoint* is basically the desktop, the laptop, or other end-user device; these days it could easily be the mobile phone or PDA/Smart Phone.

The potential problem here is inadvertent loss of these devices, especially the easily portable ones (as Figure 8-1 illustrates).

The server is not commonly an endpoint because the user isn't sitting in front of it all day (as is the case with laptops, desktops, and mobile devices). Servers tend to live in the data center, and are subject to their own risks (as Chapter 14 describes). The endpoint has the most risk because it's where the user is.

Although people are your greatest assets, they're also the biggest weakness — not because they want to make a mess of things (usually), but because information about data loss isn't shared with them nearly often enough — and that goes for both large and small organizations.

Figure 8-1:
What have
you found
in your
taxi today?

Starting your security measures at the endpoint has a couple of benefits:

- ✓ **You can start simple and build up.** You don't have to do everything at once to make a difference.

- ✓ **It doesn't have to be expensive.** That's good news when the economy is in the doghouse and the bean counters (accountants) are squeezing you for every last cent.

Threats against the user and the endpoint

Cyber-criminals know that end-users are the weakest link — and that makes an endpoint a great place to attack. But the bad guys don't confine the threat to technology; they also know about people and how to get at them — and when their attacks manipulate people at least as much as machines, it's called *social engineering* (for more about this devious gambit, see Chapter 21). Often the idea behind targeting the user is to get a piece of malware (such as viruses, Trojans, and spyware) into your network by way of an endpoint.

One of the first widespread computer viruses was sent as an attachment to e-mail ("iloveyou" a.k.a. "lovebug" a.k.a. "vbs/loveletter") and invited the user to click it. Of course, people did — even though they didn't know the sender. That's social engineering for you: The bad guys appeal to someone's inquisitive nature to get them to do what they want, or ask the unsuspecting recipient to follow a process that's made to look official (or decorated with a logo from a recognized organization).

Another aspect of the endpoint that is unique to the end-user is that end-users type. (Most servers in data centers don't even *have* keyboards.) In fact, the endpoints' keyboards are often targeted: The idea is to introduce *keylogging* malware that logs all the keystrokes that end-users make so the bad guys can get hold of usernames, passwords, and (finally) unauthorized access. Of course, users also do a lot of boring stuff (from the perspective of the cyber-criminal), but eventually they log on to password-protected systems, type in confidential usernames, and (as a bonus) might do a little home banking online — all valuable information for the cyber-criminal to resell or use.

If you aren't in *complete* control of the system you're using (anyone else can use it or has access to it), don't use it for home banking. The same is true for systems in Internet cafés! At most Internet cafés, you're unaware of who has control of the system, so checking your bank balance while you're there isn't smart.

Wayward laptops

Despite their convenience, laptops are the classic example of a portable device at risk — especially when they also serve as endpoints for a corporate network. Although people lose laptops, they're also really easy for someone to walk off with when the user isn't looking. They're small, light, common-place, and simple to hide (one looks much like another); people forget about them with the smallest distraction. If it seems unreasonable to urge vigilance toward something so common, consider what it's carrying — and the possible consequences of having your data (and your organization's data) walk away.

One military official left his laptop under his seat at a fast-food restaurant, went to collect his order, and the machine was gone when he got back.

How many times do you hear about laptops being left in cars, the car being broken into, and the laptop being stolen? For that matter, if thieves break into a house, laptops are among the most popular items to snag. In these cases, the criminals aren't (usually) after the data, just a hunk of electronics they can get $100 for at the local bar. If that's all they're after, count yourself lucky.

The physical security of IT assets remains an issue; staff need to be made aware of the risks and consequences. The organization needs to have an appropriate physical security policy that spells out what to do (and what not to do) with laptops. Here are some starters:

- ✔ When left in a car, the laptop should be out of sight in the trunk.

- ✔ While traveling, the laptop should be with the person at all times (including in the restroom).

It isn't acceptable to leave a laptop unattended in a public place. Think of standard airport-security policy — no unattended bags. The same should be true for laptops and mobile devices.

✔ While in the office, or visiting another company's offices, the laptop should be secured with a cable.

✔ At home, the laptop should be either secured with a cable or (preferably) stored out of sight.

Dealing with Lost Laptops

About five percent of corporate laptops are lost each year. This causes heartache, stress, and indigestion for those you'd expect to get upset:

✔ **The individual user**: You know— the one who lost it.

✔ **The IT department:** They have to get a new laptop to the individual as quickly as possible. They also have to think about what systems and applications the user had access to. Should all the usernames and passwords be reset? What about remote dial-in capabilities? Just how much access can you have from one small laptop?

These days data-loss and data-breach legislation brings even more people into the act:

✔ **The legal department:** They have to answer a scary question: *Do we have a full-scale data breach that we need to respond to?*

✔ **The marketing department:** If this is a data-breach incident, they have to consider what steps they need to take for damage limitation. What the competition could do with that data, and how that would that affect their campaigns? If they don't have a plan, they'll need to create one. Now.

✔ **The CEO and the rest of the senior management:** They could well end up in local or national media, responding to the incident and trying to reassure customers that all is well.

In days of yore, it wasn't a *crime* to lose a laptop. Now it might as well be; the ramifications are huge.

Have laptop, will travel

Laptops allow *road warriors* (users with laptops) to take almost *the whole office* with them. Ubiquitous network connection means they can get to the corporate network rapidly, no matter where they are in the world. Because the corporate network is also available 24/7, they can work anytime, anywhere. Unfortunately, that also means cyber-criminals have the same opportunity.

The other problem with the traveling laptop is that, well, it's *traveling*. The desktops and servers for an organization have some physical security in the office, but laptops don't. So laptops need special security treatment.

Strategies for protecting laptops

If you don't have any important or sensitive information on the laptop, you won't need to protect it quite so stringently. The big problem is that most organizations don't know what's *on* their laptops — and that "what" is changing constantly. The information could be

- Downloaded from corporate servers
- Downloaded from the Web
- Copied from other documents
- Copied from and to CD-ROMs and USB storage
- Received and sent via e-mail (both corporate and Web-based)
- Received from other applications (usually through reports)

If you don't know what you've lost, then any data-loss solution has to be able to deal with *any possible* data loss.

The most likely scenario (and the one that get you on to the front page of the news) is losing the machine or having it stolen. Fortunately, there is a simple solution to this: encryption.

Endpoint-Encryption Technologies

Encryption — essentially, scrambling the data so it can only be read if the recipient has the means to decipher it — is seen as the answer to most data-loss incidents. The reason is simple: If the data is encrypted, then in most cases, you don't have to disclose the fact that you lost the information. If the thief has no way to decrypt the goods, he's out of luck.

If your data is encrypted, but the user has written the password on a yellow sticky note and slapped it on the machine, then you've got trouble. Although you may not be legally required to disclose the loss, the data is still just as vulnerable (and the organization is just as exposed to risk) as if it hadn't been encrypted at all! Figure 8-2 shows an obvious example; most instances aren't that obvious.

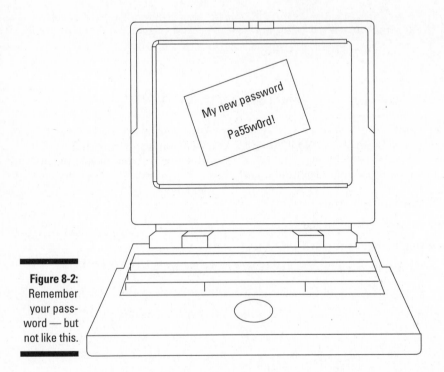

Figure 8-2:
Remember
your pass-
word — but
not like this.

We recommend considering the following general encryption options and modifying them to fit your organization's needs.

Full-disk encryption

The whole disk is encrypted — so all the data is encrypted and therefore safe. This is pretty simple. Good news.

This approach isn't just for laptops and desktops; it can also be used on mobile devices and PDAs.

Why isn't full-disk encryption *standard*? There are two basic reasons, to which (fortunately) solutions are currently available:

✓ **Manageability:** Traditionally, full-disk encryption was managed by the individual. When users forgot their passwords, that was the end of their data; the IT department didn't have any control.

Modern solutions offer centralized control by the IT department. If you forget your password, they can still get you back up and running.

✔ **Performance:** Encryption slows the system down.

Most endpoints now have a surplus of processing power (the CPUs get faster but we can't type any quicker!) so most users won't notice it.

File-based encryption

If you aren't a road warrior, and are sitting behind the company firewall then full-disk encryption is probably a little too heavy-duty for your needs. However, there may be specific information that you want protected by encryption. Perhaps it's the financial records for the quarter, or maybe an exclusive party invitation. Either way ,you want encryption — in which case, *file-based encryption* is for you: You can encrypt individual files or whole directory trees.

This method offers more flexibility than full-disk encryption; you can have different passwords for different files. Of course, that means there's more to remember, but at least everything isn't available with a single encryption key (password)!

If you let individuals encrypt files themselves — and you have no control over the encryption key they use — you can end up in further trouble. If the data is subpoenaed either directly or from an archive and you can't get at it, then you can be fined — for not being able to give access to it. It may not be pertinent to the case in point but that doesn't matter. If it's encrypted and you don't have the key you are at fault.

Why would you want to have your intellectual-property password encrypted by an employee who (potentially) may have left the company? Probably not smart. Employees create intellectual property for the company, not for themselves.

Enterprise digital rights management (eDRM)

If you don't' want to go down the file-based route but still have the need for encrypted documents then perhaps *enterprise digital rights management* (eDRM) is for you. Frequently you can integrate eDRM products fully into office applications such as word processors and spreadsheets — and you (as the user) can encrypt the document with one of the pre-determined encryption policies. The document can then be freely transferred, in the sure knowledge that unless the recipients have access to the appropriate *certificate* (encryption-key policy), they can't read it. The good news is that as a company, you can set up various policies to specify who has access and who doesn't; in real-world scenarios, no more than 10 such policies are usually needed (we aren't talking about hundreds). They can include external parties such as customers, partners, and suppliers; you can send them the information and provide them with certificates to open the document.

While the primary function of eDRM is to encrypt documents and manage them, these solutions can offer even greater control than just opening an encrypted document — all with the goal of preventing data leaks. Your encryption policies can also allow or deny individuals the right to edit or print the document, or even screen-capture it.

The certificates are handled transparently and are *cached* (held in memory). Even if you're on a plane, you can still open the document because the cached certificate is still available. The certificates are automatically renewed until such time as they're specifically revoked. Depending on the implementation, you can revoke access on a particular document, either to change who's allowed to see it or to ensure that a later copy is used.

There are two big hang-ups with eDRM:

- ✔ **Management.** How do you use it consistently, regardless of your organization's size? Fortunately, current solutions are scalable and easy to use.

- ✔ **Users are still in control.** What users think is important (or what they don't think is important) may not match the company's perspective. If that happens, documents that should be protected aren't, and vice versa.

There is a general movement in business toward eDRM; in ten years, all documents may be encrypted with eDRM just to prevent data loss. In the near term, eDRM technology will be used in combination with content-based analysis, which applies the appropriate policy automatically so the user need not worry about it. The breakthrough will come when technology is better at identifying (a) contextual changes in a document and (b) how those changes relate to intellectual property or to personal identifiable information.

eDRM doesn't prevent a malicious insider from taking a picture of the physical screen. Don't laugh; it's been done; an enterprising *insider* set up a screen on a photocopier to steal the information. This is much easier today with a flat-panel screen than it was in the days of the old CRT monitors (an ungainly but effective setup, as shown in Figure 8-3).

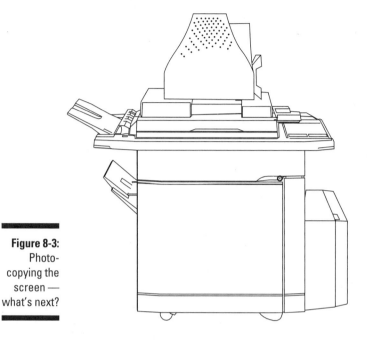

Figure 8-3:
Photo-
copying the
screen —
what's next?

So many options . . . so little time

In essence, the choice is yours. For laptops, full-disk encryption is probably the simplest and easiest approach to implement. The centralized control offered by today's networking solutions can overcome the biggest problem: users who lose their passwords.

If you're looking to implement something a little wider-reaching and include third parties, then eDRM is a great choice — flexibility and scalability, coupled with protection of your data — no matter where it is.

Here be dragons

Encryption algorithms today are practically unbreakable — but you have to use a modern one. Picking up something for free from the Web is readily possible, and a number of great Open Source solutions exist. Just make sure that the program you choose has a strong encryption algorithm at the heart of it. If it talks about AES (Advanced Encryption Standard — much better than its predecessor DES, the Data Encryption Standard) — or SHA-512 (and greater) — your data will be well protected cryptographically.

There has been some research carried out into breaking full-disk encryption. Although this is a very high-level technical hack, researchers have done it by physically reading the memory in the machine. That means it's at least a potential threat. Fortunately, there is also a simple solution: Turn off the laptop when you've finished with it. Don't just put it into *sleep* or *suspend* mode; power it down. Although the laptop will take longer to boot up, it will stay secure from this threat.

Preventing Keyloggers and Rootkits

Perhaps the two nastiest infections your computer can have are keyloggers and rootkits. Both are designed to be undetectable; they can lurk on a machine for months and the user may never notice their presence.

In one instance, cleaners were bribed to put USB sticks with keylogger software onto systems they encountered at a financial institution. They would then periodically replace them with new ones, while the criminals could look through the information at their leisure. No data was transferred across the network, which made the exploit tough to spot. Of course, the authorized users didn't notice the USB sticks poking out of their systems, because the machines were under their desks. (Well — how often do *you* check?)

Defeating the keylogger

Keylogger software is tough to fight because some legitimate keylogging applications do exist (although the vast majority aren't legitimate, nor are they used for legitimate purposes).

Legally (depends on your point of view), keylogging can be used to track what people do with the Internet (which is still *spying,* in our view) and for support purposes. As a support tool, a keylogger gives the help desk a way to check the input into your machine when you call to sort out a technical problem.

Why do cyber-criminals use keyloggers? That's how they get hold of usernames, passwords, bank-account details and other information, anything useful that a user types in. They can also collect other information at the same time, such as a history of Web pages visited. By *zippering* all these tidbits together, they have enough information to do some real damage.

Chapter 5 has more information on the fine felonius art of zippering.

There are some simple ways to defeat the keylogger:

✔ **Anti-virus/anti-malware software:** Keyloggers are just another piece of malware, so keeping your endpoint-security software up to date is essential.

You might want to exercise extra care when you're surfing the Web; a lot of malware comes aboard as a result of visiting insecure Web sites.

✔ **Firewall:** Although a firewall won't stop the keylogger from being installed, it will prevent data from being *transferred* from the computer. Additionally, it can detect such unauthorized transfers and alert you to the presence of the keylogger.

✔ **Cut-and-paste and automatic form-filler applications:** Keyloggers work by detecting and recording the key that was pressed. If you don't press a key, then the keylogger won't record anything! So, from a security perspective, using cut and paste to copy usernames and passwords from a file is a good idea.

If you have a file of your usernames and passwords on your computer, be sure it's *well secured*. One good way: Have it encrypted.

✔ **On-screen keyboard:** You can also get an application that puts a virtual keyboard on the screen, much like the one you get on mobile phones and PDAs. Then you click the virtual keys with the mouse pointer to enter the information — once again; there's no key press, so the keylogger doesn't record anything! If you suspect the presence of a keylogger, you can use this method to enter the initial username and password when you log on, and then use cut and paste.

✔ **Speech recognition:** Okay, so we're now entering into the realms of (probable) overkill, but it can be done. Of course, the password used will probably be fairly weak — due to the limited number of words recognized — unless you spell it all out. And if you sit there spelling it out ("Capital *P, a, s, s, w,* zero, *r, d* . . ."), everyone else will hear it.

✔ **Type elsewhere — at the same time:** This is the cheap method — and the easiest to forget. The idea is simple: The cyber-criminal will analyze the keylog data and pick out runs of characters that are useful. So . . . if you type one character and then move to a different window (say, an open Notepad window) and type more characters, and then back to the password window to do another character, back to the decoy window to input more gobbledygook, and so on, then the cyber-criminal can't easily figure out *which* logged characters go together to make a meaningful username, password, or account number.

Hardware keyloggers are difficult to detect unless you physically see them. The most common keyloggers fit between the keyboard and the system; they look like connection extensions. But these are only useful if the attacker has physical access to the machine. While you might just think this type of attack is the work of a malicious insider, it can also originate with basically anyone who comes into your building, including

- **Cleaners:** Or people who look like them. People usually don't ask.

- **Repair personnel:** Or people who look like them. Ditto.

- **Consultants or contractors:** Among these may be people who use the machine legitimately but leave something behind that you hadn't bargained for.

The best defense against keylogging software is not to get infected to begin with!

Defeating the rootkit

Rootkits give the underlying malware *root access* (called *Administrator access* in Windows), which makes its senders all-powerful on your computer. Then they can get your machine to can do anything they want and no one else will know about it. The tough part is that rootkits hide from the real administrator by subverting the OS into obscuring their presence and failing to report it. This happens in a number of ways:

- Concealing processes from the process monitor application.

- Evading anti-malware and other security applications.

- Hiding application files from the OS.

- Cloaking data from the OS.

When it's installed, a rootkit is hard to get rid of. It often installs an additional *backdoor* (a secret access port) through which other applications can be installed so the system can be used as a *bot* (essentially a "zombie" computer that can send out spam and viruses without your knowing).

The best form of defense against rootkits is attack. Most anti-virus applications have rootkit detection. Keeping your virus definitions up to date will prevent a rootkit from being installed. If one has been installed and detected then the system needs to be rebooted from somewhere *other* than the main boot disk (for example, a CD-ROM or USB drive) and then the system can be cleaned. If the rootkit isn't running, then it can't hide! For the details of rootkits and their devious ways, take a look at *Rootkits For Dummies* by Larry Stevenson and Nancy Altholz (Wiley Publishing).

Changing to a different OS doesn't remove the threat! Rootkits, keyloggers, and other malware have been written and deployed against all endpoint operating systems, including Microsoft Windows, Linux, Macintosh OS-X, and Symbian (a mobile-device OS).

It's a war out there

Rootkits, keyloggers, viruses, Trojans, phishing, and all the other varieties of attack are continually changing as the battle for the endpoint continues. As one mechanism is defeated by security vendors, another emerges or a variant appears. The goal is control of the system and the data on it. If cybercriminals get a foothold on the endpoint, they can then look at how to attack the entire corporate network, using the endpoint as the jumping-off point.

Connecting Securely to the Corporate Network

The opportunities for laptops and mobile devices to connect to the network have never been greater — and the bandwidth at which they can connect is also increasing. Why should you care? There are new opportunities for road warriors (RWs), those mobile end-users who work the road, hopping from train to plane to automobile, in a different city every other day, frequently needing to *synchronize* — to exchange data with the corporate network to update both the network's and the laptop's data.

It used to be that road warriors needed laptops stuffed with information — their offices-on-the-road fully equipped with the data required for any eventuality — and that was that. These days ubiquitous connection and high network speeds mean faster access to corporate networks. So how to keep the data safe coming and going? Three possible solutions: virtual private networks (VPNs), thin-client technology, and some virtualization of the client. Details coming right up.

Virtual private networks (VPNs)

Virtual private networks (VPNs) have been around for a while; the idea is that an individual out on the road with a laptop (our road warrior) can use a VPN to connect securely to the corporate network — whether sitting in a local coffee shops or at home — by creating a secure "tunnel" through the Internet to the company. All data that travels to and fro is encrypted, and so secured from prying eyes. In effect, a secure piece of the (normally insecure) Internet becomes the practical equivalent of a private network, minus the infrastructure expense.

VPNs are available as Open Source applications, so they don't cost a lot of money to install. For details, hunt up a copy of *Virtual Private Networks For Dummies* by Mark Merkow (Wiley Publishing).

Thin-client solutions

If you have plenty of connectivity and the bandwidth, then why keep data on the laptop (or any endpoint) at all? Many people have laptops so they can work at home. If they have broadband connectivity, do they need to have all the data at home too? In most casers, of course not — and that's where *thin-client solutions* come in.

You could argue that thin clients were around even at the dawn of computing (basically dumb terminals wired to mainframes in data centers), but early dumb terminals were only the ancestors of thin clients. After all the changes in the computing revolution — in particular, standalone PCs, Open Source systems, and client-server networking — those "dumb" terminals have morphed into much more advanced computing devices and interfaces than they were before. They provide a rich user experience, and seem exactly the same as if the user were running the application locally.

From a data-loss perspective, the great news is that the thin-client means *no local data.* If you have no data, you can't lose it! You have access to all the information you need (and probably more), but it's all held in the data center, safe from being lost.

A thin-client solution doesn't mean you're *automatically* safe from data loss. While the loss of the machine won't result in data being lost from that machine, the machine is now a portal into the data center. If the cyber-criminal can get into a local system and connect it to the Internet, then they can also connect through to the data center and steal your information that way. Protecting your password on a thin-client system is even more important than protecting it on a *normal* device. Thin-client computing effectively provides the baddies with a single point of access to the entire corporate network; although it makes security management easier, it also makes security more important.

Virtualizing the client

The thin-client solution can be seen as one way of virtualizing the client, but it really only applies to managing the computers (such as laptops and desktops) owned by the organization. Real *virtualization* means adding a layer of abstraction — efficient simulations of standalone systems — to simplify administration (or increase use) of a system or device. The applications running inside the virtualized environment are unaware that they're actually running in a virtual world. They behave the same as normally, caring not what goes on underneath them.

In today's environment, however, many people want to work from home. In this scenario, the company either needs to buy each employee a separate system (such as a laptop), or look at virtualization. Virtual machines are, in effect, a complete logical computer but wrapped up in a virtual container. They're being used to great effect within organizations to improve server utilization, and have now moved from just being development and test to production environments. The great thing about them is that they are

- ✔ **Standard:** Everyone gets the same copy of the system.
- ✔ **Easy to deploy:** It just looks like a file (a big file but a file nonetheless) and so can be copied around very easily.
- ✔ **Easy to update:** You just update the image and the next time a user accesses it, it's the new version not the old one.
- ✔ **Fully contained:** They can contain applications and data as well as the OS, patches and the security stack.

For the individual at home who's looking to check e-mail or run a few corporate applications, the virtual machine is ideal. You download it to your home system and fire it up. It's self-contained; it has all the necessary security and applications to connect to the corporate network. Usernames and passwords are still used (so if someone runs off with a copy of the virtual machine, it won't be much use to them). Bottom line: The individual can work securely from home.

In the same way that the thin client removes the possibility of losing data, so too does the virtual machine. Polices can be set so data can't be saved locally (and so can't be lost).

Finally, both thin-client and virtualized client solutions save management costs. Very likely the legal department will be happy with either of these solutions(no data loss), and so will accounting (cheaper to manage).

Which one for me?

Once more the choice is yours, but so is the headache. Probably the toughest objection to overcome is this one: "But that isn't fair — I can't do my job if you do that!" You may get that refrain from the old stalwarts. There is a need for education here. The introduction of new technologies or practices should *improve* the working environment, not make it worse.

You probably need to identify different categories of people and then you can tailor the solution to each of them. Here are three examples:

- ✔ **The home worker with a corporate laptop:** A VPN-plus-thin-client solution would work well here.

- ✔ **The (occasional) home worker without a corporate laptop:** A VPN-and-virtual-machine client solution that they can run on their own hardware should be considered first.

- ✔ **The truly mobile worker:** Our road warrior will probably still need a laptop, but why not streamline it with just a VPN connection back to the network? Make sure that the laptop is suitably protected with encryption, anti-virus, and all the rest because it will contain sensitive information that you don't want lost!

Products to Protect the Endpoint

Threats are forever changing and so are the products needed to protect against them.

Although all these products are available separately, many are available as combined products. For example, you can get anti-virus, anti-spam, anti-phishing, and a personal firewall all in a single package. For other capabilities, such as encryption, it's best to decide on a corporate standard before you buy.

The top 10 products (plus 1) to protect the endpoint are

- ✔ **Anti-virus:** It's as old as the hills but it still has an important role to play in protecting the users and their data. Some of the latest products include technology that looks at the way that applications interact with the Internet (a behavior-based approach), which offers protection from *unheard-of* viruses.

✔ **Anti-spam:** Many viruses are delivered through e-mail and the like. That's spam. Removing the spam before the user (or the endpoint) even sees it reduces the opportunity for infection.

✔ **Anti-phishing:** Much like spam in so many ways, phishing e-mails go one step farther: pointing users to Web sites and other Web-based malware. A simple anti-phishing filter will protect the user (and the endpoint) from the *bad* Web sites that they may be tempted, induced, or tricked into visiting.

✔ **Personal firewall with intrusion detection and prevention:** Users who are out and about and not inside the corporate firewall need to have a personal equivalent of industrial-strength protection. This is it.

✔ **Full-disk encryption:** It's simple to use and manage; if the laptop is lost, then you don't have to worry that someone can get at the data on it.

✔ **File-based encryption:** If you have full-disk encryption, then you might still want this additional protection on particular files. While this is relatively simple to do, if there are a lot of people who need this, then enterprise-wide digital rights management (the next item in this list) might be a better solution, especially if the data must be sent to third parties.

✔ **Enterprise digital rights management:** eDRM is a great way to protect sensitive information, even if it's in a document that's been copied onto a USB stick. Unless the recipient has the right key to open the document, the information will be safe from prying eyes.

✔ **USB and removable-media filtering and blocking:** This will ensure that sensitive information can't be copied onto se device and so can't be shared.

✔ **Network Access Control:** This technology is aimed primarily at protecting your network from *other* people's laptops. It also ensures that your own laptop computers are up to date with the latest patches for the operating system and applications, as well as the latest anti-malware definitions.

✔ **Content-based filtering:** This capability looks at the content of the data and applies protection policies accordingly. For example, e-mail containing sensitive information can be blocked from being sent, or uploaded to the Web. Instant messages with confidential information can also be blocked, including those with Web URLs.

✔ **Audit tool:** This isn't really concerned with protecting the endpoint as such — but it does help the IT department prove that they're doing what they say. If a laptop is lost, they can prove that the data was encrypted — and that's a big deal!

These tools, among others, can reduce the threats that can propagate internally; rogue or unacceptable devices can't gain access to the network without being approved, made safe, or both. Systems found to deviate from the defined controls can be fixed automatically and then allowed access, to ensure both the security of the environment and a transparent, rapid way to let end-users on the system get on with their work.

You can set up network-access control systems to continually monitor systems that are already accessing the environment. Then, should a major incident happen, the system can take immediate action to mitigate threats — by removing dangerous systems from the network or by enforcing a new control to ensure that the system becomes safe.

Chapter 9

USB Devices and Removable Media

*N*ever before have organizations and individuals been faced with the mobile dilemma as that they face in today's fast-moving, critical, and complex mobile environment. An organization's success revolves around information technology, whether directly or indirectly related to business process, revenue stream, or service delivery. Its survival is now entirely dependent on its own business data information — and on keeping it secure.

To remain competitive, organizations must operate on a scale to dominate their business sector, create new, leading-edge products and services, and find new and innovative routes to market. All those requirements depend on (and generate) information. Organizations must also be flexible to ride a shift in business climate, adapt to a competitive threat, or embrace new technologies and then exploit them to remain ahead of the closest competition. This flexibility is indicative of today's mobile community — which constantly generates valuable information that the competition would *love* to know.

And, this problem isn't confined to businesses. Individuals also must be mindful of what they pass on to third parties. The danger of data loss to both businesses and individuals remains one of the most poignant issues in today's global community.

One of the most significant business issues is data — the raw ingredient of information — and the means to act upon it, protect it, and ensure its security. Managing information is much more than simply putting another storage device on another server and making sure it's protected from viruses. IT is more of an infrastructure than a by-product of the business; organizations need to think carefully about how to protect it, access and share data, ensure IT availability to current and future applications, and protect against malicious threats. The goal is a robust, manageable, resilient infrastructure that really adds value to the business. And yes, it *is* possible.

Mobile working, business travel, and 24/7 operations all add to the complexity of managing and securing the end-point across the enterprise. To make that happen, companies have to undertake several big jobs:

✔ Evaluate their assets and security systems.

✔ Assess current procedures against risks.

✔ Set goals and policies for desired levels of availability and security.

✔ Identify and analyze threats — and create a plan to meet them.

The idea is not just to react, but to stay one step ahead of potential threats. Organizations that treat "proactive" as more than a buzzword can protect assets and recover from disruptions more quickly than those that don't. Here's what the more successful ones do:

✔ **Manage threats proactively and quickly.** Real-time management of security information enables IT administrators to identify, prioritize, and resolve critical security incidents — proactively. There is some pretty good technology out there that will provide dynamic correlation of security events.

✔ **Implement long-term solutions for vulnerabilities.** A good example would be host-based technology which secures against day-zero attacks, and helps maintain compliance by enforcing behavior-based security policies on clients and servers. Host-based intrusion protection stops malicious exploitation of system resources and prevents the introduction and spread of malicious code.

✔ **Regularly update data-security policies, along with the needed standards for certification and compliance.** Businesses change all the time so IT policies should do so as well. All organizations should implement, measure, and maintain security compliance with configuration standards across multiple platforms. There is some great technology that can map IT policies against security standards providing reports about where an organization does, or does not, comply.

These measures all seek to monitor IT security, keep on top of information management, and maintain a clear view of the storage system's infrastructure. Doing so gives an organization its best chance at a rapid response to any disruption.

Individuals and enterprises rely on global distribution and storage of information to govern nations, conduct business transactions, and make personal decisions. Yet it's increasingly at risk from cyber-threats, natural disasters, user errors, and system failures. Understanding and managing that risk, whether it's protecting personal information on a PC or building a global IT infrastructure that's both resilient and flexible, helps limit the risk. But another real threat comes from external devices — such as those handy USB drives. We all use them, we all love them, vendors give them away — but too often they also bring the curse of data leakage. It's estimated that half of all USB drives contain confidential information — which means they're creating risk.

Defeating USB Devices

It's a pretty weird place we've arrived at in computer capabilities. Not so long ago we could store a "massive" 1.44 MB on a 3.5-inch floppy disk and hard-drive capacity was routinely measured in mere megabytes. When we were in Cannes last year, a USB vendor showed us a USB memory chip that could hold 50 GB — that's *fifty gigabytes* (yikes) — and no bigger than a thumbnail (bitten). Here's a look at where portable data storage is going — maybe out the company door, under someone's arm or in a shirt pocket. What to do about it?

Here comes a brave new (portable) world

Things have moved on a tad these days — portable data storage keeps getting smaller and more powerful. Now we're seeing vendors roll out second-generation terabyte hard drives that use power-management techniques specifically developed for mobile hard drives, so they'll be in your laptop before you can say boo! Now, a *terabyte* (TB) is one trillion bytes — that is, a thousand gigabytes. To get a perspective, consider: A 1TB drive will hold as much data as about 700,000 of the old 1.44MB floppies. (Hey, even an iPod Classic can hold as much as 100,000-plus 1.44MB floppies!) Imagine carrying that much sensitive data around. Convenient? Yes, indeed. Risky? You bet — more so all the time.

This is a RAID!

If you don't already know what RAID is, it's a way of keeping safety copies of important data on a *Redundant Array of Independent Disks*. To break down the acronym, *redundant* means "duplicated," *array* means "bunch of," *independent* means "not depending on others," and *disks* means . . . well . . . flat, round things that store data.

RAID systems emphasize *data safety*. RAID data should remain available even if a single piece of hardware fails. (RAID storage also may be cheaper, because multiple small devices using common technology may cost less than a single large device that requires cutting-edge technology.)

So *mirroring* means copying, which is safer. If you lose a disk, you have another — hence the "redundant" in the name. *Striping* makes this operation quicker by using more than one disk to read from and write to — and *parity* is all about making the data more secure (that is, redundant) without having to make a complete copy of it.

There are a bunch of types of RAID:

*0 = Striping — no Redundancy

*1 = Mirroring with Redundancy

*0+1 = Stripe then Mirror

*1+0 = Mirror the Stripe enhanced Redundancy

*5 = Striping with Parity

*5+1 = Striping with Parity and Mirroring

Okay, why does all this matter? Because these major capabilities of a corporate network are now small, fast, and portable.

These new drives consume 43 per cent less power than their predecessors, and use three platters (not five), each holding up to 375 GB of data. This effectively cuts the number of read/write heads from ten to six, which makes for a more compact unit.

Hitachi's Deskstar drive has on-board automatic data encryption based on Advanced Encryption Standard (AES) — which is, apparently, good enough for the U.S. government. So it's probably good enough for most of us. But encryption is only as good as its consistent use.

Imation's Atom Flash Drive is a tiny, removable data-storage medium that uses USB (Universal Serial Bus). It's roughly the size of a paperclip — and from a security standpoint, potentially as irritating as the cartoon paperclip Windows put in its help files a few years ago. You can attach the drive directly to other mobile devices, so it's easy to transfer digital files. (Oops.) You see the problem: You can move any intellectual property you've accidentally stolen to another device — just like that!

Weighing under an ounce, less than 1.5 inches long and half an inch wide, this little monster can store up to 8 GB of data. (That's equivalent to everything one of your authors has created this year for work, including marketing videos!)

At least it has password protection and drive-partitioning capabilities (so you can protect what you've inadvertently walked off with and protect it from disk failure). But consider: It's as cheap as a chip (in effect, it *is* a chip, or series of them). Cyber-criminals can buy these things as easily as you can.

But if a little baby like this can hold all that information so easily, what about its big brothers? Well, for openers, the Western Digital My Book (released in June 2008) now packs a pair of disks in RAID configuration (in a package a little smaller than this book), holding a staggering 2 TB of data. Consider: If you only use one of those two terabytes, you can hold another terabyte. The My Book can *mirror* (make a complete copy of) the data on a 1TB hard drive — whether to guard against data loss with a full backup copy, or (also quite possible) to help someone walk off with an unauthorized copy.

If you copy your content to one of the My Book drives and you're using RAID, then what's written to the first disk is also written to the second disk — to ensure that if one of the two fails, you can still get your information off the other. In effect, you back up your backup. But if you really need that *other* terabyte, you can set it to RAID 0 and use both disks. So if you have a device like this, you have a powerful force for data safety *or* data loss just sitting on your desk at home or in the office — where (if it isn't chained down) it can be picked up by anyone wandering past . . . .

Careless use of portable media

Discs, USB drives, data sticks . . . you've got to love 'em. And they're everywhere. Given away by vendors and resellers the world over, portable media are as common as keychains (some of them *are* on keychains), these little babies can cause mega-havoc. Not only can you lose data, you can also introduce nasty things into your system — all inadvertently.

There is a fabulous story about a firm of do-gooders (also known as security analysts) who created 1,000 CDs emblazoned with FREE in bold red — and then stood at the entrance to a subway, handing them out to the local banking community. All the CDs had on them was a bit of code that sent a message back to the originators, telling them that someone had put the CD into his or her machine. Incredibly, something like 758 unsuspecting workers *did* put those CDs into their machines. They had no idea what was contained on the CD, where it came from, or what it could do to their machines — and if it had been malware, every one of them would have been compromised. The security analysts had shown just how simple it was to *own* corporate machines.

But the reverse situation is just as dangerous, as when removable media such as DVDs or CDs are used for backup and then just languish in office drawers. All manner of intellectual property could be lying around your office without your even knowing it's there. Or when it *isn't* there anymore.

Fortunately, technologies exist that can help stop internal people from doing silly, risky things with your data — *if* they're deployed and used intelligently. If you're an IT manager, system administrator, or other pro charged with data safety, take heart: Stopping people from being unknowingly fooled *is* possible, although it's increasingly difficult to control what those people are using from day to day.

We did come across an organization that wanted to prevent its employees from using USB keys to move their intellectual property around — and did it by putting glue in the USB port. Sealing off the port so it can't be used is simple, effective . . . and completely non-scalable. (Just try doing that to 18,000 laptops or 100,000 desktops.) Anyway, nowadays there are so many other devices and capabilities that use the USB port — many of which *don't* involve copying intellectual property — that disabling USB is a fantastic way to hamper the business (and possibly damage morale in the process). Another way must be found.

It's possible to carry *a whole computer* on a USB stick. In essence, the USB stick can hold the OS and all that's needed for a system; you stick it in the USB port and you can reboot the computer from the USB stick. You can then read the local drive (if it's not encrypted) and all the data that's there. Scary.

So what can be done to reduce the risk of losing data on portable devices? Quite a lot, actually . . . which is why the next section is called . . .

Strategies for Dealing with Removable Media

Before you can figure out your strategy to deal with removable media, there are a few questions you should ask. Do you know . . .

- ✓ Which laptops and desktops contain confidential data?
- ✓ Who is copying confidential data to USB drives or iPods?
- ✓ How to prevent confidential data from leaving endpoints?

There is pretty smart technology that can find confidential data stored on laptops and desktops, prioritizes high-risk endpoints for more protection, and prevents confidential data from being copied to USB devices, burned to CD/DVDs, and downloaded to local drives.

First, you need to find whether there is any confidential data out there. So you need to look on

- ✓ Laptops

✔ Desktops

✔ Workstations

✔ PDAs (Personal Digital Assistants) and *next-generation* mobile phones (which are essentially PDAs with built-in phones, or vice versa)

These potential harbors for data can crop up in many different places:

✔ At remote offices

✔ At home offices

✔ On the road

After you've found what you're storing on your remote devices, you can create an inventory of the intellectual property, or personal information that needs protecting.

The good news is that this discovery can be done, with minimal system impact to the end-user, through high-performance, parallel scanning in the background. In order to keep this impact to a minimum, your organization might be content simply to monitor the data on its PCs instead of enforcing a data-security policy — at least while gathering data. You can enforce the policy later, when you know the impact. You don't want everyone locked out on day one!

There are choices to be made. Some discovery technology is *agentless* — very little performance impact, but no enforcement, or you can use an *agent-based* technology. (An *agent* is a piece of technology that performs some information gathering or processing task in the background.) This tends to be very specific. Some IT professionals get uneasy about having too many agents on endpoint machines. If a technology is *agentless,* it gathers information without the agent, but this approach can be less effective).

The second you install (another) agent on the endpoint, it can have an impact on PC performance. But if someone isn't connected to the corporate network and decides to download your most important piece of data to a remote device, you're unlikely to know about it *unless* you have an agent there — which can then decide to block the copy if that's what the policy says.

We're back to getting a handle on the risks and consequences before we start deploying just *any* old technology in the vague hope that it will help. The answer may simply be to train your employees not to do foolish things and to deploy some technology to monitor and audit data movement in the network.

Most data-discovery technology provides configurations for

✔ Incremental scanning for minimal system impact.

✔ Corporate network push to — and detection of — local machines.

Push technology delivers the required technology (such as operating-system patches or corporate policies) to endpoint machines, actively and automatically.

✔ Easy agent deployment and management.

✔ Scanning of confidential data stored on endpoints (registered or not).

✔ Inventory of data by user, department, or policy.

USB ports — limit or lock down?

What it takes to limit how much data moves to USB ports — or to lock down those ports altogether — will depend on what kind of balance your organization needs between data security and enough functionality to run the business. Here are three basic options:

✔ **Total blocking of data:** You can simply block all movement of data to USB keys with the technological equivalent of sticking glue in the USB slot on the laptop, but this might be to debilitating to the business.

✔ **Selective blocking of data:** It might be that it makes more sense to simply stop certain types of data from being copied to USB keys,

✔ **Selective blocking of data plus pre-authorized devices:** In this scenario, you restrict the type or origination of usable USB keys (register all USB keys and provide scanned, secured USBs to your people). In essence, you can have *company* devices that can be encrypted — and therefore secure.

An engineering-design organization decided that its primary source of intellectual property resided in its CAD design systems. This data was "registered" in order to secure it. Technology was then used, initially to monitor and later to prevent to ensure that sensitive files downloaded to local drives were not moved onto external removable media. This technology is improving by the second and prevents employees from copying confidential data to USB devices or burning it to CD/DVDs thereby removing the risk of data loss.

More policies, more actions

You can do some pretty neat things with the discovery monitoring and enforcement policies:

✔ Use on-screen notifications to alert the end-users if they're just about to break corporate policy.

✔ Enable users to justify their actions — and either change an action or enter a circumstance for the audit trail. (Sometimes users must copy information, but a reminder makes them think about what they're doing.)

✔ If users do something that breaks company policy, notify their managers.

This technology is policy-based, regardless of whether it takes direct action to prevent data movement. Developing the management of data movement requires imagination and consistent enforcement; both can help you build a framework that unifies anti-data-loss policies and makes them effective.

Preventing data loss depends on recognizing sensitive content — and you can take this recognition to a fine level of detail. For example, if someone tries to hide a paragraph of corporate content in a document surrounded by Chapter 1 of *The Lord of the Rings,* then the technology can pick up the operation, label it as a subversive move *while it's happening*, and prevent it. Clever, huh? Of course, such close scrutiny carries its own risks . . . .

If you make your data-loss prevention policy too stringent, you can

✔ Alienate your end-user business workforce.

✔ Make your organization's normal processes so difficult that you prevent, rather than enable, its business.

If you choose to use this technology, introduce it at a sensible pace — and educate your workforce about why it's being done. Over the longer term, the policies can be tightened as needed.

Content-based encryption policies

Technology keeps acquiring new territory at astonishing rates. In this hi-tech environment, instant access to business and personal information is crucial. The capability to read business-related e-mails or browse documents in any work-related situation can save a lot of time and money. Although portable devices in various guises — a USB stick on a keychain, an iPod, a digital camera, a PDA, you name it — are a cheap, powerful, efficient way to move information around, several issues remain unsolved:

✔ What if the disk or device is lost?

✔ What if the disk or device is stolen?

✔ What if someone makes a copy of the data residing on a USB device?

✔ What if someone takes a copy of the data that resides on your PC using a USB device?

One response to these issues is (you guessed it) encryption. Routinely encrypting your data combines mobility and privacy, adding a layer of security to protect personal information from those who would love to exploit it (and you). Encryption is one tool for meeting business requirements, industry regulations, and government mandates that increasingly require all organizations to secure electronic records.

For your own peace of mind, you should make sure you aren't allowing your personal data (financial, medical, proprietary, whatever) to be bandied around the Internet. Encrypting content is a cost-effective solution that helps prevent the exploitation of sensitive information.

Encryption technology allows an appropriate degree of flexibility that puts one more security layer between your data and the bad people. To make it work, the principal requirements are as follows:

- ✔ Set it up so that you or anyone in your organization can — and will — use encryption.

- ✔ Data should be capable of being copied around the organization appropriately, so that encryption doesn't become part of the *Business Prevention* department.

- ✔ Your encryption solution should be executable from anywhere, without causing any harm to the system or losing any data — without being so easily portable that the bad people can take advantage of it and un-encrypt sensitive data.

The advantage of encrypting data on the laptop or desktop is that as you move it around you don't have to worry about the security of the information. Note, however, that encrypting your data doesn't exempt you from admitting to a loss should it occur. Or you can allow only specific applications to access the files on the encrypted disk (whether on or off the PC). This means that foreign applications will be rejected if they attempt to write or modify the data on your disk. This measure is 100 percent efficient against viruses and other sinister external factors. The safest approach is to include on the list of allowed applications only those that reside *inside the encrypted image itself.* When moving data, the rule of thumb is what you might expect: *Always check your files for viruses first.* This is important. If you don't check for viruses, *anything you copy* could potentially infect all the computers you use (or the computers someone else uses).

Policies for Destroying Data on Removable Media

Attackers are continually finding new ways to access sensitive personal or business information, but it isn't just the latest data that's at risk; they can glean old data for useful tidbits — and getting rid of old data can be surprisingly difficult. So how can you ensure that sensitive data remains secure and protected — even if somebody's throwing it away?

Well, if you shred obsolete paper documents (and what competent business doesn't?), then follow the same approach with digital documents: *Clean all data off any storage devices or storage media you repurpose or dispose of.* Organizations need to ensure that all devices containing sensitive information are thoroughly wiped or professionally destroyed. Doing anything less may leave recoverable information and create a security risk.

Most organizations don't even bother to delete old records from USB devices or portable storage — let alone decommission storage devices. There have been numerous incidents of organizations buying up old laptops or second-hand portable storage media and finding sensitive information, all of which could be a gold mine for dumpster-diving attackers. Thieves lift whatever they can from dumpsters, rooting through the trash until they find something of worth.

With the more prevalent use of increasingly sophisticated encryption, an attacker wanting access to an organization's sensitive information has to look outside the system itself for that information. One avenue of attack is the recovery of supposedly deleted data from storage media.

Three tips for destroying data

There are three common options for destroying data:

- ✔ **Cleaning:** This involves overwriting with random data on the external device to overwrite any sensitive data. This process can also be applied to any type of disk storage; in this case, the targeted storage space may include both logical storage locations and addressable locations.

- ✔ **Purging:** This is the exposure of a disk to a strong magnetic field in order to disrupt the data held on it. So, Employee A is sitting there playing with an astoundingly powerful magnet (to destroy the data on magnetic disks) next to his or her computer — with a pile of hard drives in it all whirring away. Not far away, a nice 19-inch monitor sits patiently waiting to be permanently wrecked if the magnet gets too close and the shadow mask gets magnetized. Of all the things that people *know* you're not meant to do, ever, our employee is probably doing that one right now. (Check out the accompanying sidebar for the straight goods on magnets and computers.)

- ✔ **Destroying:** To destroy most portable media, USB disks, external storage drives, CDs, or DVDs, shredding is effective — but we recommend using a cross-cut shredder for optimal obfuscation. If you're trashing a laptop, running over it with a 16-wheel truck won't do the job (we know of one such instance in which a whole lot of data was recovered from the run-over hard drive). It's best to *sand* the entire recording surface of the medium. We wouldn't bother with that; simply make

TIP

sure all decommissioned media are disintegrated, pulverized, melted, or incinerated. (Of course, you need to be able to control what USB drives are being used in the first place; make sure everyone dutifully signs them out and in.)

Consider outsourcing destruction to an organization that can do this stuff effectively, securely, and safely.

Storage-security policies

If you hold sensitive information on a local machine, then be advised: It's likely to end up on any writable storage media with which the computer comes in contact. How can IT decommission devices and media that hold sensitive information if it doesn't know how many exist or where they are? If you don't want sensitive information to turn up in unexpected places, you have to give IT some control; a storage-security policy is a good idea. Here are a few essentials for such a policy:

- Strict guidelines governing the use of removable media devices at work and at home offices.

- Consistent use of encryption software so administrators can force the encryption of all data put on portable storage media.

- Company provided removable media devices and the prevention of any others.

Can I harm a computer with a magnet?

In theory you can wave a hand-crushing neodymium-iron grungy magnet close to computing devices in perfect safety nowadays, surely? After all, magnetic field strength falls off roughly with the cube of the distance. Fairly small magnets cause no ill affects to computers and anything the size of a marble is okay if it doesn't get any closer than about 30 centimeters (one foot) away. But, even though your hard drive is protected from these sorts of effects, it does mean that a magnet the size of an iPod has be roughly a meter from your PC or your monitor and laptop will be permanently soup.

This also explains why the very small magnets in your laptop bag don't toast your laptop every

night. Magnetic fields and magnetic storage media do mix, sort of, just as long as the magnetic field isn't really amazingly strong. So is it a fallacy that magnets stew hard drives? Sort of, yes and no, magnets damage monitors and hard drives, however, they don't "zap" the data as such.

Hard drives and floppy disks store data with tiny magnetic spots on the media. When the read-head passes over these "spots," it reads the space as either "1" or "0." By placing a magnet next to the client media (not DVDs because they're optical), the "spots" will be altered, either by turning them all to "1" or all to "0" (depending on the polarity of the magnet), wherever the magnetic field reaches. But the field must be pretty strong, because it must exceed the coercivity (or the intensity of the magnetic field needed to reduce the magnetization of a ferromagnetic material to zero after it has reached saturation.) of the magnetic coating on the storage device.

Hard-drive platters have a pretty high *coercivity*, which means a magnetic field of the same strength is needed to demagnetize them. Usually, most magnets won't endanger hard-drive data, even if the drive's right next to the magnet — unless, of course, you put the magnet down right on top of the drive itself (which is,

unfortunately, what our employee did on one eventful occasion).

So, yes, magnets do damage your data stored on computer devices. But it's pretty difficult to explain to your average user why it does. In order to avoid confusion in the minds of the proletariat, we'd fabricate a more easily explained conventional wisdom, along the lines of: "Don't put a magnet near your computer, or, roughly speaking, your brain will decompose suddenly and you'll see blue."

With a caveat like that in place, most of the time we're okay.

Locking Down a Laptop

We are painfully aware that we're seeing less data saved on our file servers — why is that? Although (according to Gartner) the amount of data grows by 50 to 100 percent from year to year, organizations are seeing increases of only 20 to 50 percent on the server. Where's the rest of it? Here we have two main possibilities:

- ✔ Data capture to the servers is simply atrocious (compared to what's needed).
- ✔ IT is unaware of the growth in data.

Either way, we've got trouble.

Representatives of a customer company recently claimed that in spite of all predictions, they were seeing data increase on their servers by a mere 20 percent. This company is an enormous global concern, so we had to doubt that they *hadn't* created vast amounts of unmitigated data. That left us with the other alternative: They didn't know what they had or where it was. So where was it? That was the easy part: On the laptops of all those execs, in e-mail archive files, on external hard drives used for backup, and so on. Now, with all that data in all those places, an end-user laptop in the wrong hands — whether physically or virtually (when nasty people take it over with malware and do secret nefarious deeds) — is a disaster. Actually, that's true for *any* end-user laptop; if the user occupies an upper rung of the corporate ladder, the potential impact of the disaster is even greater.

What to do about it? Glad you asked . . .

1. **Introduce a strong password policy.** On average, the human brain can hold only five to nine "random bits of information" in short-term memory. Considering the brain's limited capacity and the sheer number of secret names, codes, and words a person needs to remember in this password-protected age, it's no surprise that the most common passwords are simple — and simply terrible:

   a. `123456`: Oh, come on. Can you count to 6? A simple numerical sequence as a "password" is depressingly common.

   b. `password`: Typing in "password" is akin to "pressing the Any key" — embarrassing, isn't it?

   c. *Favorite Football Team*: The name of your team may express your loyalty — but as a password, it's a loser.

   d. `letmein`: No, really. Some people actually use a modern-day version of "Open, sesame!" Fox Mulder's password from *The X-Files* (`trustno1`) is also popular. (D'oh!)

   e. *Your Name*: Even if it isn't emblazoned on your door or your desk, it's a bad choice. Typing in the name of a famous person is just as bad — ever wonder how many `Beckhams` there are?

   f. *Your Child's Name*: We're sure the kid is cute and smart. But *any* name is a bad choice for a password.

   g. `monkey`: Why this is one of the top seven bad passwords is beyond us. Sure, it's a six-letter word (the typical minimum length for passwords), is easily typed, and is memorable. But you couldn't call it original or hard to crack.

2. **Lock up the PC when not in use.** This is fundamental but often overlooked. Ctrl+Alt+Delete⇨Lock Computer works just fine — and if you've implemented a strong password policy locking up the machine adds strength to this policy. If a computer isn't turned on, even if it's in a (theoretically) physically secure area, it should be locked away, out of sight. Often that's enough to foil an opportunist thief. Even in an environment you consider safe, numerous people roam your corridors — and (sad to say) an increasing number of security breaches are instigated internally.

3. **Install a BIOS password and change the device boot order to prevent the system booting from anything but the hard drive.** This makes it harder for someone to boot from a CD that contains hacking tools designed to get at your data. If you ever need to boot from a CD, simply temporarily change the boot order — and then change it back. It isn't a bad idea to promote a policy where employees must remove the CD/DVD drive from the laptop when in transit (if they can), and only insert the drive when they actually need it.

4. **Encrypt the contents of the laptop hard drive.** Simple but effective. Your authors' laptops roam the world's airports, and some pretty dodgy ones at that. Every hotel, every airport, every Internet café offers opportunities for data theft. Even without the knowledge of usernames or

passwords, it's simple to gain access to private data on a machine with an unencrypted hard drive. If, however, you encrypt the contents of the hard disk, you can effectively protect against potential egg-on-the-face headlines in the press should a laptop go missing.

5. **Implement an e-mail management tool that allows you to control e-mail archive files.** You can have it remove them from the laptop altogether (which would be ideal), or at least enforce local backup and (through spot-checking) enforce a policy that saves as little data to the local machine as possible. The more data you have on the laptop, the more damage you could do to yourself when you lose it. Given the improved state of corporate and other networks, there is little excuse not to connect to a secure corporate file server instead, and upload files through the company's virtual private network (VPN). This also means that the sensitive data is protected from the bad guys, and you haven't lost any work you did on the laptop.

6. **Invest in hardware-recovery software or *ET* software that *phones home* when it's plugged into an external network.** Clever, and extraor-dinarily criminal-unfriendly; used with the assistance of the police, it claims a 90-percent recovery rate for computers that are stolen and eventually connected to the Internet. This is a great way to counter criminals who steal laptops with the goal of selling identities or credit-card details.

7. **Be wary of wireless; always disable the wireless network when it's not in use.** Carelessly used, wireless connectivity can leave open a way for your machine to be compromised. Although wireless networks provide a quick and easy way to connect to the Internet and conduct business, they also open up a huge potential for data theft when security isn't included in the network design. Turn off Bluetooth; it's pointless and insecure. In hotels, put the laptop in the safe or at the least use a laptop lock. Treat your PDA or phone in the same way as your laptop — you're 22 times more likely to lose these little gadgets than you are your laptop.

8. **Quarantine returning laptops, or enforce system scans to make sure they don't carry any viruses or spyware.** If the device has spent time outside the corporate firewall, there is a huge chance that some kind of spyware (at the least) has attached itself to the computer. At the same time enforce virus live updates whenever a laptop is connected to the Internet. Any infection like this can run in the background, which is as bad as having your laptop stolen — and more difficult to spot.

9. **Report any incidents; this is likely to become law in the not-too-distant-future.** If you don't report the theft and your computer is used to commit a crime, the owner of the laptop can end up in a tight spot that's sometimes difficult to prove one's way out of. If you do have users who are somewhat lax in their security practices and somebody's system is stolen, it's vital to change *all* security passwords and VPN account details. The goal is to protect company assets and avoid getting into the news for all the wrong reasons.

10. **Consider the thin-client computing model, at least for remote users.**
    You provide laptops to mobile workers so they can get their jobs done
    while on the road — but servers and desktops within the corporate net-
    work are almost always more secure than laptops. Because high-speed
    Internet connections can now be found in most hotels, airports, coffee
    shops, and bookstores, it's possible to set up a remote-connectivity
    solution so an end-user simply connects to Terminal Services (or Citrix)
    or uses Remote Desktop to connect (over a VPN) to a dedicated desktop
    machine within the corporate network. This prevents any work from
    actually being done on the laptop itself. Instead the laptops simply func-
    tions as a temporary terminal. Although this approach isn't feasible for
    every IT department, it can prevent data loss by separating storage from
    the device.

11. **Get some kind of endpoint protection ASAP.** Antivirus, anti-spyware,
    and other signature-based protection measures, which are primarily
    reactive, may have been sufficient to protect an organization's vital
    resources a few years ago, but not today. Organizations now need pro-
    active endpoint security measures that can protect against zero-day
    attacks and unknown threats. They need to take a structured approach
    to endpoint security, implementing a solution that protects them from
    threats on all levels, and also provides interoperability, seamless imple-
    mentation, and centralized management.

Of these measures, endpoint protection provides advanced threat prevention
that protects endpoints from targeted attacks — and from attacks not seen
before. Products used for this purpose should have some essential capabilities:

- ✔ Analyzing (automatically) application behaviors and network communications, detecting and blocking suspicious activities.

- ✔ Using administrative control features to deny specific activities deemed
  high-risk for the organization, whether for devices or applications.

- ✔ Blocking specific actions according to the location of the user.

- ✔ Repairing an infected endpoint by disinfecting or quarantining the
  system, and then deploying the necessary patch to complete the remediation process.

This approach calls for consolidating endpoint protection technologies in
a single, integrated agent that can be administered from a central management console. The goal is to increase endpoint protection while eliminating
the administrative overhead and the costs associated with multiple security
products.

Chapter 10

Mobile Phones and PDAs

· ·

In This Chapter

▶ Protecting your corporate portal

▶ Meeting the management challenges mobile devices create

▶ Controling functionality on mobile devices

▶ Using wipe and kill to make lost data disappear

▶ Preventing bluesnarfing and other Bluetooth dangers

· ·

The way we do business and work today has radically changed the way we need to approach IT security. Millions of us now do at least part of our jobs from home offices or other remote locations. It's estimated that around one in five adult workers telecommute for normal business activities. This number translates into an increasing amount of responsibility for IT managers who must keep track of all those mobile workers, their hardware, access control, and policy management. Given that mobile working has a tendency to amplify existing organizational weaknesses, IT has a huge job simply to manage the technology.

When companies extend their business IT operations to mobile employees, their risks are increased. Valuable software, data and devices are taken out of the protected perimeter of the office, and placed in the pockets, pouches, and briefcases of users.

Five percent of all business laptops are lost every year — and you are 22 times likelier to lose a phone or PDA than you are a laptop. It wasn't as much of a problem before PDAs and smart mobile phones started sprouting features; now, in essence, they offer the same functionality as a laptop. They can hold a lot more stuff that you don't want to lose. It doesn't take higher math to figure out that a larger percentage of PDAs and phones than laptops will be lost each year; the more they can hold, the greater the risk they pose.

Business processes may run more efficiently, and employer and employee have more flexibility in how they conduct the working practices, but do both parties take security seriously enough? Quite simply, no they don't. There is a tendency to believe that where there are challenges with a particular use of technology, the solution is to apply more technology. Not much benefit results if the attitudes toward using technology are complacent or irresponsible.

Efficiency and productivity are the standard justifications for adopting new technology; workplace flexibility is the top reason for interest in mobile technology (at least for most IT professionals). A company that deploys mobile technology effectively and widely has its best chance at avoiding data leakage if it adopts a corporate strategy for mobile working.

New technologies mean new problems as they create new risks. Unfortunately, for many companies the introduction of mobile devices has happened *under the radar* — and security hasn't been seen as all that important.

Even though mobile-device security policies are vital, by and large they're not implemented well. While the vast majority of IT professionals believe in the importance of security policies to cover the use of mobile, wireless, or cellular devices, a third of them don't have such policies in place. Although companies with more widespread mobile-device deployment have a somewhat better record of creating policies, still one in five of them don't. Result: Too many wireless laptops and smart handheld devices wandering around in the world without effective policies in place for mobile security.

Communicating the Risks and Benefits

Over-communication on the subject of security helps generate appropriate attitudes to user responsibilities. Intranets and e-mails are the default ways to explain policy, but many companies take advantage of two-way communication through training, employee induction, and management. All these techniques are more pronounced for larger deployments. Companies that use this approach are more likely to believe that their users understand what they must do — and that they're more likely to behave responsibly.

Even with a policy in place, however, many organizations don't set the right examples. Most recognize that security is a shared responsibility between organization and individual employee — but over a third fail to enforce security policies strictly enough. This inconsistency, along with a lack of clear leadership from the organization, can undermine security.

All types of smart handheld devices should be protected by a PIN or password. No ifs, ands, or buts, this is where security begins — even if it's annoying at times. It also means that someone who steals one of those devices can't just waltz into your corporate network or use up your expensive long-distance minutes on chat lines in outer Mongolia. Your people have to see security as more than just yak, yak, yak.

Protecting Your Corporate Portal

According to a survey by the Economist Intelligence Unit, security concerns make up the biggest obstacle to widespread adoption of remote and mobile computing in businesses — worldwide. The survey found that more than 60 percent of companies were holding back on deployment because of security concerns. About 47 percent of all respondents cited the cost and complexity of implementing security as a major inhibiting factor.

These days, the bad guys don't even need computers to go after your data. Smart phones and PDAs not only browse the Web, but also contain full-fledged operating systems with a wide variety of user-installable software — some of it sinister. Nearly one in five businesses has already experienced financial loss due to attacks launched from mobile platforms. Security-threat reports clamor about specific threats to mobile devices and mobility in general — in particular, malicious code that targets smart phones and the like. And these attacks are on the increase. But does that change attitudes? Nope.

A recent example of malicious code for smart phones is Cardtrp, which was the first cross-platform threat that could affect both the Symbian and Windows operating systems. It's an indication that cyber-criminals are getting smarter in their attacks. Another nasty little item, Pbstealer, is distributed as a file that poses as a phone-book utility for smart phones in order to entice a user to download and execute it. Then guess where all those phone numbers go . . . .

Why are these devices becoming targets? Because they *can* be targeted — but now they also hold *critical* data — business and personal — useful to the cyber-criminal. As soon as Web browser is available, people start to use it for shopping and banking — what better data for a cyber-criminal than that? After a device has been compromised by (say) a Trojan horse, information can be transmitted by a variety of means, including Bluetooth if the attacker is in range. The information they're after is nothing more specialized than what you'd normally find on a laptop:

- ✔ **Phonebook:** Remember that this feature can contain a lot of personal *and* corporate information, including sensitive contact information and appointments. (Do you keep your bank PIN number in there? Uh-oh.)

- ✔ **Notepad:** Tends to have succinct notes on all sorts of issues — some of them confidential.

- ✔ **Calendar:** Just who are you meeting and when? Oh, is your address also in there? I guess you won't be home then.

- ✔ **To-do list:** Work or home? *Call bank about loan for a car.* "Hello, this is the bank. Would you like a car loan? If you could just confirm your account details . . . ." Like shooting "phish" in a barrel.

✔ **Web history:** On-line banking, ahh . . . and there's your secret code word. How convenient.

✔ **Usernames and passwords:** Need we say more?

All these normally innocent bits of data may pose a serious breach of confidentiality. According to the Symantec Internet Security Threat Report, the risks connected with mobile data will increase as larger mobile networks become more attractive targets for cyber-criminals.

And if you need something more to worry about, consider: Hijacked mobile clients can be used to gain unauthorized access to corporate networks through an external Internet connection. The corporate network can be attacked through the smallest of portals.

As exciting new portable devices come on the market and catch on, *someone* needs to be thinking about how to lock them down and reduce the risks they pose. Preferably before someone else turns them into threats.

Additional management challenges

Bottom line: The same security requirements for external drives, laptops, and portable media for desktops apply to PDAs and mobile technology. Or should. The applications are available. Most of the issues emerge when you try to change how people view their mobile devices — get them to understand the risks that the gizmos pose. *Hey, it's just a phone* — no, it isn't — it's a direct link to the heart of the business.

Of course, security isn't the only concern for remote and mobile devices. The biggest challenge an organization faces is in managing, controlling, and securing these systems, especially because they don't maintain persistent connections. Days or weeks might pass before a remote or mobile client connects to the corporate network; when the client machine finally does connect, it has to perform a big batch of tasks to keep itself up to date. And there's no guarantee that every connection will provide the necessary quality to get those tasks done; limited bandwidth, unreliable service, and frequent disconnections ("dropped" calls) can all create havoc for organizations trying to manage those systems. Those concerns are especially evident in relation to the following essential security activities:

✔ **Software distribution and patch management:** A smart device needs the latest set of patches to fix outstanding vulnerabilities in the operating system and applications. Scheduling software-distribution or patch-management tasks to occur automatically after hours might work for the desktop systems in an organization, but those packages won't reach any of the mobile or remote clients that aren't connected during the scheduled deployment. An effective management solution must be able to deploy scheduled packages to offline systems the next time they connect. In addition, the solution must take into account the different circumstances that mobile and remote clients face. It should offer optimization features such as package compression, checkpoint restart capabilities, and automated offline completion of software installation.

✔ **Anti-virus and anti-malware protection:** Updates to counter the latest threats have to be installed in a timely manner — just as they are for laptops and other IT equipment. Most IT organizations go to great lengths to safeguard digital assets from outside threats; unfortunately, mobile systems are frequently ignored or neglected, which makes them much more vulnerable to attack. As part of an effective management solution, the security policy for mobile clients must be able to sense when a system connects from outside the corporate network — and automatically adjust security protections accordingly. Organizations can also require that all remote access occur through the corporate virtual private network (VPN), which will block any traffic that doesn't come from within the secure walls of the corporate infrastructure.

✔ **Asset management and compliance:** This is another significant concern for remote or mobile clients. Whether it's to adhere to government regulations (such as the Sarbanes-Oxley Act) or to avoid fines resulting from noncompliance with software licensing agreements, organizations must be able to track and monitor all of their systems. Solutions that manage assets must be able to recognize when mobile or remote clients connect to the network — and then execute the necessary inventory scans as needed. They must also be able to perform inventory scans offline to deal with the issue of slow, unreliable, and limited connections.

✔ **Disaster recovery:** For mobile phones, the usual disaster is the loss of the device. Solutions must be considered to make it easy for employees to readily re-create the data on their mobile device should they lose it. This means provisioning the gizmo with the right software and security stack, re-installing contacts, calendars, e-mail, and other tools, and recovering any other data that was on it. Back when a phone was "just a phone," backup wasn't an issue — there was very little *unique* data on a mobile phone. But that's changing. Mobile devices are being used to edit and work on documents — just as if they were laptops.

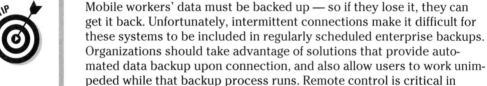

Mobile workers' data must be backed up — so if they lose it, they can get it back. Unfortunately, intermittent connections make it difficult for these systems to be included in regularly scheduled enterprise backups. Organizations should take advantage of solutions that provide automated data backup upon connection, and also allow users to work unimpeded while that backup process runs. Remote control is critical in disaster-recovery efforts — people never lose their devices when they're at the office . . . they're always out in the world when it happens!

Putting it all together

The challenges of managing remote and mobile clients touch upon various disciplines — systems, security, and storage management. A well-managed mobile infrastructure can effectively converge these management efforts and tie it all in with the rest of the IT environment.

There are many solutions that help enterprises recognize all the benefits a well-run mobile infrastructure can offer; the trick is to find one that can help simplify the complex issues associated with remote and mobile client management. The right one will fit seamlessly into your environment and promote a coherent strategy, alleviating the concerns of the enterprise, as well as helping to prevent data loss.

Controlling Functionality on Mobile Devices

If a phone were still just a phone, then managing it would be a lot simpler. But functionality creep has made the mobile device the essential business tool — and the ultimate data-loss device it is today. Devices have cameras and memory sticks (or other removable media); they can connect over any and every network type, from the GPRS network to the local Wi-Fi network — not to mention SMS, Bluetooth, and infrared. Left unchecked, this additional functionality creates a greater data-loss risk.

Organizations are experiencing an increase in the number of employees utilizing mobile devices to get their work done while on the move. Managing an ever-expanding fleet of mobile devices — and ensuring end-to-end data integrity at the same time — is a difficult task for any organization. Which means you need an end-to-end solution to manage it all. Mobile Device Management (MDM) solutions to the rescue.

MDM software applications can help you control all the mobile devices through a group policy. In effect, it helps manage a single environment that encompasses not only in-house but also mobile devices. It's great for consistency, compliance, and peace of mind. So what should you expect to get? Well, the list varies, but the core features include these:

- ✔ **Software distribution:** Let everyone have the right versions of applications at the same time.

- ✔ **Data encryption:** This is essential for main devices, memory sticks, removable media, the whole shebang. If the device is lost (but the encryption key isn't), then you don't have to worry about a data leak.

✔ **Control of endpoint functionality:** Enables or disables features, Bluetooth, SMS/MMS, Wi-Fi, Infrared, Internet access, and camera functionality.

✔ **"Allow" and "deny" functionality:** This feature can limit or prevent users from downloading and installing non-corporate software on their machines.

✔ **Device wipe and/or kill:** Gives mobile devices selective amnesia so no one can even reuse your phone.

✔ **Policy enforcement:** It's no good just talking about it. You have to walk the walk.

✔ **Inventory and reporting:** How good is compliance? This feature helps you find out.

✔ **Deployment of firmware:** The latest and greatest firmware will help fix some security vulnerabilities.

✔ **Software updates:** The latest and greatest . . . you get the idea. Frequent updates are especially important for anti-virus and anti-malware applications.

✔ **Provision devices:** The quickest way to get someone a full backup of the data on a lost laptop if they've left it in the taxi.

✔ **Adaptation and updating of user and administrator privileges:** Sometimes it's better if the user can't initiate an action that threatens security.

✔ **VPN optimization:** The goal is to protect the link into the corporate network.

✔ **Seamless connectivity:** It shouldn't matter where you are or what you're doing; if it concerns the organization, the phone should keep it all under control.

✔ **Network roaming capabilities:** The latest phones can choose the lowest-priced network, depending on where the call goes.

Encryption strategies for mobile devices

Many organizations have turned to full-disk encryption as a preventive measure for laptops — but what about mobile phones? Encryption could well be needed on those as well. But the field is getting crowded. Although encryption is a key technology for safeguarding mobile data, the challenge is how to prioritize all those mobile devices for encryption. Prioritization focuses encryption efforts on the highest-risk devices — resulting in better security and reduced cost. (What's not to like?)

It's possible to use content-aware discovery technology to build a prioritization queue — essentially a list based on insight into exactly where the most confidential data is stored. A scan can tell you which devices contain the most confidential data; focus your encryption efforts on those machines first. Take a case where a stolen or lost mobile device is known to contain personal, sensitive information or some intellectual property of the organization. These questions will help you identify what needs to be done:

- **What specific intellectual property (say, source code or design documents) resided on the device — and was it encrypted or unencrypted?** This question determines what level of action may be required to protect patents, copyrights, and other proprietary information (business plans, for example).

- **Were there any customer records? If so, how many?** This question ascertains what level of action may be required from a customer-relations perspective. Different courses of action may be appropriate for 700 records or 700,000 records.

- **What specific data types (such as Social Security Numbers and credit information) were in the files, and how much data (if any) was private?** This question establishes whether any response is needed to comply with the law, and whether federal or state regulations have been violated.

- **Was the data encrypted?** This question determines your notification strategy and potential risk. For example, some state regulations still require that you notify customers even if the data *was* encrypted.

Reports can then be analyzed to determine whether any federal or state compliance regulations have been violated, so you can be proactive in your response to government authorities and execute a focused customer-notification strategy.

If it's lost, kiss it goodbye; 97 percent of stolen computers aren't recovered, and fewer mobile devices come home if they're misplaced.

Remote wipe and kill

So your data is encrypted but you want to do more — in particular, prevent your device from being used by a cyber-criminal. There is one more piece of technology you can deploy to help you out — remote *wipe and kill.*

No, it isn't the latest item in the assassin's arsenal. In essence, when a portable device is lost or stolen, IT administrators can send out a *signal* to tell it to "destroy" itself the next time it connects — that is, delete its data and then lock itself up so the only thing a cyber-criminal can do for free is throw it away.

The other good news about this technology is that it can then report back (for auditing purposes) to confirm that the data has been destroyed. Although effectively decommissioning storage is a must, you can't take a baseball bat to any devices that are lost, stolen, or no longer under IT control — but you *can* do the next best thing: Make them useless for those who find them (or stole them).

The Dangers of Bluetooth

Bluetooth is a wireless technology for short-range (up to around 120 yards) communication; it's used to connect one electronic device to another in the same vicinity, without cables. It's pretty robust and works on little power, so it's pretty cheap to run. You probably use Bluetooth with a hands-free headset on your phone — unfortunately, it can be used for more than you might expect.

 Bluetooth security dangers are all but ignored. It's strange that no matter how many smart people rant and rave about the flaws in Bluetooth protocols, nobody does anything about it. Even in a security-aware environment, you still find people who keep Bluetooth (and other wireless) connections enabled — completely ignorant of who may be hacking into their systems via one or more of the 27 Bluetooth protocols (15 of which have already been breached and are vulnerable to attack). These flaws are accessible to anyone within 100 meters. Result: The vulnerabilities are widespread and difficult to address.

Flaws in Bluetooth communications protocols can be exploited to send malformed packets to crash systems and, depending on the implementation, can be subject to buffer overflow attacks that can lead to arbitrary code execution. Some of the reason for this is because the protocols are being used outside of the specifications for which they were originally intended.

It's a neat technology but its security is iffy at best. The risks are as intrinsic as with any wireless technology; the most significant risk with wireless is that it's open to everybody, bad and good. Short-range wireless is very vulnerable; an intruder who has the frequency to connect to your PDA could monitor your wireless activity, get mouse access, and download everything you keep on your handheld device. If the attacker's headset connects to your mobile phone via Bluetooth, then your conversations are no longer private.

A simple solution for Bluetooth vulnerabilities

Fortunately, you can take a couple of simple actions that help limit the vulnerability of your Bluetooth-equipped device:

- ✔ Don't turn it on when you don't need it.
- ✔ Turn it off when you've finished using it.

If you want to get a little more sophisticated, try these measures:

- ✔ Allow only paired devices to connect. Pairing of Bluetooth devices creates encryption and decryption for secure connections, usually consists of a PIN that is shared between devices. The devices then agree on a link key that they will use to establish a secure connection between each other. This works pretty well — so security compromises have to search for another way to gain access to the device.
- ✔ Ensure that the device won't accept *anything* requesting to connect without asking the user first.

All the vulnerabilities that exist in a conventional wired network apply to wireless technologies. The snag with Bluetooth is that malicious entities may gain unauthorized access to a PDA or mobile phone through wireless connections — *all of which bypass most firewalls*. Sensitive information that's transmitted without encryption between two wireless devices can be intercepted and stolen.

The more ambitious bad guys may usurp online identities and use them to impersonate employees on corporate networks. This also leads to the corruption of sensitive data when incorrect or corrupt synchronization occurs. Really wicked people could deploy unauthorized access points to gain access to sensitive information.

Bluejacking, bluesnarfing, backdooring and bluebugging

Here's a look at some Bluetooth-specific nefarious activities. Don't let the cute names fool you; every one of these methods produces data leaks.

✔ **Bluejacking:** One flaw in pairing a device is that this technique works on the initialization process: When a device wants to be paired, a message containing the device's name and whether you want to pair with this device is displayed. If you don't fall for it, it's harmless but — if you click to accept, the perpetrator can gain access to your mobile device.

✔ **Bluesnarfing:** As with most Bluetooth breaches, this attack method uses the way Bluetooth is implemented on the mobile device. Through the way that the object exchange protocol is implemented it can access these mobile phones contacts, calendar and pictures without the owner ever knowing.

✔ **Backdooring:** This method of hacking uses a device that should not be part of the corporate network — say, an ex-employee's computer that hasn't been decommissioned and can still gain access to corporate data.

✔ **Bluebugging:** This is possibly the most dangerous of mobile device hacks. It enables hackers to send and read SMS, call numbers, monitor phone calls, and also do pretty much everything that backdooring and bluesnarfing allow.

If, after reading this list, you start to think that Bluetooth is too much of a risk . . . well, it is. Unless you make people aware of the problems that can exist — *and* ensure that the security policy is enforced to reduce the risk — you're probably better off keeping Bluetooth switched off.

Protecting Data Against Mobile Phone and PDA Data Leaks

Security requirements are pretty much the same for laptops, desktops, PDAs, smart phones, and mobile phones. Here's a basic checklist:

✔ A security technology that can scale up and down (depending on what's needed) and is easy to deploy.

✔ Standards-based approach to Microsoft Windows, Symbian, and other mobile operating systems. Security policy should be the same across all of them so it's easier to support.

✔ Monitoring and blocking the copying of data from mobile devices to anything else (including memory sticks and computers).

✔ Automated notification of policy enforcement.

✔ Encryption for all data (main device and removable media).

✔ Integration to ensure stability, interoperability, and security for asset control, auditing, and management solutions.

✔ Integrated endpoint security suite — including antivirus, anti-malware, intrusion detection and prevention, and anti-phishing capabilities.

✔ Consistent policies for intrusion detection, remediation workflow, incident reporting, system management, and security.

Remediation workflow is a security concept that classifies each incident by level of severity and/or by the amount of data exposed on which drive(s). Such classification focuses attention on the correct company procedure to mitigate against exposure events, and ensures consistent remediation for each type of incident.

Chapter 11

Geography

· ·

· ·

*L*ocation is everything when buying a house. A good location is safe and secure. The same is true when it comes to data, except data can easily move.

The value of data varies over time and its security varies with geography. If you or your computer is in a less secure area, the risks are higher. If the risks are higher, you have to take more steps to protect the information. Likewise, if the computer is in a secure location, you don't have to take those steps.

Location-Based Access Control

The idea is simple: If you're inside the company, your access to applications and data is greater than when you're outside. This reduces the risk of something bad happening (in this case, data lost or stolen). Unfortunately, most applications aren't aware of geography, so they give full access at all times. In other words, most applications are unaware of where you're accessing them:

✔ You could be inside the physical boundaries of the corporate organization.

✔ You could be in a dodgy Internet café in Grotsville.

The anywhere-anytime application is with us. Corporate road warriors (and other employees with laptops who work outside the office) can access anything and everything, no matter where they are. That's the problem. If they're sitting in coffee shops somewhere, connected through wireless, perhaps they *shouldn't* be allowed access to everything. After all, it may not be them at all those keyboards.

When you're on the Internet, nobody knows you're a dog (so says a famous cartoon by Peter Steiner). In terms of computing access, it's tough to identify what's *actually* being accessed (or, for that matter, how) after an identity has been compromised. We have multiple ways of identifying who we are online, the most obvious being userIDs and passwords, but if those credentials are compromised, it's difficult to know who's *really* accessing company data or applications. One response would be to make applications *geography-aware*: If Employee A is accessing the network in Location X, and then the *same* employee suddenly starts to access Application M from Location Y — halfway across the globe — surely we'd smell a rat?

There is a need to change how applications work in order to reduce the risk. They need to become aware of their users and where they might be. This holds true as much for applications on end-user machines as for in-house applications.

For example, here's how that works out with a banking application:

✔ From the bank customer's perspective, all functionality is allowed from home or work. However, if the customer is coming in from a cyber-café, the quantity of money that can be transferred may be limited.

✔ From an internal perspective, running reports while in the office is allowed. Outside the office, reports with customer details can't be executed.

One health company has put a policy in place to specify what can and can't be seen on mobile devices. Any e-mail about a patient is restricted from being sent to mobile devices. They can't afford the risk of someone losing their device. This is a very technology-aware company, the devices are encrypted and fitted with remote wipe-and-kill functionality (if you lose it, you send a signal that trashes the data) but still they won't let patient data onto those devices. When we asked about this, they said a machine could be taken when it wasn't locked (although they also had auto-lock timeout policies). Although the chance of theft while the device was unlocked was miniscule, they considered even that risk too great. (Any data loss can be disastrous, but the loss of *patient* data could end up being catastrophic because medical information tends to be sensitive.)

Changing policies with geography

If geography is an important component when it comes to risk, it follows that a data-loss policy should also change according to where the user is.

One size does not fit all when it comes to data loss and geography. A blanket solution will waste time and money for you and your organization.

The easiest way to illustrate this principle is by example: When sensitive or confidential data is outside the organization's firewall, it should be encrypted. Period. When it's inside, the policy can be a little more selective; perhaps it isn't encrypted at all, or perhaps a restricted access policy is applied. Adding unnecessary encryption inside the organization wastes money and increases management and administrative processes.

Here's another example: If information is sent by e-mail outside the company, stricter data-loss policies are automatically applied. Inside there might be no such checks, or limited checks on individual users rather than on actual content (as often happens in financial institutions where the front office and the back office aren't allowed to communicate).

You could look at *endpoint virtualization* that effectively *ring-fences* (restricts) access to any application from outside the corporate network. When we spoke to some public-sector business/IT specialists on managing the lifecycle of information, one person in the audience was convinced that the only way to achieve the appropriate levels of security for his organization was to ring-fence *every* activity and keep everything within the network. In effect, that approach returns to a thin-client model — without the hassle of having to connect to the network on a dial-up line (so slow it seems powered by a tired-out hamster in a rusty wheel). Wireless technology has changed the game: Where *can't* we access the network today? (Rhetorical question!)

Merging logical and physical security

Within most organizations there are at least two security systems:

- ✔ **Physical security (p-security):** That's your electronic door-access key, or a big, burly ex-policeman who demands to see your pass.

- ✔ **Logical or computer security:** That's your username and password (or multiple usernames and passwords).

Getting physical (and then logical) about security

Physical and logical security systems can work hand in hand to make a more secure environment, but that kind of coordination isn't common practice today.

In addition to preventing random people from coming in off the street and sneaking into your building to steal stuff (including data!), physical security has some other important tasks:

- ✔ **Tracking and identifying individuals:** We know who you are and where you are! ("Winston, Big Brother is watching you!")

✔ **Tracking and identifying equipment:** RFID tags and even GPS systems can be attached to systems, so that if they're moved they can be readily tracked.

✔ **Surveillance and monitoring:** This is all the CCTV equipment that you have around the place.

✔ **Heavy-duty stuff:** Body armor, protective clothing, ballistic protection, and non-lethal munitions.

✔ **Specialist stuff:** Screening with metal detectors, explosives detectors, and equipment that checks air, food, and water.

✔ **Risk mitigation:** Background screening of personnel, executive protection, investigation, and intelligence.

While the latter items are somewhat less relevant to co-ordinating physical and logical security, they can still provide input to a security system with the (potential) events they create. For example, if an event tripped by a metal detector results in a panic button being pressed, a list of all the people in the building is useful — but such a list also affects the logical security system. For example, it could run a backup or lock people out from the system. The more interesting, and useful, cases come from tracking and identifying individuals.

If you have an electronic access card that you're supposed to swipe as you enter the building, it makes sense that you shouldn't be able to log in to the computer system through the building's company network access unless you're *in* the building. Similarly, if you aren't in the building and someone else is trying to log in as you, physical security should be able to come catch the perpetrator. (Okay, if the "someone else" happens to *be* you, on a day you just forgot to swipe your card on your way into the building, trust us, you'll catch on quickly!)

When the tie between logical and physical security is established, other policies can be tied to other systems in a similar manner and enforced in a co-ordinated way. Here are a couple of examples:

✔ Only being able to log on to machines in one building (or on one floor of a building), depending on your physical location. (You could restrict such access to just one machine, but you'd have to deal with the fact that many employees use multiple computers at work.)

✔ Configuring the Human Resources application on which you register your time off so it links access to whether you're expected in: If you're registered as on vacation, you can't access the building or log in. (Of course, there will always be exceptions; perhaps you're allowed access via VPN, so if you *really* want to work while on vacation, you can.)

The other good news about tying the security systems together is that a co-ordinated approach helps provide evidence to support your adherence to specific compliance regulations or rules.

Documenting compliance

Compliance has become a driving force in the security industry, from both the physical and logical point of view. Regulations such as Sarbanes-Oxley, HIPAA, and GLBA have resulted in the need to leverage technology (including security systems such as access control) to meet compliance and reporting requirements.

Companies must show that they physically secure assets as part of Food and Drug Administration (FDA) regulation 21 CFR Part 11, Customs Trade Partnership Against Terrorism (C-TPAT), U.S. Drug Enforcement Administration (DEA) — Security Regulation (21 CFR 1301.71-76) and others that are specific to other industries and geographies. Companies also must show that they logically secure their assets by applying appropriate security patches in a timely manner and lock down other potential security breaches (for example, unused ports).

By launching HSPD-12 initiative, the U.S. Government became a big driver for the convergence of physical and logical security. After 9/11, the subsequent creation of the Department of Homeland Security (DHS) led to the White House creating Homeland Security Presidential Directive (HSPD-12), which requires

> . . . *a mandatory, Government-wide standard for secure and reliable forms of identification issued by the Federal Government to its employees and contractors.*

As a result of this directive — and for the first time — a single, standardized credential is required for access to both federal facilities *and* information systems. Issued in 2004, HSPD-12 had an immediate impact on government agencies and contractors — and is also speeding the convergence of physical and IT security.

Risky Businesses

As the amount of control decreases, so the amount of risk increases. If you aren't on the corporate network inside the firewall, the risk is higher than it would be if you *were* inside. If (for example) you're using your computer over public Wi-Fi, in a coffee shop, the risks are worrisome; if you're using a computer in a cyber-café, the risks are much higher (and even *more* worrisome). And if you're using a computer in a cyber-café situated in a less security-aware country, the risks go through the roof and the worry goes off the scale.

Conferences and exhibitions

You're at a conference — what risks could possibly exist? After all, you're surrounded by like-minded people. Right? Suffice to say that such an assumption is inadequate protection.

Shiny toys and light fingers

Amid all the bustle of a conference, it's too easy to let down your guard:

 ✔ **Freebies, giveaways, and techie tchotchkes:** From the perspective of potential data-loss risk, those free USB memory sticks and CD-ROMs are dangerous. These *shiny* objects draw our attention but can easily contain viruses, keyloggers and Trojans. Just because it looks okay doesn't mean you should rush to pick it up! There have been instances where even these normal-looking USB keys have viruses on them (by accident); be careful.

 ✔ **Wireless connections:** The dangers of Wi-Fi are the same as those in a cyber café, so be careful.

 ✔ **Thieves:** What, thieves at conferences? Never! Well, think again. Especially during the setup and take-down periods, plasma screens and *big* computer systems are targeted — but if a light-fingered and/or "unofficial" attendee can find a quick laptop to steal, there it goes!

Apparently airports are the most likely places to lose your laptop. While you're dashing for your plane en route to and from conferences, keep in mind that around 1000 bags (including laptops) go missing from airports every month — which suggests that thieves are hanging around waiting for unsuspecting corporate businesspeople. (A total stranger asks, "Can I look after your bags while you go to the restroom?" The answer: "No, thanks.")

Keeping your wits (and your data) about you

You'll see it a lot in this book: *Forewarned is forearmed.* The old adage is true even if your "innocuous" destination is a conference. The best armament? You've heard that from us before as well: Education, education, education:

 ✔ **Tell people of the risks.** If you're exhibiting at a show, make sure that the whole staff understands the issues.

 ✔ **Be wireless-aware.** Turn off your Wi-Fi capability when you aren't using it:

   • There's usually an off switch that makes it easy; sometimes there's a physical switch on the front of the PC.

   • You may (and should) have a disable facility in your network connections. Typically you can use it like this: Right-click the Network Connections icon in the lower-left corner of your screen, right-click Wireless Network Connection, and click Disable.

✔ **If you don't need it, leave it at home.** If you don't need your laptop, just leave it at home.

If you need to take a presentation along, take it on a USB key, not on the whole computer. (Just make sure that a suitable computer will be available at the conference.)

✔ **Watch out for criminals**. If you see something strange, report it. While it may not be your equipment or data, someone else might be very pleased you noticed what was happening.

✔ **Be cautious of the free stuff.** If your anti-virus and anti-malware protection is up to date, you should be safe if you want to stick CD-ROMs and USB sticks into your machine, but be a little cautious: Make sure the protection is updated *first*.

Mergers and acquisitions

Mergers and acquisitions (M&A) result in transitional times when you're most susceptible to data loss, leaks, and breaches. The reason is unfamiliarity: You don't know anyone in the new company yet, and no one there knows you yet — or at least knows what you look like. The baddies target organizations during these transitions for that very reason.

During the M&A process, large quantities of highly sensitive data are copied and shared. Everything from financial accounts to customer lists, from product designs to technology futures. What's more, it's all shared with relative strangers. Typically, your boss says someone will come and ask you for some item of data and you're supposed to help this person. Who are you to say no? Well, you do have some reasonable and prudent precautions you can take:

✔ Ask for proof of identity when someone you don't know comes and asks for sensitive data.

✔ Never send sensitive data through to a strange e-mail account. ("Please, could you send that to my Web-based e-mail account as I can't get onto the corporate network at present?" Just say no!)

✔ Create a list of accredited people, their pictures and (if possible) their e-mail addresses. If you can see a picture of someone, it helps you know whom you're dealing with. If this is a *quiet* acquisition, including the new company's e-mail addresses may give too much away — but using picture to help employees recognize new names is always useful.

Where there's risk, there's money. M&A activities are always risky, so there's always money to be made (and not just from the two companies involved).

Internet Cafés

Hurray for Internet cafés! You can get good coffee and work at the same time! From a data-loss perspective, however, there is a more sinister side. People are often distracted ("Your double-shot skinny macchiato is ready!".) — which is a boon to the casual thief who's looking to run off with a laptop. These places are also ideal hunting grounds for cyber-criminals who use a very specific attack against Wi-Fi connections: *the evil twin*.

The evil twin

The evil twin is a high-risk attack that occurs when the intended victim is attaching to a wireless access point in a public area such as a coffee shop. The attack is simple to set up: The cyber-criminal comes into the coffee shop with a high-powered laptop, sets up near the wireless access point, and configures the laptop so its wireless connection *looks like the one in the coffee shop* (that is, has the same ID).

Unsuspecting customers waltz into the coffee shop with laptops, switch them on, and order up. Then either the computers attach to the strongest signal, or the users are asked whether they want to connect to *Free Coffee Shop Broadband*. What the heck, it looks legit, so they make the connection — to the fake access point. Then the cyber-criminal can intercept all the data traveling across the link. Figure 11-1 shows an evil twin in action.

There are a number of measures to counter *the evil twin*:

- **Study up on the subject and get the word out.** Yep, the word is *education* again. You need to talk to your employees, tell them about this threat, and brief them on counteracting it. As with many security risks, education is critical. It makes people think before doing something silly.

- **Look out for other laptop users.** *When in doubt, walk out.* Okay, so this sounds a little over-the-top — but if there are a number of other users in there and you aren't sure how safe it may be (some may look a little shifty), go somewhere else. Not very scientific, but your instinct is acute if you know what to look out for, so use it.

- **Ask whether an immediate connection is really necessary.** Do you have to connect right this minute? Can't it wait until you're back in the office?

- **Check what you're connected to.** Ensure that laptops are configured so they *don't* attach automatically to unknown networks, especially laptop-to-laptop (peer-to-peer) networks. Only allow connection to access points.

- **Use a virtual private network (VPN).** When connecting to the corporate network, use a VPN to encrypt the traffic. This will foil any snoopers who are trying to snag your data.

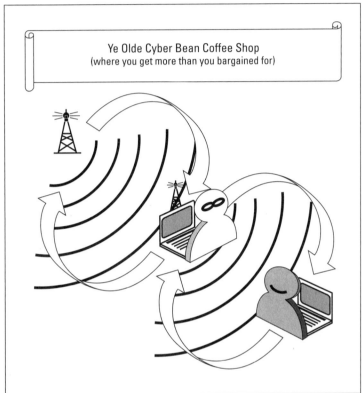

Ye Olde Cyber Bean Coffee Shop
(where you get more than you bargained for)

Figure 11-1:
The dangers
of an evil
twin.

Holiday and vacation infections

It's one thing to be careful when *at home* or in your own home area, but the risk is still there (and sometimes worse) when you go away. Nowadays people travel with laptops when they go on vacation. We live in a connected age; people want to check e-mail, connect to their blogs or social-networking sites, or use their laptops to store and display digital photos.

The problem is how they connect. While the local coffee shop has one set of risks, a visit to a cyber-café in some outlying corner of the world probably carries a lot more risk. Data security will be a long way from the owners' minds; after all, the legitimate shops are in the coffee business, not the data-trafficking business. But local cyber-criminals will know that this is a great place to pick up some useful information from the tourists!

How can you help prevent infections?

✔ **Education:** Yes, you've been here before. It's a common theme that runs through this book: *education* — informing people about the problems that can occur, so they can take steps to minimize the risks. Tell people to be wary of cyber-cafés in far-off places and bring them up to speed on some of the problems they might get if they frequent those places.

✔ **Company policy:** You could dictate that corporate laptops aren't to be taken on vacation. For that matter, you should discourage people from working on vacation anyway. The idea was for them to rest and come back refreshed. Or maybe that isn't your company policy; work them till they drop, that's what we say. (Just kidding. We think.)

✔ **Information-protection policy:** Your policies must ensure that if you do allow laptops to be taken away, the information is suitably protected. One measure you can use, for example, is full-disk encryption. If a laptop is lost, it may ruin a vacation, but there's no reason to ruin the company as well!

You're a Stranger Around Here

Suppose you're just passing through on a business trip. No one knows who you are or what you do; you don't know who other people are or what they do. You are now at risk of being compromised — and in your enthusiasm could actually contribute to a data-leak incident, even if you were *just doing your best*. It's time to be wary and get smart.

Sweets from strangers

We're taught as children not to take sweets from strangers. They might be bad people, trying to do something unmentionable. When you grow up, especially if you're an engineer (authorial experience speaks!), you're only too pleased to get something for free. Of course, sweets don't really hold the same appeal as when we were kids, but free USB memory you can drop in a pocket? That's a different story. Many of us have drawers full of USB sticks, from 16MB to 2GB models.

Unfortunately, those innocent-looking gadgets could be harboring viruses, Trojans, keyloggers, or other nasty malware. (There's precedent: in pre-Internet days, viruses spread via infected floppy disk. As document files were moved from system to system on disk, the virus went too.) What's worse, malware on a USB key can be enabled to run at the moment the stick is inserted into a machine — completely transparently to the user. Infection or data gathering can take just a few seconds — and all the time you're thinking *Great, a 2GB USB key*. Of course, it doesn't have to *be* a USB key that provides the lure; it could be a CD-ROM offering a free vacation or a DVD with "free software".

Protecting new hires

Why should new hires be singled out for protection? The answer is simple: They don't know the system. When you're an old hand, you know what to expect, what's *normal,* and what's odd. When you're new, you don't — so you can be targeted by cyber-criminals — especially if you've just put the details of your exciting new job on your social-networking page! (Please tell us you didn't do that.)

Education is important for any new hires; they need to know whom to trust and whom to ask if there is a problem or issue. Data leaks are a real problem, and new people don't yet have a handle on the risks and consequences. You need a well-documented *information-protection policy* that sets out the rules and regulations for employees. Writing it isn't enough; do your best to ensure that it's read and understood. If it's effective, it will be updated regularly;everyone on staff — not only new hires — will need periodic refreshers. As your policy evolves, its new features might address (for example) new legislation or legal regulations in your industry, a revision of password policies, or the adoption of new technology to reduce data-loss risk. It must also cover what to do in the event of a data breach; *when* (not *if*) such an event happens, it will affect everyone in the company.

New hires have a lot of stuff to master, but perhaps the most important priority to engender in them is to protect the organization's data at least as well as they would their own. (Protecting their own isn't a bad idea, either.)

Working from home

Okay, so you probably aren't a stranger in your own home, but what about other people? If you have a wireless Internet connection, is that open to attack?

If you have a wireless connection that's always on and open, then — sure enough — corporate data is at risk! Unless you live on a big, big plot of land, chances are your wireless signal will travel outside the boundaries of your property and be available for drive-by *pharmers.* (These are the cyber-criminals who drive around in their cars looking for wireless networks to use for their own nefarious purposes. This activity is known as *wardriving.*)

Pharmers can use your wireless network to mount three main types of attack:

- **Against your home computer:** Remember, while the topic of this book is essentially for business, cyber-criminals are also after your data as well. If you, in effect, *leave a window open,* they will happily climb in and take whatever they feel is of value.

✔ **Against your work computer:** To cyber-criminals, a computer's a computer, wherever it is. If they happen to get sensitive work information, they'll be happy to sell that!

✔ **Against your work network:** If they can take control of your work computer, they can access your work data. If they install a Trojan, they can disrupt network service as soon as you go back into work!

Scary stuff? Sure, but you knew that. Here are some basic countermeasures:

✔ **Buy a hardware firewall.** Don't connect to a broadband Internet connection directly; buy a broadband router with a built-in firewall. Layered security will make it tough for anyone to get in from outside.

✔ **Lock down your wireless connection point.** If you have wireless at home, make sure that it's suitably locked down so no one else can use it without your permission.

✔ **Keep your anti-virus and anti-malware applications up to date.** This is just as important for your home machines as for your work machine.

Security is only as strong as the weakest link. Make sure that your home computer isn't that weakest link, and apply that standard to all offsite computers used to handle company data.

Part III
Prevention at the Office

The 5th Wave — By Rich Tennant

In this part . . .

The traditional perimeter for IT is no longer adequate; e-mail is responsible for data leaking out of the office on a regular basis — not on purpose necessarily, but because of outdated business processes and technologies. Fortunately, this part of the book looks at how the perimeter is changing and no longer just keeps the bad stuff out, but can also be used to keep the good stuff in.

It also looks at how you need to protect the data in the datacenter and how tightening up security, authorization, and access control will not only reduce the likelihood of attacks by a hacker or cyber-criminal but will also reduce the risk of inadvertent loss by an employee.

Chapter 12

Keeping the Bad Stuff Out

At the forefront of the minds of all organizations is the security of information, none more so than . . . well, everywhere. Every business sector or organizational provider of stuff is facing a potentially damaging crisis of confidence with its customers. Worrying about what is leaving your network is fine and dandy as long as you protect the perimeter, wherever that might be. Until fairly recently, IT security was simply about a firewall and a dash of anti-virus. Not so today.

This chapter looks at how to ensure that you can keep the bad stuff out, and the bad people out. Security is not just about viruses, Trojans and spam. It is focused on keeping cyber-criminals out of the network and preventing them from taking over IT resources for subversive goals. This chapter looks at how you can ensure that at every perimeter point of your IT environment you have sufficient protection from cyber-attack.

The War Zone

Your firewall is constantly in danger of being breached. Just consider everything it has to protect (and protect against). The scene is complex:

- ✔ A proliferation of new mobile devices, phones, PDAs, laptops, and desktops.

- ✔ A welter of critical servers: file servers, messaging servers, database servers.

✔ A culture of doing business anywhere at any time, partly a response to pressures from globalization.

✔ A range of security threats motivated by cold, hard cash, as a quest for notoriety gives way to organized cyber-crime.

If your firewall lets anything nasty in, this time it isn't just the infrastructure that will suffer; it's the customer — an even more damaging implication.

Some traditional security measures are being circumvented:

✔ **Perimeter firewalls:** These can't block access to ports used for legitimate purposes. Packet scanning is only effective against *recognizable* signatures.

✔ **Network intrusion detection:** It can only reliably detect worms after they've compromised some systems and are actively spreading. It's a bit like closing the stable door after the horse has bolted.

✔ **Basic personal firewall:** It can't lock down the system enough to prevent a worm from acting like an authorized application.

✔ **Patch-management solutions:** These don't address the window of vulnerability that exists before a patch is applied. They're are also ineffective against unknown attacks.

✔ **Anti-virus (AV) alone:** Damage is done by the time the virus definition is deployed.

Okay, so you've got anti-virus wall to wall — that means you're safe, right? After all, security *is* AV *is* security, right? Well, no. Anti-virus is all well and good, but what about hackers, spam, identity theft, denial of service, and other security issues? All are on the rise.

Gone are the days when you could put up a firewall, turn on the anti-virus, and expect it to *do the job.* We're all constantly bombarded with attacks that try to discover security details that would compromise our accounts. USB memory keys and free Wi-Fi guest access to the corporate network are only the most visible and typical of the current dangers; points of vulnerability with the potential to compromise network security are constantly proliferating.

To combat increased competition, organizations have been forced to take some steps that usually involve adding or changing their technology:

✔ Optimizing and enhancing product margins

✔ Improving stock availability and time to market

✔ Increasing sales and customer service

✔ Delivering the right mix of products or services, at the right time, and in the right place.

To do all this, we've connected everything to the network and the outside world. That's good if you want to gain a competitive advantage — *and* if you want to risk losing your intellectual property or customer data and going out of business.

We're now creating huge amounts of unstructured, unmanaged information in the data center and on remote mobile devices. All this stuff is increasingly vulnerable and susceptible to security threats (data loss included), disasters, outages, regulatory compliance requirements, and the usual peaks and troughs in business.

No wonder organizations are looking for ways to

- ✔ Manage the IT environment.
- ✔ Ensure continuity of operations.
- ✔ Manage the layers of the infrastructure.
- ✔ Ensure the discovery of all IT assets.
- ✔ Ensure the protection of the infrastructure.
- ✔ Manage the information contained on all devices.
- ✔ Secure and manage the thousands of business interactions that take place daily.

Every event faced by IT can affect IT resources adversely and have a serious impact on how well an organization maintains enterprise-wide performance, availability, and reliability. IT organizations need a solution that is fast, flexible, fully automated, and integrated with the storage and data-protection architecture.

IT has a number of tasks that the business expects it to carry out:

- ✔ Make sure that the Internet is safe for business.
- ✔ Protect e-mail (the lifeblood of any business).
- ✔ Protect data from user error or system failure.
- ✔ Ensure fast data recovery from any disaster.
- ✔ Be prepared for when data growth gets explosive.

The Threat from E-mail

Increasing volume and size of e-mail leads to increase in cost of *storing* e-mail. Attachments proliferate, more messages are sent to multiple recipients, and the sum volume of a single message exponentially. Regulations obligate corporations to retain e-mail messages for a longer period time; the cost for storing e-mail increases even faster than the number and size of the messages.

In addition to the increase in legitimate e-mail volume, the biggest challenge organizations are having is a significant increase in the volume of spam — now up to 90 percent of total incoming corporate e-mail. Spam is a drag on performance of e-mail servers, wastes network bandwidth, and has an impact on employees' productivity. Also, spam e-mail is used often as a mechanism to propagate malicious codes such as viruses, worms, and spyware that can compromise customer and confidential data.

And then we also have to worry about instant messaging (IM). Most users in most organizations use IM, even if the IT department doesn't support it. As a nuisance, IM may take over where e-mail leaves off. As the rate of communication increases, we're convinced that there must be a limit to the amount of interruptions anyone has to deal with — and IM is intrusive!

Attackers increasingly target IM to proliferate viruses, worms, *spim* (yes, that's spam over IM), malware, and phishing attacks. These attacks have grown exponentially over the past few years, increasing the need for real-time threat response for IM and other peer-to-peer applications.

The move from spam to phishing

Over time, the overall impact of messaging threats has begun to be understood and measured in the following ways:

✔ End-user productivity decreases due to

- Asset damage and downtime due to virus attacks and worm outbreaks.

- Regulatory pressure to monitor and control inbound and outbound e-mail content.

- Time spent by administrators to deploy and manage a messaging-security solution.

✔ At the same time, messaging threats are constantly evolving:

- Spam accounted for 90 percent of all business e-mail traffic during November 2007. Don't expect that to go down any time soon.

- Playing on people's desperation for a tax refund, spammers and phishers have been sending official-looking e-mails bearing the logo of the U.S. Treasury Department.

- Spammers are also capitalizing on rising fuel and gas prices, promoting various dubious fuel- or cost-saving schemes.

The issue is compounded by the challenge of keeping up with growing messaging and spam volume — while keeping costs down. Increasingly, this means deploying a solution that integrates e-mail security, IM security, and outbound content-control capabilities.

Anti-spam technology can stop inbound spam (or at least slow it down, if you're required to receive all inbound messages for legal reasons) by using sender-reputation metrics to reduce the bandwidth of inbound TCP/IP streams to a single message per minute — or less. As the undelivered spam backs up on the spammers' systems, they simply give up and move on to their next target (that's the thinking, anyway). This traffic-throttling mechanism is called *traffic shaping*. It reliably reduces up to half of the overall e-mail volume.

Endpoint security

Endpoint security — safeguarding the technology that provides end-user's with their work tools — is one of the most critical computer security issues that organizations face today. But most organizations continue to be complacent about the threats posed by misappropriated data and stolen devices. *Another day, another stolen device* is a commonplace attitude we encounter almost daily An employee laptop containing personal information goes missing; a government official leaves a USB key in a taxi; a medical practitioner gets a PDA stolen with 2,500 patients' insurance numbers . . . the list seems to be endless. Will companies never learn?

Endpoint-security solutions (at both ends of the value chain) enable organizations to evaluate, protect, and remediate systems — whether managed or unmanaged — as they connect to corporate systems. Endpoint protection offers organizations and their customers a perimeter of defense to ensure that all electronic interactions are current with security software before a transaction takes place. This enforcement enables IT to address the crucial task of protecting the enterprise from the exposure of intellectual property, costly network downtime, and possible security breaches that can undermine an organization's brand integrity and affect customer confidence.

Risk with the best of intentions

Remember that these days firewalls are constantly in danger of being breached. The risk can come even from innocent directions:

- ✔ You're given a presentation from a colleague, partner, or occasional passerby (it happens) via a USB memory key.
- ✔ You allow your children to use your company laptop to do their homework.
- ✔ You work on e-mail on corporate servers via a handheld device.

✔ You utilize the free Wi-Fi at the hotel you're staying in.

✔ You provide a partner with a guest access to the corporate network to download materials for marketing.

Bottom line: The number of points of vulnerability that have the potential to compromise network security is increasing every day.

Watching all the doors

IT managers must overcome a host of technical challenges to implement successful remote operations which include bandwidth-deficient network connections, frequently changing desktop applications, user equipment physically distant from maintenance experts, and limited physical observation. Attackers are no longer focused on large, multi-purpose attacks against traditional security devices; now they're focusing on regional targets from which to steal corporate, personal, financial, or confidential information.

This combination of increased entry points and more sophisticated threats pokes holes in traditional security measures:

✔ Perimeter firewalls can't block access to ports used for legitimate purposes, nor can they lock down the system fast enough to prevent a worm infection.

✔ Network intrusion-detection systems can detect worms reliably only *after* they've compromised the system.

✔ Patch-management solutions can't prevent a vulnerability that exists before a patch is applied.

✔ Anti-virus solutions often deploy the newest virus definitions only *after* the damage is done.

In essence, all organizations need to reassess their security efforts — and focus more heavily on endpoint protection and endpoint compliance. The only solution that does this job is automation (as shown in Figure 12-1).

Automation is made up of three key components:

✔ **Policies:** What is it we want to achieve?

✔ **Configurations:** What are the configurations we need to aspire to?

✔ **Workflows:** How do we get from what we have to where we want to be, based on the policy and the required configuration?

Finally, the whole thing is driven by metrics that bring all these measures together.

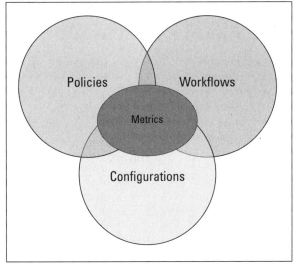

Thus endpoint security is a required component of an overall, enterprise-wide security strategy. Endpoint security emphasizes multiple, overlapping, and mutually supportive defensive systems to guard against single-point failures that can happen to any specific technology or protection method. Specifically, this security in-depth security approach includes deployment of not only anti-virus and firewalls, but also intrusion-detection and intrusion-protection systems — *on client systems*.

Endpoint-security solutions enable organizations to evaluate, protect, and remediate whatever systems connect to corporate assets, regardless of whether the connecting system is managed or unmanaged. After all, asking the security question *after* granting network access means asking too late. Endpoint protection offers a perimeter of defense to ensure that all devices are current with security software before entering the corporate network. This dogmatic enforcement approach enables IT to address the crucial task of protecting the enterprise from exposure of intellectual property, costly network downtime, and possible regulatory fines that can undermine a company's brand integrity.

Seven Deadly Sins of Perimeter Security

✔ **Assuming that all endpoints are computers.** They are not; they can be USB devices, removable storage, printers, switches, routers, and MP3 players that connect to endpoints, even a server.

✔ **Having no idea who or what is joining your network, or where.** That amounts to letting strangers in — from unauthorized, employee-owned mobile devices to rogue Wi-Fi access points, or connections from unknown remote offices.

✔ **Tying down only the endpoint and leaving the network open.** In effect, this invites abuse from hackers and information thieves who misuse the endpoints you're attempting to protect.

✔ **Setting security policies without informing your users.** Users need to know what the policies are if they are to follow them. It's a lot more effective than just telling the users what they should and shouldn't do and then using raw technology to enforce each edict.

✔ **Having no response plan for lost or stolen laptops or other handheld devices.** There is, for example, technology that will wipe stolen laptops remotely.

✔ **Having no lifecycle-management policy for your assets, especially for adding and retiring endpoints.** When a laptop is ready to go to the Great Hardware Grave, remove the computer's network name so it can no longer log on to the network. Then wipe the machine of any corporate data.

✔ **Failing to get sufficient support from upper management for security policies.** Without that support, IT has difficulty enforcing any security policies effectively. Point out to the brass how malware can get into the corporate network ("let me count the ways . . . "), what it can do to the company, and what's needed to block the invaders and patch security holes.

The Patience of Today's Criminals

Security threats are no longer focused on virus writers and hackers who attack organizations simply because they can. Instead, current threats are designed for personal (and even illegitimate corporate) gain. Examples include an increase in data theft and data leakage, and the creation of malicious code that targets specific organizations for information that can be used for financial gain. An underground economy, run by cyber-criminals who abuse hijacked company servers, sell stolen information to the bad guys, usually for later use in identity theft.

The cyber-criminal is in this game for the long term. No short-term goals or mere pranks will do. As Woody Allen said, "Just because you're paranoid doesn't mean they aren't after you." They *are* after you — after your data, in any event — and they will use what they steal at the best possible moment. That moment is *not necessarily* now. When you've just pulled off a heist in Utah, the last thing you do is start throwing around buckets of cash. Same with the cyber-criminal. Bottom line: Data loss now will have reciprocal effects *in the future*.

One recently uncovered (and unsettling) fact is that cyber-gangs have been funding local students to attend Western universities as a way to infiltrate the latest security research. Undergraduate courses in those schools usually take three or four years to complete — which shows just how long the bad guys are prepared to wait for some insider information.

Spear phishing

Spear phishing is an attempted e-mail spoofing fraud that targets a specific organization, seeking unauthorized access to confidential data. As with e-mail messages used in regular phishing expeditions, spear-phishing messages appear to come from a trusted source. Phishing messages tend to look as if they've come from a large and well-known brand. Spear phishing gets more specific; the e-mail looks like it's from a colleague inside the recipient's own company, or has more context to make the recipient believe that the fake sender is real.

Spear phishers tend to select their fake sender carefully; usually it's someone who's in authority but credible as a contact. If you got an e-mail from the president of the company (or, for that matter, the leader of the country) you might wonder why. The same e-mail from someone nearer your echelon in the company might not arouse suspicion.

Here's how spear phishing works:

✔ The cyber-criminal surfs the Web for a site that has details of employees and other corporate information that would be useful to make the attack look more authentic. (Just think about some of the information people put on their social-networking sites . . . .)

✔ They discover the domain name through the *Contact Us* link on the Web site. Only a few combinations are needed to work out the e-mail naming convention. Here are two common examples:

```
firstname_surname@company.com
```

```
firstname.surname@company.com
```

✔ Using these details, the cyber-criminal drafts an e-mail that appears to come from an individual who has every reason to ask for confidential information. This might be a fake Sys Admin or HR representative.

✔ The e-mail asks for user names and passwords, or asks the victim to visit a Web site that will result in the user downloading spyware (such as keyloggers).

✔ If only one staff member falls for the scam, the cyber-criminal still has access to the network and can do untold damage.

Shields against spear phishing

Here are some measures you can take to stop spear phishing:

- ✔ **Constantly remind employees of the dangers of phishing and how social engineering works.** The goal is to stop them from falling for the scam in the first place.

- ✔ **Keep updating employees on the latest cyber-crime trends.** This kind of education is immediately practical.

- ✔ **Run a test "scam" on your own organization.** Send out an e-mail from an appropriate source, telling staff to click a link to verify some form of confidential information. When they do, send them and e-mail telling them they've just been duped, that "this was only a test," and that their behavior could easily have resulted in downloads of spyware, Trojan horses, and/or other malware.

- ✔ **Keep your anti-virus and anti-spyware definitions up to date.** That way, if you click something you shouldn't, the updates will help block any malware deposited on your machine.

- ✔ **Ensure you have good anti-spam software.** After all, if 90 percent of e-mails delivered to large companies are spam, you want to filter out as much as you can.

- ✔ **Think about hosted mail-security services.** If you're not a specialist at looking at these types of messages, engage someone to do it who is.

- ✔ **Conduct penetration testing on your own company every year (at least once a year).** In addition to testing your defenses, it keeps your awareness heightened.

- ✔ **Use e-mail traffic shaping to protect yourself from mass attacks.** For more about that, read on . . . .

Throttling spammers by shaping traffic

Traffic shaping (sometimes called *throttling*) can reduce spam by 80 percent before it shows any impact on the network and e-mail infrastructure. There is some neat technology that can identify traffic at the TCP level, causing mail to back up on the spammers' servers instead of on yours, so *their* infrastructure has to bear the burden of all that spam. The idea is simple:

- ✔ Trusted senders get the full bandwidth inside the corporate network.

- ✔ If the sender is not trusted, the bandwidth is severely curtailed.

Traffic shaping can significantly reduce administrative overhead, network bottlenecks, mail infrastructure costs, and storage requirements. (And okay, the idea really appeals to our sense of humor. Something about hoisting a spammer with his own petard.)

Big fish and little fish

Here's an example of thinking like a cyber-criminal (always a useful exercise when you're heightening security awareness): If you're going to phish with spears, what's the best phish to phish for? It's not rocket science. But it does have levels . . . .

Whales

The cyber-criminals have worked out that aiming high reaps the best rewards and isn't necessarily a tougher nut to crack either. So the cyber-criminal is going after those with the most to lose: executives. This type of phishing is known as *whaling,* and it works like this:

1. The cyber-criminal finds the name and e-mail address of a company's top executive or handful of executives (you can find this on most large corporate Web sites).

2. The bad guy then crafts an e-mail, specific to the targeted executive's role in the organization, that attempts to get the victim to click a link.

Minnows

Minnowing is the opposite of whaling; it goes on at the lower end of the organization. This is where the cyber-criminal targets the people in departments such as Accounts Payable to get them to pay a fictitious bill:

1. Pick the company. It needs to be big enough that people in Accounts Payable don't necessarily know what has or hasn't been done.

2. Find more information about a specific individual.

   This is where social-networking sites prove to be a risk. People put all kinds of information (along with pictures) there — including where they work, the departments, and even phone numbers — on the Web for all to see.

3. E-mail to find what has happened to the fictitious payment, and then escalate from there. (The attack vector is the same as the FAX scams of old.)

   If you're impersonating a real supplier, make a quick phone call to ascertain an outstanding bill:

   > "I was just checking to see what happened to payment for invoice 1234."

   > "Don't you mean 5678?"

   > "Oh, did you get the change in our bank details for payment?"

Awareness of the threat and staff education — including refreshers for those most at risk — should be in place before an actual threat is spotted.

Wireless Security to Prevent Data Loss

Wireless networking has created a much more flexible working environment, but remember: Wireless signals leak outside the building! Unlike the fixed-wire network where you need to be inside the building (and therefore subject to the more normal physical security), the wireless network can extend to the parking lot or across the street or anywhere else. Figure 12-2 shows how easy it is to park in range of a wireless network that has extended into the parking lot — and then hack into the network whenever you're ready.

If the network is available from outside the building, then cyber-criminals can sit in the comfort of their cars while attacking the network. No has to be quick about it. For this reason, wireless networks should be locked down and scanned for on a regular basis.

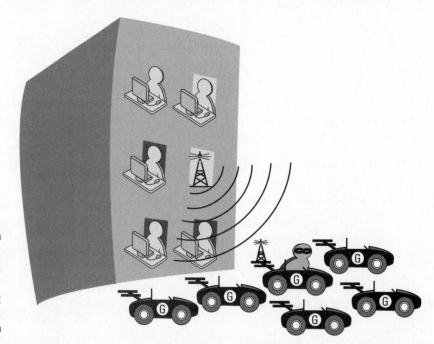

Figure 12-2: Wireless outside. Hack at leisure.

Scanning for wireless networks

This should be done on a regular basis. Anyone with a suitably equipped laptop can do it, quickly and effectively, by wandering around with the laptop looking for networks. After all, that's what opportunistic cyber-criminals do, and it works well enough that they have names for the activity: *pharming* or *wardriving*. In essence, it's finding someone's stray Wi-Fi network signal and making off with the data. But when you do it for the sake of stopping data leaks, it's a legitimate security measure.

It isn't just access points that pose a risk. Individuals with laptops pose a similar risk — not only when they're in coffee shops, but also when they're traveling. It's possible to set up the laptop for peer-to-peer wireless networking; usually, in such instances, the Bluetooth capability is enabled. Laptops that aren't sufficiently locked down will connect automatically to form a peer-to-peer network. When the machine is connected, the data is at risk. Ensure that laptops are configured so they *won't* connect automatically to the first wireless network that comes along!

Countering drive-by pharming

Make sure that your router or access point is placed well. In a perfect world, Wi-Fi signals should normally reach to the perimeter of a home or office — and no farther. A small amount of signal leakage outside the perimeter isn't an issue, but the farther this signal reaches, the easier it is for others to detect and exploit. Large campuses are really difficult places in which to manage Wi-Fi spillage, just so long as it doesn't leak onto someone else's business premises. With some wireless routers and access points, you can lower the power of the wireless LAN (WLAN) transmitter and reduce the range of the signal. Although it's nearly impossible to fine-tune a signal so it won't leak outside your building, with a wild stab at it you can often limit how much leakage you get so you can minimize the opportunity for outsiders to access your WLAN.

Invest in one of those $10 Wi-Fi locators to find out how much leakage you're producing, but also (more to the point) to find other so-and-sos who are either drive-by pharmers or some "helpful" employee who has stuck a booster WLAN router under his or her desk (or in a conference room) *because more people needed to connect to the network and this seemed like a simple solution.*

Locking down your wireless routers

Most people who set up a wireless network at home or in the office tear through the process as fast as they can so they can get their Internet connection working as soon as possible. When most people install technology, they want functionality first; security doesn't enter their thought processes. The problem is that people in the throes of techno-joy rarely consider closely what they're trying to do. That's understandable, but it's also dangerous. There are numerous security pitfalls to tumble into. Here's a quick checklist.

You can improve the security of your wireless network by developing some Wi-Fi-wise habits:

✓ **Always change the default administrator password.** The setup process for an access port or router can often entail long trails through Web pages that allow owners to enter their network address and account information. These are all protected with a login screen that requires a username and password. Don't use the default administrator password.

All default logins for any piece of equipment are simple — and well known to hackers on the Internet. Change the passwords before you do anything else.

✓ **Turn on some form of encryption.** All Wi-Fi equipment supports some form of encryption. This can be WPA (Wi-Fi Protected Access) or at least WEP (Wired Equivalency Privacy). Although you will want to pick the strongest form of encryption that works with your wireless network, make sure that all Wi-Fi devices on your network share the same encryption settings. WEP encryption is easier to crack; WPA or WPA2 provides better protection and is easier to use.

✓ **Turn on MAC filtering.** The *MAC address* (sometimes called the *physical address*) is unique to each Wi-Fi component. Access points and routers keep track of the MAC addresses of all devices and each of their dependents. Most Wi-Fi products can restrict the network to allow connections only from those devices listed in the MAC addresses. This sounds like really good but it can be limiting: you need to find and enter the 12-character MAC address of every system that will connect to your network. This can become tricky if you're working on a large installation. MAC addresses can be *spoofed* easily by bad guys who know what they're doing. MAC filtering isn't a guarantee of security, but at least it adds another hurdle for the cyber-criminal to jump over.

✓ **Change the default SSID.** Access points and routers all use a network name called the *SSID.* Manufacturers normally ship their products with the same SSID set. *You should change this.* It won't stop the average well-versed hacker from breaking into your network, but it does put cyber-criminals off because they tend to assume that *a default SSID equals a poorly configured network.* If you show them you're not an easy target, they have more reason to look somewhere else.

While you're at it, turn off the SSID broadcast. Most WLAN routers continually broadcast the network's name, or SSID making it dead easy to set up wireless clients because you don't need to know what it's called but also dead easy for occasional passers-by to see your network.

✓ **Pay attention to your firewall.** Most network routers nowadays have firewall capability; this means that you can turn on firewalls for further protection. That also means someone could turn them off too:

• Ensure that your router's firewall is turned on.

• Install and run personal firewall software on each computer connected to the router.

✔ **Take care how you use dynamic IP addresses.** Most home networkers use dynamic IP addresses via the Dynamic Host-Configuration Protocol (DHCP). This capability uses a pool of IP addresses — and cyber-criminals can snag that resource pretty easily. Turn off DHCP, at the router or at the access point, and set a fixed range of IP addresses; configure each connected device to use a matching private IP address range. Th idea is to prevent your computers from being reached directly via the Internet. A couple more Wi-Fi safety hints are in order:

- *Turn it off when you aren't using it.* This is the most obvious, the most effective, *and the least used* method of protecting yourself:

    If you own a wireless router but are only using it wired (Ethernet) connections, you can sometimes turn off Wi-Fi on a broadband router without powering down the entire network.

- *Always disable the wireless network when not in use.* If you don't, the wireless connectivity leaves your machine vulnerable to being compromised.

- *Turn off the Auto-connect option that opens Wi-Fi networks.* It doesn't discriminate among wireless networks, which can expose your computer to all sorts of security risks.

✔ **Turn off Bluetooth.** From a security standpoint, it's pointless and insecure.

✔ **Consider disabling remote administration.** You should use this feature only if it lets you define a specific IP address or limited range of addresses. Otherwise, almost anyone — anywhere — could potentially find and access your router.

If you're doing all this to make your workplace more secure, then do it at home, too. After you hone your wireless security skills at work, home should take about ten minutes. It's well worth the time.

Utilizing Hardware Appliances

Hardware security appliances come in many flavors, traditionally security appliances have been pre-built high performance operating systems with dedicated applications on dedicated server hardware. The advantage of hardware appliances is that your security is all ready to go. The following sections go into the pros and cons of appliances (virtual or otherwise).

All-in-one protection isn't a bad idea, but make sure any all-in-one solution you consider covers the basics. It must still enable administrators to

- ✔ Stop spam, denial-of-service attacks, and other inbound e-mail threats.

- ✔ Analyze global and local sender reputation, which can help you reduce e-mail infrastructure costs by restricting unwanted connections.

- ✔ Filter e-mail content to remove unwanted content, demonstrate regulatory compliance, and protect against leaking intellectual property and data over e-mail.

- ✔ Secure and protect public IM communications, using the same management console as e-mail.

- ✔ Obtain visibility into messaging trends and events with minimal administrative burden.

While messaging threats in general are on the rise, they also fluctuate in their intensity. That's why many organizations demand the capability to adjust their spam- and virus-filtering capacity instantly, without having to add or configure physical infrastructure. The quickest way to attain this instant ajustment is through virtualization, which can scale message security up or down, quickly and incrementally. An added benefit is improved efficiency in utilizing resources efficiently — and there's no need to do massive installations of special-purpose hardware that can't be used for other applications when the spam waves recede.

A virtual defense system for messaging can centralize your control of security provisioning so you can increase or decrease the scanning of messages instantly, for all your servers and appliances. Such a system can synchronize configurations automatically, which helps you not only improve efficiency but also meet compliance standards and regulatory mandates for your industry.

Plug and Play gateway appliances can provide you with some built-in advantages:

- ✔ Anti-spam, anti-virus, and advanced content filtering.

- ✔ Sensitive data control.

- ✔ Effectiveness greater than 97 percent.

- ✔ Automatic compliance with regulatory mandates.

- ✔ Scanning capability for messaging infrastructures, with automatic removal of unsolicited messages from network and mailbox servers.

- ✔ Scanning and filtering capabilities for e-mail and IM.

Chapter 13

Keeping the Good Stuff In

. . . .

. . . .

Keeping the good stuff in is about preparation. News of data breaches bring home the reality that organizations are seriously vulnerable to e-criminals mugging their digital assets, malicious insiders deliberately leaking information, and other employees losing data on laptops and CD-ROMS. Worldwide legislation that forces companies to disclose data breaches has elevated what used to be whoops-we-blundered-again mistakes to headline news.

To make matters worse, what looks like a cybercrime may be an honest mistake or run-of-the-mill carelessness. A typical instance of a careless data breach starts when someone obtains copies of someone else's identifiable personal information or company intellectual property. But there's no guarantee that the person who appropriates that data

- ✔ Will know what it is
- ✔ Was after it in the first place
- ✔ Can use it

If (for instance) an employee leaves his or her laptop in the back of a car in plain view and later finds it gone, it's regrettable but not all that surprising. It doesn't necessarily mean that an e-criminal has been stalking this individual.

For every $1 spent today preventing bad things happening, you will spend $10 fixing the immediate problem and $100 shoring up the long-term issue.

Global organizations and government agencies require more than network security to guard their confidential data and sensitive information. They must protect the data itself. Yet most organizations have little insight into where their confidential data is stored, and where it's going. They rarely have any idea of these basics:

- ✔ Who is accessing what
- ✔ What their data is
- ✔ Where their data is
- ✔ How the data is being used

They may also be unaware that data leaks fall into four basic categories:

- ✔ Unauthorized or illegal access
- ✔ Hardware loss, theft, sale, or disposal
- ✔ Employee error
- ✔ Employee abuse

Whatever else one might say about it, the adult entertainment industry is tops at keeping its customer information safe. If that data were lost, it could cause huge embarrassment and a lot of cancelled subscriptions.

Protecting Intellectual Property

Many industries don't have nearly so much awareness of what their data can do in the "wrong" hands. This lack of understanding forces security-conscious organizations to carry out a number of top-line changes in how they do business:

- ✔ Identify and protect data appropriately
- ✔ Deploy comprehensive data-protection solutions
- ✔ Ensure appropriate network-access control
- ✔ Achieve regulatory compliance (save money)

Although many businesses cite compliance and external regulations as what drives their pursuit of protecting sensitive data, the best at this are more likely to identify *data-loss prevention* (DLP) as a top priority. Compliance tends to be the excuse for making sure that the organization has appropriate security measures in place.

Considerations for keeping the good stuff in should include these:

- ✔ Definition and enforcement of data usage policy
- ✔ Discovery of sensitive data
- ✔ Training in data use and compliance requirements
- ✔ Monitoring, auditing and reporting of data use

Also consider the following technologies to give your company both a higher level of general security and specific help in preventing data leaks:

- ✔ Data-loss prevention solutions
- ✔ Endpoint security measures
- ✔ Anti-spam
- ✔ Anti-phishing, anti-pharming, and anti-spyware solutions
- ✔ Web filtering
- ✔ Endpoint encryption (at the file, folder, and device level)
- ✔ Encryption and key-management solutions
- ✔ Enterprise rights-management solutions
- ✔ Network access control
- ✔ Personal- and network-level intrusion detection and prevention

Messaging systems

You should know that 90 percent of all IT security attacks come from messaging systems. The number-one messaging system is e-mail, specifically corporate e-mail. Other messaging systems include instant messaging and Web-based e-mail; there is a lot of crossover now, as Voice over Internet Protocol (VoIP) solutions enable files to be sent and instant messaging allows speech. Messaging systems can be the bane of our lives as well as an extraordinary way to reach friends, business partners, and new customers. Today's organizations depend on enterprise-wide messaging applications — used by everyone from employees and customers to suppliers and partners. These applications support key business processes such as e-commerce and business intelligence, but they also create a mountain of information that must be successfully harnessed, securely stored, continually accessible, *and* safe from leakage.

Organizations that don't protect this data — or don't have a comprehensive data-protection plan — are under threat from data loss, with all its implications for potential loss of revenue, customer loyalty, share value, brand equity, and market share.

The threats are real. Just pick up a newspaper on any day of the week and in any part of the world to find an (in)appropriate story on a data-loss incident!

Today's turbulent, networked world presents many risks to corporate information: security breaches, blended attacks, terrorist threats, floods, and power outages, not to mention earthquakes and other natural disasters, can devastate businesses. Actually, human-caused disasters are topping the list:

- ✔ User and operator errors account for more than 32 percent of permanent data loss.
- ✔ Cyber-crime and computer virus attacks are the fastest-growing cause of business disruption.

Although server and storage hardware continue to improve, IT infrastructures are growing more complex, adding new potential points of failure.

Organizations require rapid, secure, and continual availability and integrity of their information. Watertight data protection is therefore critical. But as organizations rely more on the rapid, continual availability of information, the means of keeping it that way become more complex.

Nonstop, 24/7 operations require data-protection solutions that can deliver robust, scalable storage management, backup, and recovery. This protection must be available from desktop to data center, for a mix of data environments — and delivered from a single location. Not only does this approach take the onus of data management off the shoulders of end-users, it can also streamline, scale, and automate backup throughout the organization.

Twenty years ago, we didn't have e-mail or any type of electronic messaging solution and still the world went around (maybe more slowly, but it still went around). Nowadays, it seems we can't even remember our names unless we have e-mail running. Every transaction through our small corners of the commerce world is done through messaging systems.

We still can't restrain ourselves from checking e-mail. Every two or three minutes that silly little box appears, telling you that you have unread messages — and you can't resist checking to see whether it's that Really Important Message (which may not be all that important or interesting), or someone trying to push some performance-enhancing drug. And after you've accessed your new messages, have you lost the thread of the task you were doing?

Perhaps you're exhausted by the time it takes to manage your in-box each day. Even if you have a technological/business, love/hate relationship with your e-mail, you still have to manage your in-box.

It's like a drug — you can't resist it:

"I'll just check my e-mail."

"Let's see if I've got any messages."

"Just logging in, darling, to see if anything's come in."

And your partner replies:

"Why can't you leave that alone?"

"You're becoming distant and withdrawn."

But, you can handle it — it's only 200 or 300 e-mails a day:

You can stop whenever you like.

It's a social thing.

You only do IM at parties in the kitchen and e-mail on the weekend.

It isn't as if you can't stop!

Okay, let's just assume that you *won't* stop using e-mail. How do you protect it?

Protecting e-mail from accidental (or not-so-accidental) loss

The big-picture issue surrounding electronic messaging is its management and security. As e-mail has become an indispensable application for conducting business, electronic messaging has evolved and taken on new functions. It went from being a communication-only channel to a repository that contains business records, customer's confidential information, corporate documents, and business transactions — which it was really never designed to do. Small wonder that corporations see more challenges cropping up around managing e-mail.

These days, e-mail is not only a vital communication tool, but *also* home for up to 80 percent of your organization's records. Its indispensability for these purposes represents a significant risk to your confidential information. Whether the upshot is a small-scale embarrassment or a major financial disruption, the use of e-mail entails plenty of risk for confidential data loss.

Fortunately, data-protection technologies available for e-mail can sit neatly on top of your current messaging systems. These technologies usually work in one of two ways:

- ✔ Forwarding e-mails from the *mail-transfer agent* (MTA) to the data-loss prevention software for inspection, which then reflects them back to the same mail-transfer agent. (An *agent* is usually a program that performs some specific task that's designed to have minimal impact on performance.)

- ✔ Receiving messages from an upstream mail-transfer agent, analyzing the messages, and reflecting them back to a downstream mail-transfer agent.

Make sure that your chosen technological solution works with your e-mail system. In particular, make sure that its application programming interface (API) is compatible with your messaging infrastructure or mail-transfer agent.

Ensuring compatibility will allow you to use your existing infrastructure rather than having to throw everything away and start from scratch. Compatibility can even save you from having to add another step in the outbound Simple Mail Transfer Protocol (SMTP) messaging flow.

If you're using encryption, make sure that your data-loss prevention technology will work with your encryption product.

Basically, the policies set up in any data-loss solution worth its salt are designed to integrate with your mail-transfer agent(s) to block, reroute, or alter e-mail messages in response to specific content or other message attributes. If an e-mail is approved for sending, it's returned to the MTA to be sent into the e-mail process. If an e-mail breaks a policy, however, the technology can modify the e-mail header and send the message back to the originator — specifying that the message is in violation of policy. Depending on the policy violation, the MTA can return the message, send it to a quarantine folder, or forward it to an e-mail-encryption gateway.

Any e-mail that must be redirected can be routed by adding appropriate keywords, either to the subject line or to the subject header. Using these changes, MTAs can forward the message appropriately and include any additional message formatting necessary for processing (whether through encryption gateways or other downstream message systems). This type of technology holds the inbound message stream open until the outbound message stream closes; doing so ensures that the message is never lost: The sending MTA holds on to the message until the receiving MTA holds a second copy of the message.

Web-based e-mail

Web-based e-mail is an e-mail service that is accessed via a Web browser, as opposed to through an e-mail client, such as Microsoft Outlook. Most of us now have a variety of Yahoo! Mail, Hotmail, or Gmail accounts. The advantages of this system over Outlook or Lotus Notes are that you can access your e-mail through any Web browser or any machine connected through the Internet.

You might think that the employees never use Web-based e-mail for work. Wrong. There are a number of reasons for them to use it, and this is why it must be considered and protected. Here's a sampling:

- ✔ **Corporate e-mail is down.** Suppose an employee has a contract that needs to go out, and the corporate system is down. Guess who used a Web-based account to send it off.

- ✔ **They don't want work to know.** Perhaps some are going on job interviews elsewhere — or maybe they want to send some work they did to someone else. (By the way, that's a misuse of company intellectual property!) This is not necessarily always a subversive situation; possibly they might need to work at home after hours or while traveling.

- ✔ **By mistake.** Lots of people have colleagues who are also friends — and they send data via the wrong e-mail system, by accident .

- ✔ **They're malicious insiders.** Okay, so this won't be everyone — far from it — but you can't rule out the possibility of a few insiders who send sensitive information out through their own personal accounts!

In general, most Web-based e-mail is unencrypted — anyone can see it, from the service administrators to someone who's using packet-sniffing software on the Internet! (*Packet-sniffing* programs are normally used for legitimate functions related to network management. But tools have illegitimate uses as well.)

Messages sent via Web-based e-mail use the Hypertext Transfer Protocol (HTTP) or Hypertext Transfer Protocol over Secure Socket Layer (HTTPS), and File Transfer Protocol (FTP).

Hypertext Transfer Protocol (HTTP) is an information-transfer protocol for the Internet. HTTPS is a secure HTTP connection; identical to HTTP which is used in the same way with another encryption/authentication layer between the HTTP and TCP. This system was designed to provide secure communications across the Web. TCP provides reliable, ordered delivery of a stream of bytes from one program on one computer to another program on another computer — in this instance, e-mail.

In this case, data-loss prevention requires a technology that can integrate with Internet protocols to queue outbound data transmissions. The idea is to scan the content before sending. If the data transmission doesn't violate the data-loss policy, the e-mail is released and sent as normal. If the Web-based e-mail violates a policy, then the e-mail can be terminated, or the program can just remove the confidential data. If it removes the confidential information, the e-mail continues on its merry way and the Web browser is unaffected. That's just as well; sometimes the interruption of a process can crash the browser — and this wouldn't prevent data loss so much as prevent business process.

Most data-loss technologies now capture the action and enable a new Web page to pop up, informing the end-user that the message has broken a data policy and that the e-mail was blocked. Some go farther than this, allowing the policy to send the notification *and* the blocked e-mail to the individual's manager for appropriate action.

These technologies also enable other Web-based communications to be monitored and controlled, including blogs, message boards, and wikis. To be on the safe side, look for a solution that covers *all* aspects of Web-based communication.

Instant messaging

Many of us use instant messaging (IM) systems to see "who's online" these days. In effect, IM is where e-mail was five years ago: a good way to "ping" people (check to see if they're out there), send jokes, and share the odd silly picture. So far IM is absolutely useless for business documents such as proposals, requests for information, and contacts. But for how long? And as if IM isn't enough of a distraction — all those colleagues and friends sending you great big KISS pings, right? — you can now add *content* to IM systems. That means you can send all sorts of stuff that perhaps you shouldn't send via IM. Oops!

In theory, the same process can be applied to IM as to Web-based e-mail, although it's a little tricky to do. It depends on whether your network recognizes all the IM ports used by such instant-messaging systems as Sametime, Yahoo, and Live Messenger. At the moment, IM simply interrupts business with irrelevant stuff — but if you must have it, tie it down!

Technology exists today that can interrupt IM messages if they violate your data policies. You can use technology to manage, secure, log, and archive IM traffic, consumer IM networks, and enterprise IM platforms. By providing policy enforcement and security controls for text messaging, file transfers, audio, video, VoIP, application sharing, and other real-time communication capabilities, you can manage content and create regulatory-compliance policies to govern IM use.

Riding herd on IM can help to protect your organization against the loss of sensitive information or intellectual property over that route. What's needed is an appropriately detailed policy to control internal IM use and set standards for the real-time monitoring of users. IM management technology can aggregate all the IM ports to give you a single point of control. With this technology in place, you can scan IM content for IP or PII data, and archive any such data you find (for compliance purposes). By intercepting data transfers at this point, you can also strip out URLs to prevent the data from leaving the corporate network.

If you use IM internally, consider getting your own corporate IM system. That way all communication remains behind the firewall, safe from sniffers and other nastiness.

If you don't think you have IM in use in your organization, think again. There are a number of freeware IM monitors out there. Pick one, install it, and just watch the traffic. This will prove two things:

- ✔ **IM is in use inside your company.** Don't be surprised if that's true, even if it's against your corporate policy.

- ✔ **IM is insecure.** You will see all the data flowing back and forth with no encryption, no nothing.

The wrong Dave

We do this sort of thing all the time: Who hasn't sent an e-mail to the wrong person, or received one from someone who thought they were sending the message to someone else? *The wrong Dave* refers to that darling of functionality that fills in the e-mail recipient's name for you, basing its guess on previous addresses you've used. Even with extreme names like "Guy" or "Gareth" there are potential problems here. Example: There are, at the time of writing, eight "Guys" and ten "Gareths" in our organization. If you're a fore-finger (rather than four-finger) typist who doesn't look at the screen as you fumble around the keyboard, then you have eight — or ten — chances of writing to the wrong Guy or Gareth. Messages that go to folks with common names like Dave are much more likely to go to the wrong person; they're a bigger problem. Figure 13-1 shows how easy it is to write to the wrong person.

How do you stop employees from sending confidential information to the wrong *internal* recipient — let alone an external one? The easiest way is to turn off the automatic address-search function in the e-mail system. That will at least make people think about whom the message is supposed to reach, instead of picking the first name in the provided list!

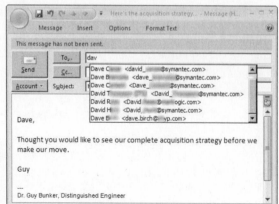

Figure 13-1:
The wrong
Dave.

In Microsoft Outlook, follow these steps to turn off the automatic address-search function in the e-mail system:

1. **In Outlook, click Tools⇨Options.**

   The Options tool box appears.

2. **In the Preferences tab, click E-Mail Options.**

   The E-mail Options Message Handling box appears.

3. **Click Advanced E-mail Options.**

   The Advanced E-mail options box appears.

4. **Un-check "Suggest names while completing To, Cc, and Bcc fields," and then click OK.**

   The Advanced E-mail options box closes.

5. **Click OK.**

   The E-mail Options Message Handling box closes.

6. **Click OK.**

An HR person (not for long after this particular event, alas) sent a list of salaries of the board to the CEO. Unfortunately, the poor HR employee picked up the CEO's alias and hit Send before the e-mail was distributed to (as it turned out) around 3,000 disgruntled employees. Oops! To compound the problem, the HR employee tried to recall the message. Instead of a few hundred employees reading the e-mail and opening the attachment, *everyone in the organization* opened it up to take a look!

To prevent this type of internal disaster from happening, companies are locking down large corporate e-mail lists so that only specific people can send to them. While this wouldn't have prevented this poor person from sending to a smaller list, at least the wrong message wouldn't have gone to the whole company!

A better solution

Although you can take a number of simple steps to regulate e-mail, nothing beats technology as a way to prevent *the wrong Dave*. The same device that prevents spam from coming into an organization can also be used to prevent the good stuff from going out.

The idea is straightforward:

1. Classify the data.
2. If the data is sensitive, prevent it from being sent outside the company.

There is, of course, a *policy engine* (a set of automated rules stored in the data-loss prevention application) in there as well, so people who are allowed to send data outside the company can do so — but this system will also catch large numbers of mis-sent e-mails. Each of these security events can also be logged, and other actions applied. Perhaps senders are warned that what they're doing is against company policy (so they can change their minds, or just realize the error before it becomes a problem), or perhaps an e-mail goes to the sender's manager as a notification of what's going on here, and the e-mail in question is quarantined for review before being released.

The key here is that the actions are based on the content of the e-mail. So if you want to send an e-mail to a friend about lunch, that goes through — but the message about acquisition targets does not.

Developing Consistent Data Classification

As an issue, the importance of data is actually as old as the hills. But understanding how we deal with electronic data — and managing its *lifecycle* — is a relatively new discipline, forced upon us through the advent of new data-compliance legislation, industry directives, quality codes of conduct, and a simple truth about data: We've got too much of it. And that's one reason we lose too much of it.

Of the data we have, too much winds up in the wrong places:

- ✔ One in 50 network files contains confidential data.
- ✔ Four out of five companies have lost confidential data when a laptop was lost.
- ✔ One in two USB drives contains confidential information.
- ✔ The average cost of a single data breach is $14 million.
- ✔ Companies that incur a data-breach experience a significant increase in customer turnover (as much as 11 percent).
- ✔ Laws in over 35 states, in addition to several federal mandates, require organizations to protect confidential information.
- ✔ Insiders are responsible for 70 percent of security incidents that incur losses.

What to do with all that data? Well (for openers), figure out what you have, classify it, sort it out, and then decide what to keep and what to pitch.

The meaning of life (-cycle management)

Many records must be retained for specific periods: from 3 months to 99 years. But simply retaining information isn't the point; easily *retrieving* the information is the issue. Simply, our ability to cope with data management isn't possible without new technologies, such as lifecycle management for your data or information, storage networking, and storage resource management (SRM). Issues such as data-loss prevention have compelled companies to reshape their storage infrastructures and start to look more carefully at how administrators plan and implement storage capacity. A vital step in this process is examining the lifecycle of data and determining how it can be effectively managed as it ages.

What to keep and for how long?

Although organizations can approach the problem with a wide-ranging statement that all data must be kept forever, that isn't always practical; *not all data is equal*. Some data is more important than other data. Data-retention legislation suggests that all data is important to all organizations, forever — but here's a reality check: Data is actually less inherently valuable to a business as it gets older.

Managing the lifecycle of data and information effectively depends on the awareness that data has different values at different moments in time. Figure 13-2 shows the lifecycle of data held in the data center. When an e-mail first arrives in your in-box, the information may be urgent (even vital) for securing a business deal or transaction. After two or three days, the information held in that e-mail may be of little significance. The longer it's in there, the less importance it has for the recipient.

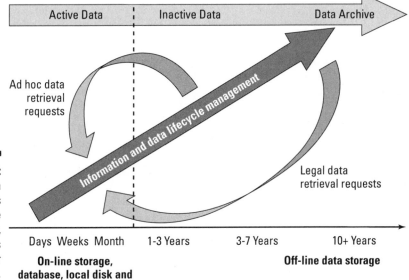

Figure 13-2:
Data remains vital to the business, but loses value over time.

If you don't need to keep it, don't! Remember, however, that information can still have value to the bad guys even if it's no longer useful to the originator.

Classifying data by its stage in the lifecycle

The lifecycle of data begins with a basic business need: *acquiring* data. During day-to-day business operations, active data must be available to decision-makers on a regular basis; they refer to it often. Over time, this data loses its importance and is accessed less often, gradually losing its business value. It becomes inactive data and eventually ends up in an archive or disused. But even then, data still has inherent value to a criminal.

As data moves through its lifecycle phases, companies can develop a strategy of policy-based management to map usage patterns and send the data to appropriate storage media. This minimizes risk in storing data and optimizes the company's storage assets. Here are some general pointers for developing such a strategy:

- ✔ Classifying data as it's created means that as it goes through a cycle of interest to the business (surely anything that isn't of interest to the business shouldn't be captured?). Data needed frequently for an active business process can be stored on fast, easily available storage devices.

- ✔ Deciding which data to store in relational databases depends on how often the data is needed. After data ceases to be active, it becomes (you guessed it) inactive. This data is no longer critical to the business, so it can be migrated to cheaper storage. After it's migrated, the number of people who have access to it diminishes — and so does the risk.

- ✔ Inactive data tends to be old files that may be useful in the future but are no longer accessed on a regular basis. The inactive stuff tends to be one to three years old; the organization still needs to be able to access and retrieve this type of data (mainly for compliance purposes) but the data itself is likely less valuable to the business.

- ✔ Archived data is no longer of immediate use to the business. If data reaches the point at which it's no longer accessed, it should be deleted (if it can be without regulatory repercussions). If it's deleted, then it can't be lost, or breached, or leaked.

Data classification and ILM as a business advantage

Data classification is the first crucial step toward managing the lifecycle of your data. Data/Information lifecycle management (DLM or ILM) offers your organization some practical advantages — including more efficient compliance with industry regulations and more efficient use of in-house resources.

DLM/ILM as an aid to compliance with regulations

While you're working on policies to cover data retention, you should consider regulatory compliance as a major factor. The following requirements are typical of industry regulations:

- ✔ All personal data must be connected to some definite term, beyond which storage and processing are not allowed. If that term is three years, then the data can't be altered in any way for the remainder of the term that it has to be kept — say, seven more years.

- ✔ All persons about whom data is held or archived must be made aware of what is contained in that electronic archive and have access to their personal data.

✔ E-mail and instant messaging content must be retained in its entirety, and must be managed and treated in the same way as personal data.

✔ All data held must be correct.

✔ All data held must be kept secure with appropriate access restrictions confined to those with legitimate reasons for having access to it.

Most countries have legislation that gives individual access to data, sets up data-management practices, guarantees security of data, ensures that individuals can request copies of their own data and gives a right of privacy to individuals. So, an organization's first act should be a look at its current electronic data/document retention policies and abilities.

Managing information lifecycle is an important skill for storage administrators because

✔ It provides a framework within which they can understand the value of different records.

✔ It helps them build storage infrastructures that reflect those determinations.

Figure 13-3 shows how data storage requirements will change over time.

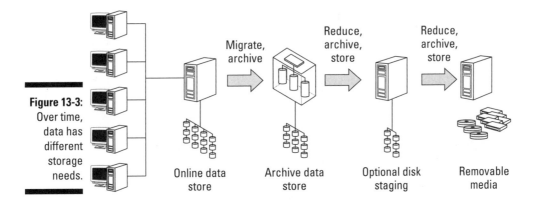

Figure 13-3: Over time, data has different storage needs.

Migrate, archive — Reduce, archive, store — Reduce, archive, store

Online data store — Archive data store — Optional disk staging — Removable media

DLM/ILM as a money-saver

It's no accident that information lifecycle management (ILM) exists in most organizations. The key benefits of software-based ILM include savings in total cost of operation, as well as indirect enhancements to an organization's business process. Here's an overview:

✔ D/ILM lowers total cost of ownership (TCO) per unit of storage capacity by

- Eliminating unnecessary copies of data to aid in hardware consolidation

- Reducing data-protection backup-and-recovery times

- Reducing the consumption of storage media

- Improving the utilization of appropriate storage resources

✔ D/ILM improves hardware utilization, uptime, and performance by

- Enabling hardware consolidation

- Eliminating disk and mailbox quotas

- Moving the most critical data to highest-performance storage with the highest level of protection

✔ D/ILM improves the efficiency of IT management by

- Providing common central administration for all aspects of data management

- Automating the use of specific classes of storage and media types for data and data copies

- Using automated, policy-based management engines to enable "management by exceptions"

✔ D/ILM improves data retention by

- Automating the retention and appropriate disposal of data to reduce the risk of regulatory non-compliance.

- Providing seemingly infinite — but appropriately managed — disk storage for users and applications.

- Storing data where appropriate, with no impact on user or application workflow.

✔ D/ILM delivers value to the business process over time by

- *Improving performance:* The most critical data remains accessible as needed, residing on the highest-performance storage as long as necessary.

- *Improving uptime:* Copy most critical data with highest level of protection resulting in a higher average uptime for data for which uptime counts most.

- *Improving — even guaranteeing — data retention:* Automated retention and disposal provide a higher degree of more verifiable compliance. This applies to both industry-specific regulations and the requirements of internal corporate governance.

Consistency counts in classification

ILM that works depends on good, consistent data classification. Done right, content-based classification can be used at multiple places in the IT environment to prevent data leaks. Inconsistent classification can create more risks; it's essential to use this technology across the entire IT environment. Figure 13-4 shows a bird's-eye view of how consistent data classification works.

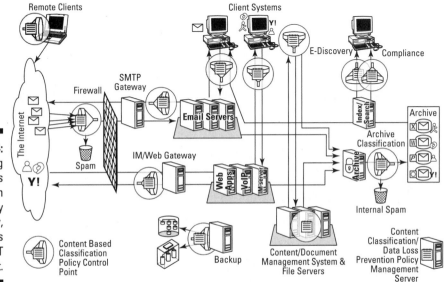

Figure 13-4: Applying data-loss prevention technology consistently, across the IT environment.

If your data definitions — or implementations — are inconsistent, you've got trouble. For example, if a file is classified as *Company Confidential* and prevented from being sent outside the organization through the corporate e-mail system, but *can* be sent via Web-based e-mail, that inconsistency has created a potential data leak.

Done thoroughly and consistently, content-based classification for data-loss prevention ensures that the system will work at all points in the IT network. Here are some especially critical areas:

- ✔ **At the e-mail gateway:** Prevent good stuff from going out by e-mail.

- ✔ **At the Web gateway:** Prevent your intellectual property and sensitive data from leaking out through Web-enabled applications.

✔ **On the client (endpoint):** Don't let confidential data end up on CD-ROMs and USB sticks.

✔ **Policy push:** Ensure that centrally created and managed policies can be pushed automatically to the various places in the network.

✔ **Automatic operation:** The system needs to be fully automatic; it should not depend on connection to the policy server. The system needs to work even when a user is outside the firewall and not connected to the internal network.

Recognizing Potential Security Holes

Publish, to all employees, your IT policy and departmental procedures for managing privacy and security of data, as well as your records-retention policies. The next subsections outline the issues your policy should address.

User-level security issues

Here's a quick checklist of security issues for users to think about:

✔ Determine the level of confidentiality of the information you handle.

✔ Collect only what you need and keep it only as long as you need it.

✔ When you give information to others make sure that they know if the data is confidential and how it should be treated.

✔ Assume that what you're working on should be kept confidential.

✔ Don't leave sensitive documents in clear sight in work areas (desktops or by the side of printers).

✔ Store physical confidential material in locked drawers.

✔ Shred sensitive documents when they're no longer needed.

✔ Protect sensitive materials when using office equipment such as photocopiers and fax machines. (Destroy any "extra" copies you're not using, and don't leave the originals behind when you walk away.)

✔ Don't prop open doors that lead into secure areas.

For that matter, you might want to check with company security to find out the approved course of action if you see someone you don't recognize (or someone who has no company ID badge) in supposedly "secured" work areas. You might ask the person whether you can be of help. (If the person runs, then guess who probably shouldn't be there.) At any rate, you should know whom to call.

Securing individual computers

Be sure that you use appropriate protections on computers, and consider whether they have a role to play in your security policy. Here's a basic list:

- ✔ You can set password protection to kick in when you leave your desk (even for short periods of time). Here's how:

  1. On the desktop right-click and select Properties⇨Screen Saver.

  2. Select a screen saver.

  3. Set how long the computer can sit without password-protecting itself.

     Two to three minutes is usually pretty good.

  4. Put a check mark in the "On resume, password protect" box.

  5. Click OK or Apply.

     Now you can password-protect your computer by pressing Ctrl+Alt+Delete and choosing Lock Computer.

- ✔ Protect the passwords you use to access e-mail, databases, Web sites, and other electronic resources.

  - Don't use default, easy-to-guess, or other foolish passwords.

  - Don't write them on sticky notes and stick them to your computer.

  - Don't use the same password for your bank account and your social-networking account.

- ✔ Be sure that your organization has sufficient deletion processes to get rid of any confidential information on computers when they're disposed of or change hands.

  Specialists can routinely recover "erased" data. Make sure they can't.

- ✔ If your company allows you to store personal information on your work computer, make sure that you keep it separate; create a folder called "Personal" but keep something else in mind, namely . . .

  Any data held as "personal" isn't really. Nowadays nothing is personal. Don't expect privacy in your Personal folder.

- ✔ Immediately notify a manager/security guard/someone/anyone if you suspect that either personal and identifiable customer information or company intellectual property — or other confidential or sensitive information — is missing, has been accessed, or has been altered illegally.

Managerial security issues

It never hurts for IT managers to think about security. A lot. The most important concerns that crop up in the IT realm include, but aren't limited to, these:

- ✔ Conduct periodic security-awareness training and education.

- ✔ Do regular security assessments.

- ✔ Include security-awareness topics in your regular instructions to end-users.

- ✔ Periodically review IT data practices and determine what new security measures should be implemented.

- ✔ Review data-management practices after any changes in the working environment, such as relocations and new technology.

- ✔ Review equipment and software. In particular, ensure that end-user machines have adequate data protection in place (such as appropriate security and software configurations and current patches).

- ✔ Review end-user machines to ensure that users have access to the correct or appropriate information.

- ✔ Establish company-wide procedures to ensure compliance with IT, industry, and governmental policies.

- ✔ Ensure that end users (including partners, suppliers, and all those to whom the organization supplies information) are familiar with the privacy and confidentiality policy and laws that apply to your organization.

- ✔ Create an inventory of — and classify consistently — all data created and held in your organization. (This both helps with compliance and can assist with creating tiered storage capabilities.) If you know how your information or data is being used, you're in a better position to establish procedures for handling information in ways appropriate to its classification.

- ✔ Ensure that all users are aware that the organization has the right to access any information maintained or created on workplace machines; the methods you will use to access it and the policy about that access.

- ✔ Identify personnel who are authorized to access networks, systems, or applications and ensure that appropriate authorization controls are in place.

- ✔ Identify which applications have access to which data sets or storage resources. Make sure that you retire applications that are no longer in use. (That helps with costs too — how many applications just sit around with no one accessing them?)

- ✔ Enforce secure password management.

✔ Put policies in place for controlling the lifecycle of IT hardware — including its reassignment, decommissioning, or final disposal.

✔ Ensure appropriate session termination.

✔ Determine the event-logging practices that serve your organization's security needs without hampering business processes.

✔ Review procedures for physical entry to your site. Consider the appropriate use of locks, badge readers, or access cards.

✔ Ask periodically: *Is your data safe?* Check and update your backup policy for applications, networks, server systems, and end-user machines.

Chapter 14

Protecting Your Data Center

*T*he *data center* is where your data lives — or at least where it *should* live. These days, the data center is usually a dedicated server (or array of servers and storage devices) that receives, stores, and makes available the data it receives from across the enterprise. As such it's an invaluable resource, and well worth protecting.

A central location for an entire organization's data may seem old-fashioned — wasn't it chucked it out the window along with the Open System years ago? — but these days it's actually *under*used. Although the overall amount of data is growing at disproportionate rates, only about 20 percent of this data is *structured* — generally that's the stuff that actually resides in the data center. Semi-structured data (like e-mail) can sometimes be captured within a data center, but often not. Unstructured data (usually documents, spreadsheets, slide presentations, music, and pictures) is rarely captured.

Two things must happen before you can look realistically at managing data protection in your data center:

✔ You must have the data *in* the data center (not everywhere else).

✔ When you've got data control back, index everything.

There is a perfectly reasonable argument to suggest that in today's connected world we could actually keep everything we create *within the network environment* and never let any of it out onto the fat-client machines that we go to such lengths to protect and manage.

Really what you're talking about is risk — not just IT risk, but also information risk — and the management thereof. Doing business means dealing with a huge raft of risks, often tied to immovable objects that can trip you up.

The goal of *information risk management* is to keep data in its appropriate bucket for the right length of time, with the correct access provided to the correct people, with the correct levels of security, at the right time. This requires planning to mitigate against the risk or impact or disruption to the organization's information — a disruption that inevitably affects staff, facilities, processes, reputation, brand, customer relationships, applications, data, IT infrastructure, and value-creating activities.

As the information-driven organization evolves, the demands placed upon the data storage infrastructure become stronger. Despite the massive growth of the data storage industry, many organizations have preferred to invest in solutions that address their specific areas of pain. Result: a jumble of different tools, each with its own internal view of the storage infrastructure and its own administrative capabilities. In fact, such mix-and-match storage-management solutions reflect the same weakness that organizations have been working to get rid of.

Just as an organization needs a meaningful information strategy, it needs a storage-management strategy. To create one, you need to understand what you're trying to manage.

The Curse of Unstructured Data Files

Most organizations try to manage their information somehow but have no idea how to go about it right. The goal of an efficient data center seems distant, mainly because generating data and information is not enough; unless you structure it, it just accumulates. A heap of unstructured data is nearly unusable, as the accompanying sidebar full of practical oxymorons points out.

Most of this chaos has been created by an accumulation of unstructured data — and a lack of awareness: Does anyone know (for example) what IT has and doesn't have? Or why nothing in IT ever seems to get retired, be it hardware, software, data, or networks?

The trick to answering such questions is (first) to understand what you're trying to deal with — your data, before and after it evolves into information — and then to impose an order based on that understanding.

Top 10 oxymorons in IT

In the absence of a clear and accurate sense of what information is, some basic IT concepts look more like contradictions in (impressive-sounding) terms:

✔ IT management: You can't manage what you don't know you have. Even if you know what you have today, what you have — and what you need to purge — probably will be different tomorrow.

✔ Storage management: With utilization rates as low as 10 percent and as high as 35 percent, not much management going on there.

✔ Information lifecycle management: "Copies of everything the world has ever created" seems to cover it (and the world), piled up somewhere just in case.

✔ Security management: Lots of security measures, securing lots of *something*, but no operations center to manage all that activity — with nothing to generate reports on the mess, and no visible security posture for the organization.

✔ Network access control: Lots and lots of access, not much control. Some organizations have more contractors and partners accessing their networks than they have employees.

✔ Device management: Loads of devices — but no one's sure how many, what kind, who's running them, or (for that matter) what's running *on* them.

✔ Asset management: How much stuff does your organization own that's actually listed somewhere as an *asset?* Of what's listed, how much has been junked, thrown out, switched off, or left humming along with no users?

✔ Server management: Lots of servers everywhere doing what? No one's got an iota of a clue how many — or even where they are.

✔ Network management: Lots of stuff sent everywhere, with no clear idea of where it came from, where it might be going, or (for that matter) whether it actually got to its alleged destination.

✔ Application management: How many applications do you run, who uses them, which ones are critical to the business — and how much of that is known?. Are any applications running that nobody is accessing? Have you checked recently?

For openers, data does not structure itself. Unstructured data is really difficult to classify because you don't know what's in the file or document without taking a gander at it. Without much trouble, you can get *25 million* structured records onto a couple of CDs that hold 25 pop songs each. The secret is in how you use the capacity of the storage device.

Unstructured data takes up huge amounts of space — and it's difficult to understand which bits are important and which bits are not.

Managing your data's lifecycle is traditional

The concept of Information Lifecycle Management (ILM) is, in effect, a later evolution of Hierarchical Storage Management (HSM) techniques that date back to the early days of mainframe computers. The idea behind HSM is to move data between high-cost and low-cost storage to conform with business needs, policies, and priorities. Files needed most frequently reside in high-speed storage; data kept over the longer term migrates to lower-speed, lower-cost storage. Managing your data's lifecycle offers a range of benefits:

- Reduces the total number of expensive RAID disks an enterprise needs.

- Makes storage use more efficient.

- Improves performance.

- Performs some routine storage housekeeping tasks.

ILM gives organizations a consistent scheme for moving data automatically from expensive hard drives to less expensive optical media or to tape, according to specific policies — while making any needed changes to the security value of the data. Users don't have to know that their data has migrated to less-costly storage media because ILM products track data movement and create paths for data retrieval. When a user or application retrieves a file that has moved down the storage hierarchy, the ILM product automatically returns the data to the top level of the storage infrastructure.

For more about the benefits of ILM from a data-classification standpoint, see Chapter 13.

The content defines the value

By understanding how specific data sets are utilized — and what their retention and security requirements are — IT departments can route data to the appropriate company resources. The idea is to match data with the levels of performance, protection, availability, retention, immutability, and cost that make it most effective at each stage of its lifecycle. The content of a data set determines its value, and affects how the company handles that lifecycle.

Information lifecycle management (ILM) provides an integrated, automated approach to the overall management of information. It includes such tasks as preventing data loss, keeping data available, managing the protection and retention of data, as well as the discovery of data as it is required, and maintaining the transparency of applications as well as the uniformity of end-user technology (frequently through common federated data classification and policy management). Big job? You bet.

Administrators who master information lifecycle management can meet various goals:

- ✔ Deploy the best combination of storage devices, media types, and network infrastructure to meet the organization's needs.

- ✔ Create an appropriate balance of performance, data accessibility, easy retrieval, and data reliability, based on the relative value of the data.

- ✔ Examine data capture, transfer, processing, analysis, storage, backup, retrieval, archiving, and deletion.

- ✔ Determine whether to store data online, near online, or offline.

  Making data available in *near-online* or *nearline* storage (for example, on tape) means it's accessible in a short time but not instantly.

- ✔ Decide when data should be deleted.

  Deletion is part of your data's lifecycle (see the accompanying sidebar).

Minimizing the number of copies

Why minimize copies? Well, try a thought experiment: Suppose you build a 96-slide presentation, full of high-resolution files, and send it to a colleague because you think he might be interested. And, hey, he is — and then he thinks of another ten suckers on whom he can fob this off as his own work, without mentioning you ("oops, accidently on purpose"). So he sends it off, and hey — all those miscreants do the same thing. Works like a charm in large organizations! The only downside is that if it's *really* good, it tends to come back to you, the originator, and — game over — you know somebody has waltzed off with your hard grind.

Now let's add up the existing copies of the aforementioned presentation:

- ✔ You created *one* on your desktop, and . . .

- ✔ Sent it to your colleague (that's two, because it also lives in your sent items), and he . . .

- ✔ Has it in his e-mail system (that's three) but he also . . .

- ✔ Saved it to *his* desktop (that's four), and then . . .

- ✔ Sent it to ten people, so there's one in *his* sent items (that's five), and it then . . .

- ✔ Arrived in ten inboxes (we're up to 15), and everybody . . .

- ✔ Saved it to their desktops (whoops, that's 25), and . . .

- ✔ Sent it to ten of *their* colleagues, so 125 copies exist now . . .

  . . . and so far those colleagues haven't saved the wayward presentation to their desktops — or (for that matter) sent it back to *you* for your thoughts on "their" outstanding creation!

- ✔ Then one or two of those folks actually runs a backup from their local machines — and makes sure that they have copies of the presentation on the file servers, just in case. (This is getting way out of hand.)

Now we get into the realms of disk-to-disk-to-disk-to-tape backup, mirroring one huge clump of stuff in one set of storage arrays to another storage array somewhere else. (How much total space *does* that one presentation take up? Hand me that aspirin bottle, will you?)

The point is that even though data is created equally and has different requirements throughout its life — requiring different levels of performance, availability, protection, migration, retention, and disposal — there is rarely any need to stash and keep the same item in 125 places. Even so, most organizations store individual documents or data sets 50 to 500 times. Even a storage geek would call that a trifle excessive.

The rapid growth of storage across the enterprise — both inside and outside the data center — has challenged traditional backup approaches. For the most part, data backups still wind up on tapes that are sent offsite to a secure storage location, there to await retrieval in case of a disaster. Disk-based backup helps organizations address some of their backup challenges but can add complexity by generating a pile of corporate data-backup policies — that probably haven't been reviewed in a few years at least.

Without a policy to control what gets copied, you create huge numbers of copies of files — again and again. This happens even with disk-based backup — unless you use *data deduplication,* a technology that reduces the number of duplicate copies you keep, which in turn reduces the overhead of managing your storage and backup systems.

Data management has four main segments that require attention:

- ✔ **Storage management:** This segment manages the storage resource that contains your data, and includes volume management (in other words, managing disk partitions and logical volumes on storage media):

  - Data allocation

  - Data availability

  - Data growth

- Data migration
- Storage resource management to view, track, analyze, report, and (de)-provision

✔ **Protection and security management:** This segment uses multiple methods to protect data (and prevent data loss) for various recovery purposes:

- External data-extraction attacks
- Internal data leaks
- Corruption of single data items
- Corruption of data sets
- Storage or server failure
- Disaster recovery

✔ **Retention management:** This segment is typically associated with archiving, though not exclusively. The focus is on specific data retention and all aspects of near-term and long-term data preservation, across a variety of media and through successive generations of media technology. The most important archival functions include

- Data organization
- Navigation
- Search
- Retrieval
- Export
- Collections/grouping
- Location management
- Data-quality management
- Security, integrity, immutability
- Disposal

✔ **Content management:** This segment's focus is the discovery and retrieval of content and data. It provides in-depth search capabilities, as well as data organization (both dynamic and static):

- Content management for online/primary data
- Offline content management
- Version management
- Protecting content against tampering

Data Availability for Good or Bad

Keeping stuff available is critical to most organizations — but it's also handy for the cybercriminal. These days an effective security strategy requires a full arsenal of tools to protect the IT environment. Each tool is a response to a specific security question that IT must be able to answer to ensure full and successful protection from potential threats in all their forms.

As entry points proliferate and threats become more sophisticated, many organizations are reassessing their endpoint security efforts. Even a cursory examination of today's threat landscape is enough to show how thoroughly the situation has changed. Threats are more frequent and devious these days; it's no surprise that traditional enterprise-level security measures are being circumvented.

Working 24/7

The 24/7, work-from-anywhere world of road warriors and Wi-Fi has a persistent problem: Today's data center holds too much valuable data that can be grabbed too easily by powerful mobile technology. To protect the LANs of yesteryear, you could deploy a firewall and anti-virus (AV) product wall to wall, and you were safe — right? I mean, security *is* AV, right? *Was.* AV is all well and good — for what it is — but it doesn't deflect hackers, spam, identity theft, denial of service, and the other security issues that have been on the rise for years. You can't just set up a firewall, turn on the anti-virus, and sit back.

These days security is the biggest obstacle to widespread adoption of remote and mobile computing in businesses — worldwide. These days, 60 percent of companies hold back on deployment because of security concerns; nearly 47 percent cite cost and complexity as a major obstacle to deployment. Nearly one in five businesses has already experienced financial loss due to attacks launched from mobile platforms.

So hold it right there, mighty IT czar: You need answers to some basic questions before your organization goes any farther into 24/7 mode:

✔ How do you ensure the safeguarding of your intellectual property (such as confidential business data, proprietary designs, and IT assets)?

✔ What does your current security infrastructure look like? Is your network too complex to keep track of? How do you plan to address growth or change? Do you want or need to expand your network environment?

✔ Do you have multi-layered protection at every tier of your network? Does your company have a current plan to address intrusion protection?

✔ Do you — or will you ever — need to conduct security audits? Do you need to comply with industry-specific laws, regulations, and/or standards? For that matter, how well do you comply with your own security policies? Have you ever been involved in an HR or contract dispute? How easy is the retrieval of data or information for legal purposes?

✔ Do you know who is connected to your network? How about who has network access control? How many endpoints are you trying to manage/protect? How many remote users do you have? Do you enforce restrictions on who gains access to your network?

✔ How many e-mails do you get per day? Is the volume and size of e-mails and/or file shares increasing? Have your messaging storage requirements gone up?

✔ Do you allow the use of PST files? If so, how are they managed/stored? Do you have regulations that force business messaging retention? Have you considered categorizing your e-mail or other unstructured content?

✔ Is instant messaging allowed or blocked? Is there more than one type of IM used in your organization? Is IM unmanaged in your organization?

If the answer to any of these questions makes you wince, then you need to revisit your security, put in place some new policies, processes, and technologies, and then re-ask the questions!

Intrusion detection

An *intrusion-detection system* (IDS) inspects all inbound and outbound network activity, identifying suspicious patterns. Such patterns may indicate a network or system attack from someone attempting to break into or compromise a system. There are several types of IDS:

✔ **IDS misuse detection:** That is, detection *of* misuse. The IDS analyzes the information it gathers and compares it to large databases of attack signatures. Essentially, the IDS looks for a specific attack that has already been documented. As with a virus-detection system, misuse-detection software is only as good as the database of attack signatures against which it compares the contents of data packets.

✔ **IDS anomaly detection:** This type of IDS requires the administrator to define some network baselines — such as the normal state of the network's traffic load, how often the system breaks down, what protocols are in use, and the typical packet size. After that's done, the anomaly detector monitors network segments to compare their states to the normal baselines, looking for anomalies.

✔ **Network-based IDS:** Also known as NIDS (Network Intrusion Detection System), this approach analyzes the individual packets that flow through a network. The NIDS can detect malicious packets that are designed to be overlooked by a firewall's simplistic filtering rules.

✔ **Host-based IDS:** These products examine the activity on each individual computer or host (server).

✔ **Passive IDS:** This approach detects potential security breaches, logs the information, and signals an alert.

✔ **Reactive IDS:** These systems respond to suspicious activity by logging off a user or by reprogramming the firewall to block network traffic from the suspected malicious source.

An IDS differs from a corporate firewall in its placement in the network. A corporate firewall sits at the border of the network and examines traffic going into or out of the enterprise. An IDS system sits *inside* the enterprise network and looks for suspect traffic patterns there, regardless of whether they're entering or leaving the network via the Internet.

Advanced intrusion-detection systems can also correlate the activity detected by several different IDSs at different points inside the network to identify an overall attack. Originally, IDS systems detected attacks by using a more sophisticated pattern-matching capability than was available on endpoint machines. These days endpoint security has caught up; the best endpoint-management and security solutions offer the same kind of pattern-matching as IDS systems. Using these capabilities, an IDS evaluates a suspected intrusion after it has taken place, signals an alarm, and watches for attacks that originate from within the system on which it resides.

An *intrusion-prevention system* (IPS) is an IDS that can fight back, so to speak; it can drop packets that it determines are part of an attack. For full security effectiveness, organizations should look at having a combination of IDS, IPS, firewall, and endpoint-security technologies.

Protecting Server Infrastructure

Businesses rely on enterprise networks — and the endpoints connected to those networks — to manufacture products, keep employees productive, and receive orders from customers. Those business-critical systems are constantly under attack, and a successful attack results in denial of service, theft of sensitive information, or exposure to regulatory penalties. As you might imagine, the data center is considered a prize target.

Traditional perimeter-focused security architectures fail to secure the network because they allow insecure endpoints to connect to enterprise networks.

Most security systems only stop attacks after it's too late and allow infected computers to infect the rest of the network. All those little devices we can plug into the corporate network that were never protected — or compliant with any policy — should be protected (and limited as necessary) to protect networks, enforce business policies, and automate security practices. Unprotected access by unmanaged devices such as home computers, kiosks, and guest laptops exposes enterprise assets to data theft or loss.

Critical system protection

Critical system protection (CSP) provides host-based security against day-zero attacks (an attack that takes place before the application, hardware, or security vendor patch is released), and helps maintain compliance by enforcing behavior-based security policies on clients and servers.

A host-based CSP capability meets a range of goals:

- ✓ Stops malicious exploitation of system resources
- ✓ Prevents the introduction and spread of malicious code
- ✓ Protects against threats launched from many standard interactive applications
- ✓ Blocks inbound and outbound connections by port, protocol, and IP address, and also blocks network-based threats
- ✓ Prevents buffer overflows (which helps protect against denial-of-service attacks)
- ✓ Protects file systems and OS code against unauthorized modification
- ✓ Prevents unauthorized executable files from being introduced and run on the OS, in high-risk applications, and against databases

Critical system protection can surround OS system functions with a security shield, continuously hardening the operating system. When CSP software is installed on servers and clients, security events are managed centrally from a secure console. Among other capabilities, administrators have the option to prevent data and applications from being copied to and from removable media (such as USB drives and CD-ROMs) to help ensure that data isn't misused or stolen.

Servers, endpoints, and thin-client computing

Back in olden times (2004), thin clients simply hampered the drive towards mobile computing. A *thin client* (as opposed to a fat client) is a network computer or PC without a hard drive; a fat client includes a disk drive. When you connect a gaggle of thin clients to a server, the infrastructure ends up looking like a mainframe with a brood of dumb terminals that happen to be attached to a network. (For mainframe lovers longing to bring back the days of the vt52, all is forgiven!)

Okay, that makes sense, but we're so used to having a fat client to do with as we please, do we really *want* a thin client? Probably not. However, even that reluctance can be overcome by desktop virtualization.

Virtualization is a nifty technique that can *ring-fence* an application and data set — that is, run them from the network but set them apart in a dedicated space so they seem to run on your machine. You can modify the data as appropriate, but the data never leaves the server. In fact, the activity you're running from the network *exists only as long as you're connected to the network.* When that session has completed, it shuts down completely, simply because it doesn't exist on the laptop at all. Result: That data is protected from silly mistakes such as leaving the laptop in a car where a thief can walk off with both hardware *and* data.

The argument for desktop virtualization goes like this: The more your information resides centrally — and the less it resides on a laptop or desktop — the more secure that information is. If you haven't got it, you can't lose it! The dumber the terminal, the more your sensitive company data is protected from the dreaded "dumb user" who might lose or do silly things with the data. Virtualization is a boon to organizations that run large production applications, manage call centers, or have to ride herd on long chains of partners in their business processes to ensure against fraud (as when a bad guy pretends to be one of those partners). This added safety is welcome in such lines of work as manufacturing, local and central government, finance, and energy.

Other benefits of using thin clients and desktop virtualization include these:

  ✔ **Boot-image control:** Controlling the boot image is much simpler when a virtualized application is being used. A single boot image can accommodate a wide range of user needs. In a virtualized desktop environment, only mouse movements, keystrokes, and screen updates are transmitted from (and to) the end-user. The image can be easily updated and rolled out the next time the user accesses it.

✔ **Central management:** Lower IT admin costs result when you do administration almost entirely at the server. There will still be calls from users, but the fixes (other than *Are you sure you switched it on?*) will be done at the server and then transmitted to the user over the network.

✔ **Fewer points of failure:** Not only does the hardware infrastructure have fewer points of failure, but it's also much more efficient with its use of resources. The downside is that the central server represents a single point of failure; in effect, you're putting all your eggs in one basket (relying entirely on your server); providing a high degree of availability and security for your server infrastructure becomes even more important (if that's possible).

✔ **Better control of data leakage:** Potential data loss is easier to manage because no application or data ever resides on the client (which only controls what's running on its assigned part of the server). Result: centralized malware protection.

✔ **Improved security:** This is especially true if the local environment is highly restricted (and often stateless), providing protection from malware. Anything ring-fenced through desktop virtualization is protected within the network. If all applications and data are centralized, then switching users on and off becomes a lot simpler to manage, as does controlling who uses what. As a result, viruses are also easier to deal with and it's easier to manage compliance with IT policy and regulations.

  • Thin clients — or, for that matter, restricted fat clients — are particularly useless to the bad guys. A thin client doesn't do anything outside the server environment; a desktop-virtualized environment doesn't hold any sensitive data.

  • Given how many laptops get stolen each year, it's perhaps no surprise that companies are looking for more ways to secure their corporate data. Thin clients are both less valuable to the bad guys and much harder to sell on the black market. They're nearly useless to anyone but their legitimate users. Ring-fenced, desktop-virtualized clients are now sexy devices that look like laptops but don't contain any of the data you'd normally find on your average lost or stolen notebook PC.

These days, thin clients are better able to handle mobile working than in the past, largely because of

✔ Better server-based hardware and software

✔ Higher security through virtual private networks (VPNs)

✔ Improved connectivity

Thus, where thin clients were hardly an option in the dark ages (2003), all this innovation means enhanced versatility, configurability, and usability for network-centric computing.

For example, I can work through my corporate network anywhere in the world as long as I have VPN connectivity (an encrypted "tunnel" through the Internet that keeps your data safe from snoopers). In practical terms, what real difference does it make whether the data is held in the local machine or centrally on the company network? The only place I may still have to struggle is on an airplane — and even the airlines are looking at Internet connectivity options these days. (Of course, if I'm flying hanging-on-the-wing class to save money, the work environment isn't exactly ideal; even with a fat client, I won't do much work if I don't have room to open my laptop, let alone fend off the screaming, marauding children next to me.)

Just because the data isn't on the laptop doesn't mean you can't get at it. The client functions as a portal into the corporate network. The same security considerations are needed to prevent sneaky malware such as keyloggers and rootkits from getting into your machine and stealing your information; without them, stealthy data leakage could go unnoticed for a long time.

Why centralized backup is a good idea

The recent history of data protection, retention, and retrieval is spattered with business faux pas and major "security events" (a tactful way of saying "security breaches") — showing that companies need effective document-retention policies, and too often don't have them. A decent data-retention policy avoids vast fees in future litigation; utilizing intelligent software to implement the policy can save storage space and costs.

Centralize your backup efforts to ensure that you've secured all your intellectual property as well as your customer information. Unstructured data has a bad habit of ending up on external devices without proper protection.

External storage devices — don't have them if you can possibly avoid them. Put everything in the data center and you don't need them.

Here are just a few questions you might ask yourself and that can be a signal that you have data-protection issues:

- ✔ Is data at your remote offices protected consistently?
- ✔ Is critical data not backed up or backed up too infrequently?
- ✔ Are backup tapes sent offsite in a timely manner?

✔ Do your backup jobs often fail to complete on the first attempt?

✔ Do you have to delay backup jobs until a more convenient backup window becomes available?

✔ Can you quickly retrieve data such as files or e-mail from online and offline sources in audit situations or recovery emergencies?

✔ Do you frequently test data recovery as well as your state of disaster-recovery readiness?

✔ Do you know how much money you spend to protect different types of data — and whether your most important data has the highest level of protection?

✔ Can you quickly recover both applications and data in the event of human error, system failure, or disaster?

✔ Can you effectively demonstrate and report on protected data across business units, locations, and applications?

A combination of over-duplicated files and old backup policies or technology can easily end in tears; it would be good to ensure that you gather all your data into the data center *as soon as you can.*

Protect your backups. The backup contains a copy of everything you think is important — all your intellectual property and customer details, for openers. If a backup wanders off into the wrong hands . . . well, you know the refrain, and it isn't pretty. Keep two principles in mind for your backups:

✔ Backups must be physically protected, even if they're onsite.

(What are they doing onsite anyway? Just asking.)

✔ If backup tapes are going offsite, then they need to be encrypted!

Denial-of-Service Attacks

A *denial-of-service attack (DoS attack)* is an attempt to overload and stymie your network so its computer resources are unavailable to its intended users.

A *distributed DoS (DDoS) attack* is parceled out to multiple attackers; a notorious example was launched against Estonia a few years ago. (Yes, Estonia — the entire country!) This was done by hiring computers controlled by cybercriminals — malware-compromised machines called *bots* — and using them to launch the attack from multiple locations. The attack itself is relatively simple: Flood the network with requests until the servers can't cope; then they either crash or grind to a halt. If something like this hits you, then to the outside world, you have *gone off the net.*

In the case of data theft, the motives — and targets — for a DoS attack are fairly straightforward: sites or services hosted on high-profile Web servers — such as those for banks, credit-card payment gateways, and even DNS servers at the root, or administrative, level. (For more about doing awful things to the Domain Name Server, see "Poisoned DNS as a method of stealing data," a little later in this chapter.)

Variations on the flooding attack

One common method of attack involves bombarding the target (victim) machine with so many external communications requests that it can't respond to legitimate traffic — or responds so slowly as to be rendered effectively unavailable. These attacks, known as *flooding*, effectively prevent an Internet site or service from functioning efficiently (or at all). Simple flooding stymies the target; the more ambitious version of this attack goes after your data by temporarily or indefinitely taking over the target resource, or diverting traffic to a false site in order to extract data from unsuspecting users.

A *smurf attack* is a variant of a flooding DoS attack on the public Internet. It relies on misconfigured network devices that allow packets to be sent to all computer hosts on a particular network via the broadcast address *of the whole network*, instead of a specific machine's address. The network then serves to amplify the smurf attack. In such an attack, the perpetrators send large numbers of IP packets with the source address faked to appear to be the address of the victim. The network's bandwidth is quickly used up, preventing legitimate packets from getting through to their destinations.

Computer systems that control power stations, water utilities, and banking systems are obvious targets for DoS attacks, but Internet service providers could also be tempting targets. To combat these attacks, there are organizations thae have given network service providers the ability to identify misconfigured networks and to take appropriate action (such as filtering).

Poisoned DNS as a method of stealing data

The *DNS (Domain Name System)* acts as the intermediary between humans and digital machines, making reliable communication possible between them. DNS allows us to enter a comprehensible name (say, www.wiley.com), rather than an obscure digital reference, into a Web browser's address bar or an e-mail address bar. One nefarious type of DoS attack "poisons" the DNS with fake information — in effect, making the go-between untrustworthy.

Using DNS when it works right

If I want to go to a Web address, my computer will take several steps I don't actually see:

1. I type, say, `www.wiley.com` into the Web browser.

2. The Web browser asks a DNS application to convert `www.wiley.com` into an IP address.

3. The DNS application checks the hosts file and the local cache to see whether the IP address I want is available.

4. If it's available, the IP address is passed to my computer's network protocols to set up a connection. If the DNS application can't find the address, it asks my ISP for the IP address.

5. The search for the IP address begins.

   - If the ISP's name server has that information in its cache, it immediately returns the IP address to the DNS application, which then sets up a connection. All this time my computer is relying on authoritative information.

   - If my ISP takes over the search for the domain name, it joins a queue searching for the top level (in this case Wiley) by the authoritative name servers.

6. The root (administrative-level) name server returns the IP address for the appropriate .com name server to my ISP's name server.

7. My ISP's name server queries the .com name server.

8. My ISP's name server queries the `wiley.com` name server for the IP address associated with `www.wiley.com`.

9. Now that my ISP has the required IP address, it returns this sought-after tidbit to my computer so it can establish a connection.

10. When the connection is complete, the Web server sends specified Web pages back for me to view in my browser.

If all this seems like a good deal of running back and forth just to view a Web page, well, it is — but it takes only milliseconds to carry out because of some handy features like these:

- ✔ **Caching:** A dedicated space in memory holds information locally so it takes less time to access, which makes finding the IP address much easier.

- ✔ **Time to Live:** This property controls how long a server will cache the IP address, and helps to keep cached information up to date.

- ✔ **Out of bailiwick:** In effect, the software kicks out anything irrelevant to the query (such as like names).

Poisoning the DNS

DNS is a trusting application — so attackers can play tricks on DNS to redirect users to go to places they didn't want to go — as when cyber-criminals redirect users to spoofed (fake) Web sites with the hope of stealing personal information. If (for example) the attacker knows the Transaction ID number used in the victim DNS server's latest query, the attacker can send malicious DNS query responses that use this authentic Transaction ID. For this to work, of course, the attacker has to be patient and wait for the intended victim's DNS server to send out a query when the Time to Live has expired.

But suppose I'm a fidgety attacker who doesn't *want* to wait until the Time to Live expires. If I wanted to poison my ISP's DNS record right now, well, I know the domain name of my target — and I can get hold of the IP address of the authoritative name servers. I can also get the IP address of my ISP's name server and what port it's using for DNS queries.

So I get the needed address and port, and then send a query for a fake computer — say, nastyjack — and because my ISP's server has no machine with that name, its name server must send a DNS query to my target (intended victim — bwahahaaaa!). At the same time, I construct a bunch of DNS query-response packets. Each one includes a spoofed source IP address that makes it look like it's coming *from the target,* along with the correct port and the IP address of a server that I control. This makes it appear as if the return query is coming from the requested IP address — when it's actually coming from my rogue server. If I can trick the target into trying to find a non-existent computer, the data is as good as stolen.

To overcome this problem, you can randomize your query ports or make sure that you're running a Secure Sockets Layer (SSL) certificate (SSL creates a secure connection between a client and a server, over which any amount of data can be sent securely). These attacks can't work if your URL displays only secure Internet protocols such as https.

Encryption in the Data Center

The sheer volume of news stories in the press regarding data leakage and encryption might fool you into thinking that encryption is everywhere. Unfortunately, it's not. At least it isn't particularly well done even when it's in place. Encryption is a critical piece of information security, but it's easy to do badly. Try to avoid falling to any of the six classic snags that await unsuspecting IT organizations on the road to implementing encryption technologies.

If you want to protect your data at rest *and* your data in transit, heed the sections that follow.

Why outright encryption might cause more problems than it solves

The first mistake is assuming that encryption is easy. The technical aspects of encryption are easy, but the key-management part is *really difficult.*

Encryption is easy. Key management is hard. But here are some starting points for going about it right:

- ✔ **Don't hard-code the very stuff you're trying to protect.** The whole point in encryption is that it doesn't depend on its secrecy but on its key. If you leave a key lying around embedded in code, configuration files, or other *hidden* files, you're just making keys available for attackers. This mistake has lead to many disasters; passwords *hidden* in files help the attackers that snag the files to extend their control over the compromised network. You can only really *secure* a password by encrypting it and then your problem doesn't go away because then you need a new key to unlock the password key to unlock the data.

- ✔ **Don't use encryption when it has already been done for you.** Most of the messaging protocols, FTP and HTTPS are the most obvious examples of ready-made encryption. There is no excuse for not encrypting data in transit when you can use those protocols; it's easy and doesn't cost extra.

- ✔ **Database and data-center encryption is the new black.** Just encrypt all the stuff in your data center and you'll be all right. Now, where should we put the keys? Stick them in a database somewhere. There is little point in going to all that trouble of encrypting stuff in a well-implemented encryption algorithm if you leave your keys in the front door.

  It has been known that a few organizations (of the financial variety) who when implementing a protection policy for all those critical 16-digit numbers encrypted the appropriate tables and then stored the key in another table on the same database server. To really protect the keys, put them somewhere where they won't leak into swap files, crash dumps, logs, and other areas that attackers might pry their way into.

- ✔ **Don't invent your own algorithm.** Leave it to the cryptographers. Math is hard!

And then there is the encryption that is so secure that when the guy who holds all the keys (excuse the pun) doesn't turn up to work one day then the very process of encryption prevents you from ever getting your data back. (Oh, good job! Otherwise known as *employee-hit-by-bus test.*) If whoever knows the keys to data is hit by a bus, can you get your data back? If not, then the data would be as good as gone dead-y-bye-byes.

If you have an enterprise encryption strategy check who has access to the keys and, equally important, ensure that no single person can change them without the other's knowing. Else you could be held to ransom by a malicious insider or disgruntled employee who leaves a last-minute "goodbye gift."

Content-based classification and protection

Find out what you have, if it is important to you and/or a criminal and nail it down if it is. To do this you need

- ✔ **Data-matching technology** for protecting data that is typically in structured formats, such as customer or employee database records.

- ✔ **Document-matching technology** to protect unstructured data, and can include file types such as `.pdf`, `.doc`, `.ppt`, as well as CAD drawings.

- ✔ **Content-matching technology** to detect data with common characteristics such as keywords, regular expressions, filename, file type, file size, validated data types, and sender/recipient/user combinations.

- ✔ **Education** and a pile of goodwill from your employees.

Here's a quick look at each of these requirements:

Data matching protects structured data that is generally stored in a database. It will identify the values such as First Name, Last Name, Social Security Number, Account Number, and Phone Number as a string or any combination occurring together and is designed to protect large numbers of structured records. Data matching bases detection on particular combinations of columns in a given row of data. This capability of defining rules is required to identify incidents that violate state data-privacy laws (such as California SB 1386, which requires a first name and last name in combination with any of the following: SSN, bank-account number, credit-card number, or driver's-license number). For extremely high-security environments, this technology offers an encryption tool that allows users to create the cryptographic index directly on the storage system.

Document matching helps detect unstructured data stored in documents such as Microsoft Word and PowerPoint files, PDF documents, design plans, source-code files, CAD/CAM images, financial reports, mergers-and-acquisitions documents, or even music files (perhaps you don't want these to end up on your network servers). This type of technology creates document "fingerprints" to detect extracted portions of the original document. For example, if a literate bad guy extracted two paragraphs of the company sales strategy and tried to send it out mixed up in the text of *Hamlet,* this technology can detect the ruse. Partial matching can trigger appropriate responses: It creates different versions of protected documents (or segments of documents) and can spot configurable matching on

- ✔ Derivative documents, such as revisions and versions
- ✔ Passages, such as chunks of protected content that are pasted into other documents

Content matching locates data when it's difficult to get a copy of the information for indexing, or when the precise content can be described but is unknown. This technology can match both structured and unstructured data by using keywords, registered lists, network-protocol information, file types, file sizes, senders, recipients, and usernames. It also uses pattern-matching capabilities to identify sensitive *pattern-based* data — such as credit-card numbers, Social Security Numbers, National Insurance numbers, telephone numbers, or Payment Card Industry (PCI) data; it can match any word or phrase, including word delimiters.

Content matching helps you discover your data and find out if something has been copied from something else. (Even clueless malicious insiders can figure out how to cut and paste!) After a system is involved and content has been classified, you can take some technological steps to protect it:

- ✔ **Access control:** Who can see the data can be restricted by using access-control lists.
- ✔ **Storage location:** Sensitive information can be moved to a more secure location, perhaps with more secure backup and replication policies.
- ✔ **Restriction from being copied:** If you know a particular data set is sensitive, then your data-loss prevention solutions can prevent it from being copied onto removable media, or even printed.
- ✔ **Encryption:** If you don't want people to see the information, then make sure that they can't, even if they get hold of a copy of the file. The only way to do that is to encrypt the data and keep strict control of the key.

Managing digital rights across the enterprise

Okay, if you're going to do business, then at least some sensitive or confidential data must go "outside" — not just outside the data center but also outside the organization. In this case, you have two options:

✔ Live with it. It's out of your control.

✔ Find a solution that keeps you in control of your data.

Here the solution is *enterprise digital rights management* (eDRM) — encrypting your documents and enabling the key to be shared with anyone, including those outside the organization. The key has a time limit; after a predetermined amount of time, the key has to be renewed before the document will open. The good news is that if employees leave the organization, then any documents they might take with them will be useless without the key. Likewise, if you send information to a partner, it will be useless if it's sent to someone else or left on a USB stick in a competitor's conference room (perish the thought). eDRM solutions also protect against simple cut-and-paste pilfering — or even against taking screen images.

Chapter 15

Authorization and Access Control

. . . .

In This Chapter

▶ Considering technology that can reduce and manage data access

▶ Tracing the phases of automatic Network Access Control

. . . .

*A*fter you've defined security policies for your network, you need tools to put them into practice. Network Access Control (NAC) is a system that enforces security policies throughout the entire network — on managed *and* unmanaged endpoints (the stuff you own and control as well as the stuff you don't). NAC protects networks from insecure endpoints by continuously enforcing compliance with security policies at the point of network connection. The idea is simple: If you can control the devices that attach to your network and limit the functionality of those you don't trust, then your network is safer.

The world has changed since the days of limited network usage; now you have all sorts of people connecting to your network:

- ✔ Employees (okay, no change there)

- ✔ Contractors

- ✔ Visitors — including customers, competitors, and (yes) would-be hackers

- ✔ Suppliers and partners

If so many people want (or need) to attach to the network, then you need a way to control it. Otherwise a data leak, loss, or breach is bound to occur.

Network Access Control protects access to a range of network types — VPN, wireless, wired-switch, DHCP, and home — by desktops, laptops, servers, guest systems, and embedded devices. By automatically quarantining, correcting (and applying access controls to) noncompliant systems, the software prevents the propagation of malicious code, eliminates disruptions to business-critical systems, and ensures regulatory compliance.

Sounds wonderful, doesn't it?

Network Access Control can help organizations define how secure a particular endpoint must be before it can access specific network resources. (Which makes absolute sense. Why have a laptop riddled with viruses connecting to your network and offloading a pile of bad things?) NAC can automate several essential security-related processes:

- Discovering endpoints
- Determining an endpoint's compliance with security policies
- Enforcing Network Access Control
- Monitoring endpoints continuously for compliance

Used effectively, NAC can help to increase network availability, reduce malicious code propagation, and ensure regulatory compliance.

It's an approach to computer network security that unifies endpoint security technology (such as anti-virus, intrusion prevention or detection, and vulnerability assessment), with authentication of users or systems and the enforcement of network security. We can't blame you if Network Access Control seems like some kind of panacea: a technology that can

- Authenticate who's using your company's network.
- Ensure that users' methods of access are virus free.
- Ensure that all access fully complies with your company's corporate security policies.

Marvelous!

A large manufacturer of an unmentionable thing (which must remain unmentioned because to name it would make us unpopular with its makers) now has more non-employees connecting to its network than it has employees. Sounds a bit drastic, but in this day and age, partners, contractors, suppliers, and even customers (especially in manufacturing) all must be part of the same process. Otherwise all those horror stories you hear about in the news start to happen (like that famous mistake somebody made when a crash-landing on Mars resulted from using imperial instead of metric measurements . . . don't ask). Collaboration is a good way to make sure that everyone's on the same page, as long as it's done securely.

Tightening Control over Access to Data

No doubt all organizations need to tighten up their data-access control as well as their ability to manage all those who have access to their systems.

The larger the organization, however, the tougher it gets. Network Access Control aims to put some steering gear on the juggernaut — to regulate access to a network with policy-based management that can include quarantining endpoint devices and checking for compliance with security policy before allowing access. The aim is to ensure that (a) the persons and devices trying to access your network are who (or what) they say they are and (b) any hardware seeking access is up to the rigorous security standards you've set for your organization.

If you require a certain standard of security on the endpoint, then all of its virus, spam, and other malware definitions must be up to date before the NAC system allows the device onto the network.

In essence, Network Access Control is a bunch of protocols that define how to secure the network from such dangers as security breaches, hacking, and data loss. NAC can accomplish this goal by

✔ Integrating an automatic remediation process — in effect, fixing security shortcomings in devices that don't meet network requirements before allowing them to access the network.

✔ Allowing endpoint devices, routers, switches, and firewalls to work together — provided that all aspects of the network are secure before the network allows itself to interoperate with those other systems.

Reducing data access

We all have at least some access to data that we don't really need to get at. Why? *Just in case*. That's why. Of course, *open data access* has also been a mantra of the open-systems movement, but the concept was misunderstood: It was more about providing the *right data* to the *right people* at the *right time* than about giving *everyone* access to *everything* at *all times*. Although the latter happens simply because it's easier to go that route than to think about how to segment your access authorization.

In the age of implicit trust (see Chapter 25), all this access was fine; people were trusted to do the right thing. Today, with data losses on the front page of the news every day, it's time to tighten up a bit. That means reducing access to data; if fewer people have access to it, then it's less likely to be lost.

When you find sensitive data (or determine that, sure enough, it's sensitive), do a check to see who can access it. Then see if all those folks *really* need access to it. If they don't, look to do something about it:

✔ Move it to a different share or partition that has better security.

✔ Remove unnecessary access-control list (ACL) entries. All too often, whole groups of people are added by default, when only one individual actually needs access.

✔ Encrypt it to make it really secure.

✔ If it's really old stuff, you may even be allowed to delete it.

Check with your governance-and-compliance people *before* you start deleting. Just because something's old doesn't necessarily mean you don't have to keep it for a while.

The trick here is to do something *when you find a problem* instead of letting the problem propagate.

Reducing network access is a lot of work, but worth the hassle. Organizations that do it effectively and appropriately can

✔ Reduce propagation of malicious code such as viruses, worms, spyware, and other forms of malware and crimeware.

✔ Lower their risk profile through increased control of unmanaged and managed endpoints accessing the corporate network.

✔ Improve network availability and reduce disruption of services for end-users.

✔ Verify organizational compliance information through near-real-time endpoint-compliance data.

✔ Minimize total cost of ownership as a result of an enterprise-class centralized management architecture.

✔ Verify that endpoint-security investments such as anti-virus and client-firewall technologies are properly enabled.

What are the alternatives?

There are a number of techniques you can use to reduce access to your data. Here's a basic list:

✔ **Agent self-enforcement:** Uses an agent on the host to enable and disable network access, using the host's firewall rules.

✔ **Peer-to-peer enforcement:** Distributed enforcers watch network traffic and identify systems that don't have the appropriate agent in place.

✔ **DHCP Enforcer (plug-in):** Controls which IP addresses are given access.

DHCP Enforcer is easy for the bad guys to work around *unless* the switch fabric (the switch fabric is the interconnected infrastructure between network segments) is aware of exactly which IP addresses correspond to which MAC addresses.

✔ **ARP poisoning:** This approach uses ARP to manage the MAC-to-IP mapping. Like DHCP, however, it can be easily got around.

✔ **In-line blocking or In-line NAC:** This technique uses purpose-built hardware designed for packet processing; it's like deploying a network firewall on each switch port. Be wary of performance claims, however; the closer to the access port, the better the control.

✔ **LAN 802.1X Enforcer (appliance):** This protocol is for IEEE port authentication. It authenticates a device to the network. Enforcement is through switch-port control or VLAN steering. Used mainly in wireless networks.

✔ **VLAN steering:** Puts hosts and switch ports onto specific virtual LANs. This means a visitor can be given access to the Internet, but nothing else. The command-and-control application has to integrate with the switch.

Network Access Control: What's In It

Network Access Control architecture comprises four key components:

✔ **Endpoint evaluation technologies** assess the state (checks whether they're compliant or noncompliant with policy) of endpoints attempting to access the network.

✔ **Enforcers** act as the gateway that permits or denies access to the network.

✔ **Policy management** creates, edits, and manages the rules or policies that control network access via a central management console.

✔ **Monitoring** makes sure that a validated endpoint stays that way.

The enforcement and evaluation technologies report to — and receive their configuration policy information from — administration. That's where policies are created, edited, and managed. If the endpoint-evaluation technology determines that the endpoint isn't in compliance with policy, it will block the endpoint from accessing the network.

NAC technology can also perform remediation tasks (in effect, bringing non-compliant devices up to snuff so they meet security requirements before logging on), validate and enforce for all types of endpoints on all types of networks.

Data on the move

When data gets used, it moves — a lot — and if it's sensitive, you need to know where it's going. All organizations should be monitoring all data usage and stopping sensitive data from exiting any network gateway or endpoint. To do this you need to work out which are your exit points. E-mail is only part of the problem; 50 percent of incidents occur via Internet protocols other than e-mail, such as those for instant messaging or blogs. In addition, USB devices and CD/DVDs all need to be monitored and (more to the point) blocked to prevent sensitive data from being lost.

So it's all about a combination of letting the right people have access to the right stuff at the right time — and then making sure that they don't waltz off with it, either by accident or "accidentally on purpose." Your shiny new technology should accurately prevent security violations for all data types and all network protocols — including e-mail (SMTP), instant messaging (AOL, MSN, Yahoo), secure Web (HTTP over SSL), FTP, P2P, and generic TCP sessions over any port.

Data at rest

When data's at rest, it's just waiting for someone to use it; you need to have control over who that "someone" is. Why not create an inventory of all the stuff you *don't* want lost — and prioritize high-risk data and its probable exit routes? That would be a good starting point.

In addition, make sure that your solution can stop data movements that infringe acceptable use, security, or privacy policies — *before* the data leaves the network. Even if your plan is to introduce prevention capabilities gradually over time, your software vendor should offer both monitoring and prevention today, giving you the flexibility to expand according to your requirements.

Data isn't fixed; its importance can change with circumstances. So what's okay for anyone to see one minute can become sensitive (and a candidate for restriction) the next. Systems looking to keep your data compliant with security policy must be proactive about hunting for changed files and re-checking them to make sure their contents are still aligned with your access policy. If those files aren't compliant with policy, remediation must occur quickly before any damage is done.

Comprehensive Remediation

In the most current offerings, NAC happens in four phases:

- ✔ **Discover:** Endpoint devices constantly change during use, so your NAC solution must make continuous or periodic assessments. With some NAC products, "continuous" isn't *really* continuous. Be careful. Most products use passive monitoring (IDS) which determines when a host needs a reassessment according to its behavior.

- ✔ **Enforce:** The types of enforcement vary widely. The most versatile provide a variety of in-band (using regular channels, usually Ethernet, for device management) and out-of-band (using dedicated channels to manage devices, and allowing policy based enforcement management of a device) enforcement but do depend on the network infrastructure already in place. Any enforcement means major changes to your infrastructure; even plug-and-play appliances get security evaluations.

- ✔ **Remediate:** This is the crux of NAC; after the endpoint device is validated and assuming all the defined policies are okay, we're away. But what happens when they fail the validation? At this point you realize how users' computers are much more varied than you might like to admit — so the wider the criteria your NAC system can use to assess and validate a host's condition, the better. The way it's supposed to work is that your organizational policy kicks in and decides which patches or remediation may be required.

- ✔ **Monitor:** Security-posture information is validated as it's gathered. How data is gathered depends on the NAC product and on the integration points between products. Assessments are passed to the policy server, using standardized protocols. The Policy Server validates a host's condition according to a defined policy, and then either sticks the device in remediation mode (where it's quarantined) or okays it and allows it onto the network — where (don't forget) it's being monitored at the same time.

These four phases are a continuous cycle, as shown in Figure 15-1.

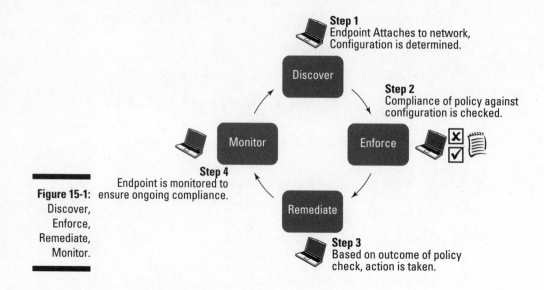

Figure 15-1:
Discover,
Enforce,
Remediate,
Monitor.

Authorization strategies to reduce data access

You can use patch-management or software-distribution solutions that usu-ally work on a schedule. These can bring endpoint devices into compliance. Be wary of users with administrator privileges thinking that they're exempt from corporate NAC and data-access policies.

Be careful of solutions that use some iffy techniques and

- ✔ Increase the number of agents installed on the endpoints. This can put a strain on the endpoint device's OS.

- ✔ Create more complexity, which in turn increases risk.

- ✔ Create too many disruptions to the IT infrastructure.

- ✔ Don't deliver effective enforcement and remediation.

- ✔ Don't integrate with the technology you already use for endpoint secu-rity or management.

- ✔ Aren't appropriate for your particular business requirements.

Using NAC agents

There are two major types of *agents* (programs that act as a go-between when a user logs on to the server) out there. Here's a quick look at their functions and differences:

- **Persistent agents** allow permanent employees to access the network. They tend to check the status of anti-virus/anti-spyware technology, as well as installed patches. They're the most effective and reliable agents and should be the starting point for your NAC solution. They access and examine software installation, patches, and Registry entries. Solutions that aren't based on agents don't give the network administrator sufficient access to make the necessary modifications to your endpoints to bring them into compliance with your security policy.

- **Dissolvable agents** are designed for all those people who have access to your network but aren't employees. They're usually partners, temporary staff, suppliers, and such. Unfortunately, handling dissolvable agents can be a nightmare. Productive input from all these folks, as well as more network requests, can bombard administrators if you don't get this right. The last thing you want to do is block users' access. Effective Network Access Control solutions must have the ability and flexibility to verify that a new or temporary endpoint doesn't pose a threat to the network — *and* determine what level of network access should be granted to the endpoint. Dissolvable agents dissolve (spookily) at the end of the session.

By itself, Network Access Control isn't enough. To beat the data-loss phenomenon, you need a variety of tools in your arsenal. Figure 15-2 shows the complex requirements for a comprehensive loss prevention strategy.

A comprehensive data-loss solution combines data discovery, data-movement blocking, and host-based security technologies with tools designed to eliminate vulnerabilities from home computers, kiosks, and guest laptops — in particular, desktop firewalls and policies to control the use of peripheral devices.

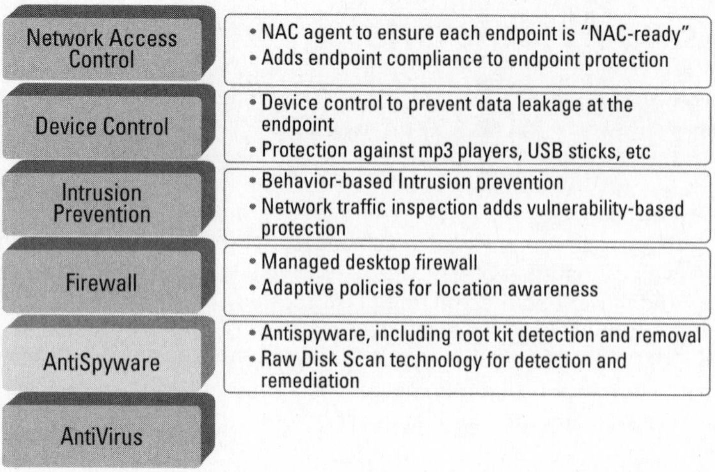

Network Access Control	• NAC agent to ensure each endpoint is "NAC-ready" • Adds endpoint compliance to endpoint protection
Device Control	• Device control to prevent data leakage at the endpoint • Protection against mp3 players, USB sticks, etc
Intrusion Prevention	• Behavior-based Intrusion prevention • Network traffic inspection adds vulnerability-based protection
Firewall	• Managed desktop firewall • Adaptive policies for location awareness
AntiSpyware	• Antispyware, including root kit detection and removal • Raw Disk Scan technology for detection and remediation
AntiVirus	

Figure 15-2:
Network
Access
Control isn't
enough. You
need all the
help you
can get.

Part IV
Applications

"We found where the security breach in the WLAN was originating. It was coming in through another rogue robot-vac. This is the third one this month. Must have gotten away from its owner, like all the rest."

In this part . . .

There are a number of critical applications that need to be considered when it comes to data loss. This part looks at the special requirements needed for backup and archive applications as well as how you can protect your Web-based applications.

It also provides information on how you can begin building data loss prevention into your applications, as well as examining some of the other places and ways you can lose data which you probably haven't thought about.

Given that all information is of value to someone, processes and polices, which have been around for years, need to be revisited in order to prevent data loss. So, the final chapter in this part tells you how to redesign processes and successfully implement them.

Chapter 16

Backup and Archiving

· ·

In This Chapter

▶ Identifying the issues of data loss in terms of backup

▶ Using encryption with offsite backup data

▶ Appreciating where data loss can occur in a backup environment

▶ Recognizing how an archive can help ameliorate data loss

· ·

*B*ackup is a simple idea: You regularly take a copy of the information that's important to you and store it somewhere safe. In the event of a disaster, you can recover the copy and continue to work.

Backup technology has changed over the years; while the data is still stored on tape, it's also stored on inexpensive disks and on other media such as CD-ROMs and DVDs. Either way, the outcome is the same: The data is safe and secure, and can easily be recovered.

From a data-loss perspective, backup is a potential nightmare. This chapter looks at ways to exercise due care and pay some security-aware attention to the backup environment.

Backup: The Easiest Way to Lose Critical Data

It used to be said that the easiest way to carry out corporate espionage was to steal the backup tapes. Nowadays, the same is true, but general data loss has become a much more pervasive issue — and losing customer data has consequences that are just as bad as those of losing corporate information — if not worse.

Backup is designed to capture all the company's important information and keep an easily managed copy for use when needed. The change in technology — from tape to an interim backup on disk — means end-users are now allowed to restore their own files whenever they want to instead of submitting a job for the IT department to do it. Convenient? Maybe. But it's also the first problem: *Individuals can have access at any time.* In addition (and increasingly) the content is fully indexed; finding a particular file is becoming easier. Individuals who have administrator (or backup) access can search the entire backup catalog for files. Using regular pattern-matching techniques, practically anyone can search for (say) credit-card numbers and other highly sensitive pieces of information.

When looking for backup software, make sure that it has an audit feature. That way you can look to see who is requesting information to be restored — and spot anomalous behavior.

Tapes are used for backup because they store a lot of information, are easily stored, and are easy to transport. All three of these characteristics are also useful to the cybercriminal. Loss or theft of a backup tape is similar to loss of a laptop; if you're in the U.S.A. and you mislay a tape or it's stolen, full public disclosure is required. Similar laws are cropping up around the world. Result: The stakes are higher than ever if you experience data loss.

Backup tapes . . . under lock and key?

Offsite storage is frequently used for backup tapes. In fact, storing tapes offsite is basic to business continuity. The data is backed up onsite and then transported elsewhere so the company can request the data and restore the files if a disaster trashes the main office. Historically, data on backup tapes was not encrypted (and often is not, even today). If you could obtain a tape, you could use a copy of the backup software that made it to read the tape and restore the files — even if you were an unauthorized user. It was really that simple. No wonder a protection strategy is needed.

Internally, backup tapes need to be stored in a physically secure manner. Processes should be in place to ensure that individuals who store and retrieve the tapes are who they say they are, and aren't impersonating the people who have legitimate access. *This is equally true of data being stored or held offsite.*

If data goes offsite, it should be encrypted. Even if the tape is being stored at another company location, the data should still be encrypted *before* it's in transit, just in case the truck it's riding in is in an accident and the tapes are lost.

Additionally, there should be an audit kept of the tapes and other backup media, including their physical locations (both internal and offsite). At the end of its life, a tape should be suitably destroyed and disposed of. In some cases this might just involve shredding. If the information is particularly sensitive, it may require incineration.

It's not just the tapes

The backup application tends to be all-pervasive in the network — so the tapes (or other removable media) aren't the only parts of the system that must be secured. In fact, you should take even more care at a number of other places in the backup environment.

Figure 16-1 shows a typical backup environment: Data is sent from the client to the media server — and control happens at other points.

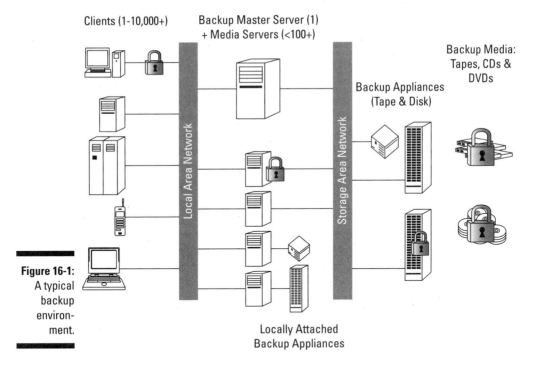

Figure 16-1: A typical backup environment.

Clients (1-10,000+)

Backup Master Server (1) + Media Servers (<100+)

Backup Media: Tapes, CDs & DVDs

Backup Appliances (Tape & Disk)

Local Area Network

Storage Area Network

Locally Attached Backup Appliances

Because all the data on a server (or laptop or desktop) has to be backed up, the backup application has access to all the files — even if an individual user does not. Unencrypted communications can be snooped en route between backup client and media server, and that means stolen information. This is particularly true if some of the data being backed up is outside the firewall.

If data is being backed up over a public network, be sure to encrypt the data so it isn't lost to possible snoopers listening in on the connection.

Disk-based backup protection

Although tape has a strong future in backup solutions (largely because it's inexpensive), technology has advanced and the humble disk has taken center stage. With it come new risks — including physical loss of the disk array.

Thieves broke into the data center of a financial institution and made off with disk arrays. Maybe they wanted the valuable hardware rather than the data, but no one can be sure. As with backup tapes, backup disks contain all the company's confidential and important data; they need to be secured. Carefully consider encryption for the disk arrays in your data center.

Hardware encryption to protect offsite data

While software on the server can be effectively used as an encryption solution, a new breed of devices for backup can encrypt the data in hardware. It can happen, in transit or in the tape device. In all instances, the encryption key management can be the toughest part. Data on backup tapes can be valid for many years, so the encryption keys also must be managed for many years.

Figure 16-2 shows where encryption can occur in a backup environment.

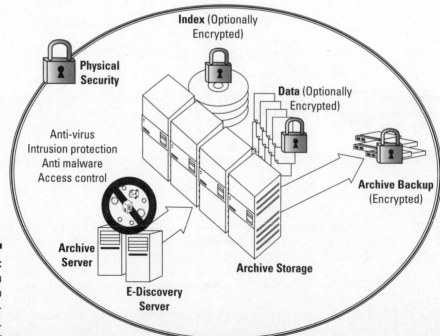

Figure 16-2: Encryption in a backup environment.

The two most popular ways to encrypt data to tape are

✔ **Inline encryption appliances:** An *appliance* is a dedicated hardware system. With encryption appliances in place, the backup system doesn't have to interact with the encryption key-management system. (For more on encryption, see Chapter 14.) These appliances are also useful when used with an existing backup infrastructure (for example, with existing tape drives). Inline encryption can come from a number of vendors, including Decru, NeoScale and Cisco.

✔ **Tape drives with embedded encryption:** Vendors include Sun/ StorageTek, IBM, HP, Quantum, and Spectra Logic. Several of these manufacturers have their own key-management systems; others enable backup vendors to provide the keys.

Embedded encryption is likewise a good idea for organizations that are replacing their backup infrastructure in a hardware-refresh cycle. This happens every few years; accordingly, it's a great time to match new business requirements — say, *preventing data leaks* (hint, hint) — with the new technology.

Compress and then encrypt

Encrypted data, by its nature, is difficult to compress. So, just as the barbarian hordes had to remember to pillage *before* burning, remember one of the rules for encryption (especially for tape): Compress the data and *then* encrypt it. For example, if you start with a file that takes up 28,980 bytes and you encrypt before compressing, its size is *still* 28,980 bytes. But if you *compress before encrypting*, the size shrinks dramatically — to 304 bytes!

When looking at encryption over the wire, from the client to the media server, consider *transient encryption* (encrypting data before it's sent and then decrypted when it's received). It can be readily compressed and written to tape, or in some cases re-encrypted with a different key that resides in the backup-management system.

Managing encryption keys

Management of the *encryption keys* (the small programs used to encrypt data) is the hardest part. The backup process has special key-security needs that must be understood from the outset.

If the encryption keys are lost, so is the data, because then it can't be decrypted. There are no backdoors! In the event of a disaster, you have to recover the keys *before* you can recover the data.

For these reasons backup encryption shouldn't be taken lightly — even with potential data loss looming. A phased deployment should be carried out, with extensive testing of the key-management and disaster-recovery facilities.

Third-party backup management (SaaS)

Some companies turn to external organizations to back up their data (whether structured or unstructured) — those third parties provide storage or backup *as a service;* what they do is called *Storage as a Service (SaaS).* If you're planning to use that approach, be sure to take appropriate steps to ensure that the organization you're using has sufficient safeguards against data loss, and can handle your disaster-recovery and business-continuity requirements.

Although Storage as a Service does take some administrative tasks away from your IT organization (or, for that matter, from individual users), you're potentially putting all your customer-data and intellectual-property eggs in (effectively) one basket. Consider whether the saved labor is worth the risk.

Any organization offering SaaS must be able to prove it can protect your critical data. All too often, data loss is the result of third parties' mistakes. Take the example of the U.K. Driving Standards Agency that lost 3 million records when a hard drive went missing in Iowa. Details of the driving candidates in the U.K. were sent to the U.S., to Pearson Driving Assessments in Iowa. The records were then sent to another state before being returned to Iowa. And that's where the hard drive (in effect) disappeared.

Although the U.K. government made formal statements that the data was not "readily usable or accessible" by third parties, this data-loss incident happened at the worst possible time: During the same month, the U.K. government had admitted that Her Majesty's Revenue and Customs lost discs containing tax details for (oops) 25 million people. The U.K. government's promise of data protection suffered (to put it kindly) a *big* loss of credibility.

The Importance of an Archive

Unfortunately, most organizations don't understand the data-loss impact of losing specific files, or the impact of a mis-addressed e-mail. Avoiding such loss is one major advantage of having an archive.

Identifying risk

Enterprise archives are created for various reasons that range from simple storage management to compliance with regulations and laws. While archives can contain data from multiple sources, e-mail is where they can be most useful in data-loss incidents.

Depending on the type of data-loss incident, the archive can provide a picture of what information has been put at risk. If an e-mail was sent to the wrong recipient, then the archived copy will have all the relevant information, including the attachments. Only affected recipients need to be notified of the potential breach, not everyone in the database. (Ideally you don't want the wrong e-mail to be sent to the wrong person. The data-loss prevention technologies described in Chapter 22 can help stop that.)

You can use a backup in much the same way as an archive when you want to find what information has been put at risk. If a laptop is lost and the data on it isn't encrypted, recovering the last backup enables you to find which confidential information has been put at risk. Even so, this method isn't foolproof after all; it depends on the laptop having been backed up recently — and on the owner remembering (in effect) all work done on the machine since the last backup.

Protecting the corporate memory

Ultimately the archive will contain all the unstructured information that's important to an organization. It will also contain a lot that isn't, but because archives are usually fully indexed, finding the wood from the trees isn't too difficult.

Having all this information in one place offers cybercriminals (especially malicious insiders, if you're unlucky enough to have them) a great opportunity for mayhem. Thus an unsecured archive itself offers the organization a significant risk. The main difference between a backup and an archive is how the data is organized; in an archive, it's been indexed and so it's readily searchable. In many cases, access to the original isn't required in order to obtain the information needed. For example, you could search for credit-card numbers and they would be returned in a list ready for cutting and pasting into a different document. Depending on the way the archive is organized, it might *also* return other sensitive information along with the credit-card number — say, the account holder's name — quite possibly all the data needed to commit fraud.

Security is therefore of critical importance — both physical and logical. From the physical perspective, the archive will probably be located in the data center. At least there it will have the same physical constraints as other critical corporate infrastructure, which is good. But that's only a start.

Logical (that is, software) data protection is also needed here. Be sure to give your archives endpoint protection such as anti-virus and intrusion detection. In fact, if you archive a significant amount of e-mail data, some of it may contain viruses — so it's important to scan all data retrieved from an archive — especially old e-mail and attachments — and to make sure that your anti-virus software is up to date at all places of risk.

Managing access control is the other side of security that must be strengthened to reduce opportunities for evildoers (whether outsiders or insiders) to gain access to company secrets. Figure 16-3 shows the various points in an archive solution that must be protected to prevent data loss.

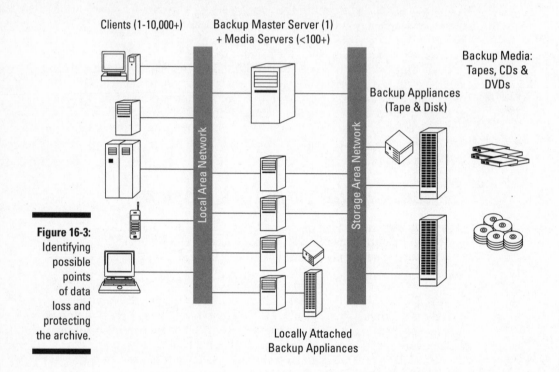

Figure 16-3: Identifying possible points of data loss and protecting the archive.

Chapter 17

Protection through Web Applications

....

....

*H*ow do you do business? It doesn't matter how big or small you are, the Web is now a valuable portal for you to reach your customers and for your customers to reach you and buy stuff. If your Web site is down, then it probably hurts your business. Unfortunately, the cybercriminal has also realized the potential *monetary* benefits of your Web site — sure, a few years ago it used to be fun to deface or disable Web sites, but these days the threats are much more subtle; most people don't realize they're happening! That's because the bad guys are after bigger game. So some caution is in order: Just because the Web page *looks* okay doesn't mean it hasn't been hijacked; understanding that is a good start. So let's look at how cyber-criminals can *use your Web site* to attack *your customers.*

Attacking Applications through the Web

The Web is now the *de facto* way to do business. Even if you don't take orders for goods or services through a Web application, chances are that you do collect information from customers via the Web so you can send them information and market their socks off. If you do take orders online, then you're collecting data such as credit-card numbers, names, and addresses. That's nectar to the cybercriminal. So imagine: If you were a cybercriminal, where would you focus your efforts, on the individual (where you might get one set of information that is useful) or on a corporate Web site (where you could end up with *millions* of records)? No contest there — especially if you have a ready-made pipe straight into the data center. And you do: the Internet.

SQL injection attacks

Businesses take and hold customer information in databases, also known as *massive repositories of structured data* (MRSDs). In the good old days, order processors would enter orders received on paper into applications that would then populate the database. Reports could be generated, orders fulfilled, and customers satisfied. The world was a happy place. The application would enter and retrieve the data through a language called SQL (Structured Query Language). Great.

Along comes the Web: Organizations decide to *cut out the middleman* (that is, the order processor) and have the customer enter the data directly over the Internet. Cool. Nothing really changed — with one major exception: What people hadn't realized was that you could send a *different* SQL statement over the Web interface, and — guess what? — you could get back *all the data*. Rather than just your record, you could get back *everybody's* records, along with credit-card information (names, addresses, and expiration dates). In fact, a cyber-criminal could harvest all the data out of the entire database. Such criminal bonanzas — disasters from the victim's point of view — are called *SQL injection attacks*.

The worst thing about the SQL injection attack is that unless you're set up to spot it specifically, it's difficult to detect. So, far from being a one-off, it can happen over and over and over again — silent, stealthy attacks you never even know about.

Several retailers have fallen foul of this attack; one lost more than 40 million credit-card records. What was worse: They didn't know when it started. The first attack could have been six months ago, two years ago, or even longer. As data leaks go, that's a gusher.

To stymie SQL injection attacks, you must have two capabilities:

- ✔ Prevent the *possibility* of losing data to an SQL injection attack.
- ✔ Spot when an SQL attack is happening.

The second of these is a good place to start, for one good reason: The attack can come from the inside — the malicious insider — and be hard to spot.

Malicious insiders have a great advantage over "outside" cyber-criminals: They know where the data is — and they probably have legitimate access to it. Implicit trust: You give employees/partners/suppliers access to the network and then trust that they'll do the right thing. Unfortunately, too often this trust proves misplaced. One insider stole intellectual property worth an estimated $400 million from his employer (for the grim details, see Chapter 25).

How can you solve this problem? Behavioral analysis. The idea is simple, you monitor normal behavior and then detect if something strange happens. When it does, you alert someone in authority to look into it. For example, if an order-fulfillment clerk who usually accesses one record at a time suddenly decides to create a report on the top *1,000* customers — including their credit-card details — the appropriate person can be alerted to go and question our friend about why this unusual report seemed necessary. There may be a legitimate reason, so don't assume the worst! (There is more about this technology in Chapter 25.)

The good news is that this technology can *also* spot SQL injection attacks. For the moment, however, let's be a little more proactive, shall we? As in . . . preventing them from happening in the first place.

Preventing SQL injection attacks

The solution to prevent an attack is relatively simple: Don't allow raw SQL to be passed to your database. Of course, in practice, this means that the simple port of the application that was Web-enabled must be overhauled. Here are the basics:

- ✔ **Don't allow *escape* characters.** This will help prevent potentially unsafe additions to the SQL statement. All input needs to be properly filtered.

- ✔ **Handle *types* correctly.** If you're expecting a number, then check whether it's a number, don't blindly pass anything. That can cause a problem in the database and result in a successful attack.

- ✔ **Use parameterized statements.** Basically all the input data is filtered according to specific parameters, and then assigned appropriately — with checks on the expected data type. Problems are resolved by the application before they can be sent to the database.

- ✔ **Use code reviews.** The changes needed are relatively simple when you get the hang of making them, but it's always a good idea to review the code. Two pairs of eyes looking at the problem (and solution) are better than one.

The Dangers from the Internet Browser

How do you get to the Internet? Chances are you use a Web browser and download Web pages that show you the information you're looking for. In the interests of making the experience better for the user, the Web browser enables a rich interface — which allows you to see pictures, videos, and all sorts of other information. The interface makes you think you're in an application rather than a simple interface. My how the browser has evolved from the text-only days! And it's still changing; in the brave new world of Web 2.0, the browser is making possible even more access to content of all sorts — and one of the essential items in Web 2.0 is the *plug-in*. However, the plug-in brings with it an enhanced opportunity for cyber-attack.

Think of the browser as a building that started off as a garden shed. There was a door, so everything came and went through the one door. Now think of it as a building with multiple doors, windows, and a basement. Air-conditioning units on the roof are like a *plug-in* — they're installed by a third party, maintained by someone else, and (hopefully) *do what they say they do* (which in this case means cooling the air). But what if there is problem? Or, what happens if someone were to tamper with the unit to make it do something different, or knew how to circumvent security to make it do something *really* different? Now think of the browser as an apartment block — lots of people coming and going, lots of air conditioners, satellite systems, and all sorts of devices — most of which have vulnerabilities and are beyond your control.

Browser plug-ins

How many browser *plug-ins* (or *add-ons* as they're also called) do you have? Those available to your browser will be listed in its *Options* or *Preferences* section. Chances are you have half a dozen or so when you start — but that balloons as soon as you start installing stuff. Media players, search engines, document viewers, download accelerators, they'll all be there. The problem is that you don't know what they all do or whether they're okay to use. Furthermore, when you go and visit Web sites, often they ask whether you want to download and install a plug-in. What to do? Do you trust the site? What if you know nothing else about it?

Regularly delete browser plug-ins. If you need it, then it will reload itself with the latest version. If you don't need it, not only will you not miss it, but it will also reduce the risk of attack.

Speaking of attacks, the upcoming sections profile several such nasty exploits that make use of standard capabilities used online every day: cross-site scripting, clicking a mouse, and the use of session cookies.

Cross-site scripting

Back in the good old days, when a Web browser basically went to a site (same origin) and downloaded the information it found, there was no concept of *cross-site scripting* (also called *XSS*). Today the data for a Web page can come from multiple sources — typically images and ads can come from different Web sites — but from the end-users' perspective, the data is all visible on whatever Web site that they're visiting; it all *seems* to come from there, but doesn't.

So, to set up an XSS attack, the cybercriminal just sneakily attacks a Web site and adds a small piece of code into the Web page that redirects the user to visit a Web site that hosts malware. The malware is then loaded into the browser and infects the browser and the users' computers. Because the attack is transparent, the users don't know which data is genuine and which isn't. They're duped into accepting the malware and installing it on their systems. Increasingly, the bad guys are targeting sites with well-known brands — especially social-networking sites — and the infection rates are growing at a frightening rate (as shown in Figure 17-1). Over the same period, however, the time needed to fix the problem decreased from 57 days (in the first half of 2007) to 52 days (in the second half). So countermeasures are getting better slowly. But however long it takes is still a long time for customers to be put at risk.

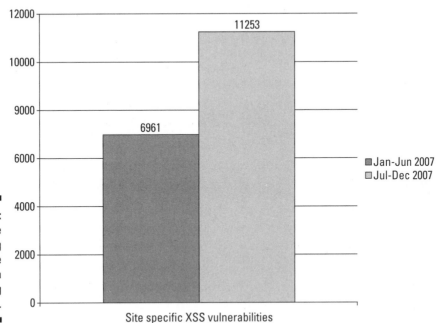

Figure 17-1: Cross-site scripting attacks are growing at a frightening rate.

There are a number of approaches to preventing XSS attacks:

✔ **Educate your users.** Tell people not to accept browser plug-ins unless they're sure that those things are genuine. Only download and install plug-ins from the actual site where the plug-in originates — for example, from Microsoft or Adobe. Don't trust browser plug-ins from other sites, especially social-networking sites.

✔ **Disable scripting.** This is feasible within an organization. The IT department ensures that the version of the browser installed on users' machines has scripting disabled. Of course, this won't work well for customers — and even the employees might find this impossible to live with because many applications require scripting.

✔ **Check your own Web site regularly.** See whether it's been hacked and whether someone's introduced an XSS vulnerability. It's no good just *looking* at a page, however; have your IT people look at the *code* that creates the page on-screen. A number of companies can monitor your site for you, or you can program a script to can check for changes automatically.

✔ **Remove the need for scripts.** If your Web site can run without scripts, then instruct the users who are concerned about the risks of scripting to switch off scripts, but make sure they still can (and still know how to) access your site.

Clickjacking

Clickjacking is a recent phenomenon (it surfaced in mid-2008); it's a clear example of how cybercriminals are upping the stakes against anti-malware companies. In essence, the vulnerability takes over control of all the links on a Web page. *All* clicks are hijacked; the cybercriminals can get you to go to wherever they want you to. Of course, when they have that kind of control, they can then *force* you to download malware and infect your machine — all without your realizing it.

Currently there is no easy solution to clickjacking. If you really want to avoid it, you can disable browser plug-ins and scripting altogether. The good news is that doing so fixes the problem; the less-good news is that browsers now *depend* on plug-ins to help them provide the rich user experience that people expect online.

Session poisoning and hijacking

Session poisoning is, perhaps, the most insidious of browser exploits. A cyber-criminal steals a session cookie, complete with its security-authentication data, and pretends to be the user. If (say) you've just logged on to your bank account or a corporate application with access to customer details, the cyber-criminal can use that account with your name and network privileges. (Worse, it will look to the network as if it really *is* you!) In effect, you've just had a piece of your identity stolen.

Preventing session hijacking generally means a major revisit to the application being built. However, if you're a bank — or any e-commerce player — then this prevention is an essential task to prevent data loss:

- ✔ **Encryption:** Many sites use only Secure Socket Layer (SSL) encryption for their login Web pages. So, the information during login is encrypted, but all traffic after that is *in the clear*. This makes it simple for the cyber-criminal to steal the cookie by sniffing the packet traffic after it has been created and then impersonating the user.

- ✔ **Large and random numbers as session keys:** One of the ways a cyber-criminal gains access is to guess the *session key* (the encryption key that allows access to the session). If the key is a large and random number, it's much harder to guess.

- ✔ **Secondary checks:** Some applications make more secondary checks on who is requesting what. For example, is the request coming from the same IP address as the initial login? If not, then chances are way above average that a cyber-criminal is at work.

- ✔ **Rapidly changing cookie information:** This is one way to impede a cyber-criminal. If the cookie is only valid for a short period of time before its information changes (and that change happens rapidly and regularly), the bad guy's window of opportunity is a lot smaller. Change the cookie and reduce the risk.

The Internet browser is the window that your customers have on your business. It's also the window that your employees have on your applications. It's the key to the future of IT and applications. If you don't protect your applications and your users — whether they're customers or employees — then your reputation is at risk. Build secure applications and educate everyone to the new risks — it builds confidence in everything you do.

Chapter 18

Making Applications Safer

*W*ith data loss at an all-time high, it seems everybody is selling technology to prevent it. Surely there has to be a better way? The answer is *yes:* Instead of making a specialized application do all the hard work of protecting data outside its bailiwick (which it really knows little about), the application can be tasked with keeping its own data safe.

Okay, so this isn't really practical for applications that currently exist. They do their work in the way they always have — so you *do* need those specialist applications to protect you. But what if you have a new application? Wouldn't it be great if the newcomer *reduced* the risk of data loss instead of increasing it? With that in mind, this chapter looks at how you can build data-loss prevention into your specialized applications.

Data Corruption: Worse than Data Loss?

Applications are built with one priority: functionality. Software engineers don't think about security of that application enough and certainly don't think about data loss.

Engineers who design applications are (or should be) trained to take into consideration every aspect of that application — including how and where it will be used. This isn't just about software coding; it's about business issues and other considerations that are best addressed when designing the application. This is all about security — in this particular case, why it's important to prevent data loss.

The best way to get through to engineers is to provide examples and ideas that they might like to think about. They will then step up to the plate and come up with suggestions on how they can achieve what you want. So let's start with a question: *What's the worst that can happen?* Well, suppose . . .

- ✔ **The code crashes.** Okay, so the application doesn't run. At least you know about it.

- ✔ **The code crashes the machine.** This is a bit worse; if the machine has completely died, all the applications that were happily running aren't running now.

- ✔ **The code crashes the network.** Perhaps a little farfetched, but not unheard of. If a distributed application environment doesn't talk nicely over the network, it can saturate the network and cause widely distributed problems.

- ✔ **The code runs but the data is corrupt.** This is the worst possibility: The application appears to be running just fine, but the data isn't right — and the problem may not be noticed for weeks or months.

  And there is one more:

- ✔ **The data has been copied and lost, and the information compromised.** This is the *obvious* one and is the one to which the average developer would say, "Not my problem" — to which you must ask, "How would you *prevent* it from happening?"

All these problems can be overcome. After all, *it's only software*. The trick is to know that the problems can happen. Forewarned is forearmed.

Guarding against data compromise

Perhaps the hardest problem to test for is data corruption — especially if you don't know where the compromise is. Here we have to ask some questions:

- ✔ **Can the data be changed outside the application?** If the data is in a database, could database tools be used to access and alter the data?

- ✔ **Is the data coming from outside the application?** In the world of Service Oriented Architecture (SOA), data could be coming in from anywhere.

- ✔ **Is the data coming from outside the *organization*?** Once more, the world of SOA means that the data might be coming from a third party — in which case the data feed could be compromised.

✔ **Is the functionality being provided by a third party?** In some transactions, you send your data outside the organization, someone does something to it, and that party sends you back a response. One example here is credit checking, which is done by specialized agencies.

Understanding the potential problems helps you think up appropriate solutions and select them according to their applicability. Solutions might include these:

✔ **CRCs or hashes:** Cyclic Redundancy Checks (CRCs) mean that when you write the data out, you create a unique number out of the data. Then you can use this number to make sure the data hasn't changed when it's read back in. This approach works with files or with database records.

✔ **Check data feeds:** Is there *example or test* data that can be sent and received on a regular basis to check that all is well? You can also check that the data is being received on a regular basis — and perhaps use a hash to verify that its contents haven't changed en route. Be sure to check internal as well as external data feeds.

✔ **Check functionality hasn't changed:** If a legitimate third party is manipulating data, then it's a good idea to send test data on a regular basis and check to make sure the result is what you expect. For example, if you request the data in miles and it returns it in kilometers, then it's good to know sooner rather than later! At the same time, you can check performance: Knowing that the data should take 50 milliseconds to send and finding out that it's taking *an entire second* means you can take action before that lag starts to affect your customers.

✔ **Check whether callers are who they say they are:** If you're providing a service, ensure that the persons (or applications) calling you are the right ones. Check to make sure you aren't being *spoofed* by someone or something that's faking a legitimate identity.

The good news is that these checks will make your application better; the bad news is that sometimes all this checking reduces performance. However, if you know about this trade-off from the start, you can order a higher-performance machine as the target production server.

Taking the performance hit

This is sometimes the tough part. If you want to be secure, you must do extra work within the application. More work needs more processing, which slows the application down. So there is a compromise here between security and performance. Security can also affect usability (which can also be categorized as "performance," but it's at a different level.)

The Payment Card Industry Data Security Standard (PCI DSS) has been designed to protect against data loss from credit and debit cards. While this may not be relevant to you directly, the ideas and method are useful — and good to go through with engineers. The idea is simple:

✔ Identify sensitive information.

✔ Identify the applications that are using the information.

✔ Identify processes that use the information or applications.

✔ Identify the people involved and their roles.

✔ Reduce the amount of data and and/or or people who have access.

✔ Protect the data. (In the main, from a technological perspective, this means *encrypt* the data.)

Engineers are creative people, so having worked out the various issues they can then come up with some solutions, such as these:

✔ **Encrypt the data on disk.** If the data file is copied it can't be easily read — and the data can't be easily extracted.

✔ **Only show users what they need to see.** Improve granularity for role-based access. If a user doesn't need to see bank-account details, then don't show them. This means replacing general-purpose screens with more specific ones.

✔ **Apply restrictions on reporting.** Perhaps limit the number of results someone can get back at once (depending on their role.) This ensures that it isn't simple to run off with the customer list.

✔ **Prevent reports from being saved to disk.** This might not be practical — but if it is, go for it.

✔ **Prevent database extracts that include sensitive data.** If you have sensitive data in a database but some of the data (not the sensitive stuff) is needed in other applications, then prevent sensitive data from being in the extract, or zero them out.

✔ **Encrypt database extracts.** If you have a database extract application, have one final step that encrypts the data before it goes to disk.

✔ **Use audit logs to track information.** While this won't necessarily prevent loss, it will help you find out who did what.

Not all these ideas will be applicable, so it's worth going through them and looking at how useful each one may be in your situation. You don't want to spend a million dollars in extra development costs to prevent access to ten dollars' worth of data.

Poor Code Results in a New Threat Vector

Why is data loss such a problem? One quick answer is because applications traditionally can't look after their data on their own — and *people* (often the weakest link in any security story) are involved. In this new era of cyber-criminals targeting information, no new application should *create* more problems than it solves. Okay, the average programmer isn't expected to be interested in anything but application functionality — that has to change: Security in all its aspects should top the list of these considerations; to that end, *data integrity* is a new-but-indispensable part of application security.

Data has a high degree of integrity if it's strong in these three areas:

- ✔ **Availability:**. Is the data there when you need it?

- ✔ **Performance:** Can you get at the data fast enough? Is it consistently reliable and free of corruption?

- ✔ **Security:** This is the big one . . . .

  - • Can it be tampered with?

  - • Can someone else see it unintentionally?

  - • Can it be locked down so only the right people can see it at the right time?

Automatic code checkers, such as those provided by Coverity, IBM's Purify, and the Open Source FindBugs, are a great help when you're looking for potential security flaws in new code. These programs aren't perfect, however; like automatic spell checkers and grammar checkers, sometimes they miss the nuances. If you spell the wrong word right, it won't be picked up by the spell checker; if the coding is checked for a buffer overflow (the most popular potential security threat in application development), the checker may not find access-control problems in the code. The checkers are great and catch all the common problems, but they can't read your mind. Only you *know* what you want to look for, so you must stay directly involved in the checking.

Of course, there's a lot of *free* software out there. It's called Open Source. It's a great resource for application developers; they can use the code (or even whole applications) as part of the applications they're designing. As a rule, the developers are only interested in functionality — but they should also be concerned about security. Help them think a little differently about it — especially when they're about to use code that they don't control and may not fully understand. Here's a closer look . . .

Open Source software

Many companies now see Open Source software as a viable alternative to more "mainstream" commercial applications. It's a great way to get some great software. Just keep your eyes open when you choose. There are tens of thousands of Open Source projects out there; a few are bound to be close to what you want.

Open Source software isn't as easy to maintain, or as secure, as commercially developed software. Here's why:

✔ You may not get the support you need when some part of it goes wrong.

✔ The functionality may not really be what you want.

✔ Security may not be emphasized. (Engineers like to put functionality into their applications, without worrying much about security.)

When someone says it's time to "go the Open Source route," be sure to ask about security in the application. Here are some starting points:

✔ **What does the application do about security?** Do the support forums and the program's documentation even mention security?

✔ **How fine-tuned are the program's security controls?** Is there a concept of specific roles that can help secure data from the application?

✔ **What if a security issue shows up in the program?** How often and how quickly does the application get fixed? What patches or updates are available?

✔ **Is the data stored encrypted?** It may not have to be — but think about how the data might be copied or lost, and consider this additional measure of safety.

✔ **Does the Open Source application depend on other Open Source applications?** If it does, then be sure to ask these questions of *all* those other applications.

✔ **Does the application have many (or any) other users?** With Open Source, the user community is vital to support; it's better to be one of many than one of one.

✔ **Who runs the project?** If there are only two people developing the application, then the chances are neither of them gives top priority to security. If it's a small group, often the group members check each other's work — which is great, and some of those folks may be security-minded. There is some risk, however, of Open Source projects being infiltrated by hi-tech cybercriminals bent on putting *backdoors* in the applications so they can get illicit access later. If this has happened, then when you try to protect the application with usernames and passwords, the bad guys can still get in — and compromise the application, your data, or the system it's running on. It's unclear whether this kind of backdoor exploit has happened in the past or is happening now, but sooner or later, it will happen in the future. It's worth knowing a little about the project team, as well as their development policies and practices.

If you want to know about security, ask the developers. The great thing about Open Source is that you can ask questions of an application's development community and get responses back really quickly. By and large, the Web is a wonderful place to work.

Don't fret about seeming awkward if you broach the subject of security. The developer may think you're being difficult, but focus on the practical concerns: It's all about *not* making an avoidable mistake. Providing education about the risks and consequences is critical in winning over developers.

Developing data-loss testing

When a new application is being developed, the common approach is to develop a test plan at the same time. This should also hold true for data-loss applications: They, too, need testing.

There should be a set of data-loss prevention tests with check boxes you can use when the issues are adequately addressed. Here are examples:

- ✔ **All stored data that is sensitive or confidential is encrypted:** Can we say honestly, "If it's lost, we don't care — no one can read it"?

- ✔ **Role-based access control is used:** Are we sure that the right people — and only the right people — can access the data?

- ✔ **Minimal data display for task at hand:** Are we sure that the right people can *see* the right data — and only the right people?

  Be sure to run this check on each screen in the application.

- ✔ **Data-source checking:** Are we sure that no one is faking, spoofing, modifying, or otherwise messing with our data?

- ✔ **Data-feed checking:** Are we sure that no one is interfering with the data we're getting?

- ✔ **Third-party functionality checking:** Is the service we rely on still working as expected?

Putting it all together

Getting security into the forefront of a developer's attention is tough — because there are so many different aspects to the problem. You can pull all these facets of security together and make them part of a periodic review of your code. (Figure 18-1 shows this process.) Nothing focuses an engineer's mind like the thought of a review; usually developers will be expecting code reviews anyway. One more won't faze them — but it will make them think.

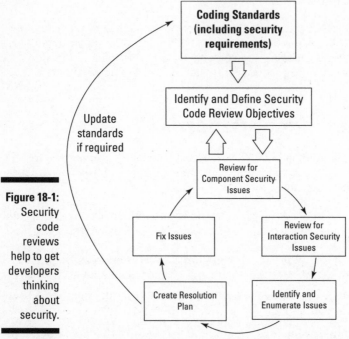

Figure 18-1:
Security
code
reviews
help to get
developers
thinking
about
security.

A security-oriented code review needs the right expectations. Here are some starting points:

- **What are you looking for?** The answer is security issues — not functionality per se. Don't get dragged down a rat hole into arguments over functionality. There are other reviews for that purpose.

- **Create a checklist or two.** Give the developers time to review and answer the listed points well in advance of the review meeting. It will save a lot of time.

✔ **Ensure that you have the right people in the room.** You'll need some system architects and other Big Picture people at the review meeting. You're looking for folks who can see how the particular module or functionality under review interacts with the rest of the system.

✔ **Review regularly.** This is especially important for junior members (or new members) of the team so they can get a grip on what needs to be done. At the outset, this will be a learning process for all.

✔ **Follow up.** If the review uncovers some unresolved security issues, be sure you follow up on them after the review. If no actions are taken as a result of finding issues, then the developers will tend to ignore the review. Set a time limit for the fix and hold another review.

✔ **Update.** Security reviews are one more way to benefit from experience. Condense what you've discovered and pass it on. Update the checklists, coding standards, and expectations. If necessary (and it will be at the start), hold training sessions to go through the security-review process with the developers.

Software as a Service: Who's Watching the Watchers?

Software as a Service (SaaS) is a very trendy way to provide functionality these days: In essence, you use applications that someone else develops and pay for them as you use them — but you have to be sure you can trust your applications. The idea behind SaaS is that this sort of outsourcing is cheaper than developing and running in-house applications — and you get access to applications normally found only in *big* enterprises, even if you're only a small business. One great example is a product from salesforce.com: a Customer Relationship Management application delivered as a service. It's so good that even large enterprises use it so they don't have to develop and run one themselves. Even with a relatively big SaaS provider that has a great reputation and an excellent product, it's worth asking some questions.

The issue of implicit trust crops up here. You're assuming that the developers will always do the right thing, have the appropriate experience, debug and test their applications sufficiently, and so on. Unfortunately, this assumption isn't always valid. Deadlines are deadlines; shortcuts are sometimes taken. More often than not, these shortcuts aren't a threat, but they could be. Even within the biggest teams, the issues are the same, so if you're looking to implement SaaS, take extra care when you're selecting a service vendor. After all, you're about to trust another company with your most valuable asset: your data.

Identifying threats in SaaS environments

Most data-loss threats in SaaS environments are the same as those you find with in-house application development. The major difference: You aren't in control. Although it may seem a little rude to inquire about the development practices of a service provider, it isn't. After all, you want to use their products, and the questions are legitimate from a security standpoint.

When looking for SaaS providers, draw up a list of questions to ask about their development processes — specifically, how they prevent data loss. Here are some useful questions to start with (practice asking them in a friendly, matter-of-fact tone):

- Do you have a development process?
  - Is it written down?
  - Is it available for your clients to see in action?
  - Does it follow a consistent methodology?
- Do you have security code reviews?
- Do you look specifically at data security and integrity — particularly at preventing data loss?

If you get answers you're happy with, then that's as good as it gets. If you don't, then it might be time to look at another vendor!

Securing your data from tampering

One of the biggest concerns when you hand over your data to a service provider is that it will be compromised.

A few years ago, a new airline was just starting up; it needed some IT to run its booking systems and the like. Instead of buying and running a whole new IT infrastructure, the startup decided to use another airline's IT; the second airline provided their software as a service. All was well until the new airline had grown big enough to run its own IT. After the data was dutifully migrated across to the new IT department and all was well — or *seemed* well. Then a letter went out to the new airline's customers, offering deals — from the airline that had provided IT capabilities earlier. The new airline's data had been compromised — in this case, copied and used for someone else's marketing campaign.

You need to protect your data, no matter where it is. Look at how the service provider handles it in all stages of its lifecycle. Ask questions; if you don't ask, you won't know — and if you don't know, then you don't understand the potential risks and could be putting your business at risk.

Focus on the data and the security that surrounds it:

- How is it created?
- How is it stored and managed?
- How is it deleted?
- Is there an audit trail? For example, if someone deletes records will you know about it?
- Where is encryption used?
- Who has access, why, and when?
- Will you know if it has been copied?
- Are the backups encrypted?
- If you hold the encryption keys, how will you protect them?

Chapter 19

Losses from the Unlikeliest Places

. . . .

In This Chapter

▶ Accidentally helping cyber-criminals

▶ Destroying electronic data

▶ Safely selling and repairing equipment

▶ Finding data in unlikely places

▶ Dealing with the printed word

. . . .

*W*hether you've been jumping around in the book or reading straight through, by this point you're probably familiar with data loss (whether by leaks or by breaches) as a threat to electronic data and in an everyday working environment. But these days data lives in a lot of other places — and they all need protection. If that isn't something you think about much (or regularly), this chapter is aimed at helping you to remember.

The good news is that in all these cases, securing your data is often as close as making a simple change in company policy and/or procedure, followed by bringing the staff up to speed about why the changes are necessary. We start with an obvious situation: How often have you walked past a pile of old computer equipment sitting in the corridor and thought, "I wish someone would remove that" — and then find it gone one morning and think, "About time"? Sometimes, of course, as the old junk leaves the building, so too might the company's data — and reputation.

Is That Your Data Walking Out the Door?

In the same way that stealing backup tapes will give you access to all the important company information, so too would stealing the machines. Now there is a way to *steal* machines without actually stealing them. In fact, people will *help* you if you offer to take away their old machines.

We can hardly go on a customer visit without seeing old computer hardware sitting in a pile waiting to be collected. The hardware is ancient — two or even three years old (!) — of no real use to the business anymore. It's a pain to remove, especially under the new WEEE directives.

A quick aside on WEEE: The E.U.'s Waste Electrical and Electronic Equipment (WEEE) Regulations include IT equipment and aim to do lots of good things, including these:

- ✔ Encourage separate collection of WEEE.
- ✔ Encourage treatment, reuse, recovery, recycling, and sound environmental disposal of EEE.
- ✔ Make producers of EEE responsible for the environmental impact of their products.

More often than not, the old hardware sits in the corridor for several months before it's removed and discarded. But even if the hardware is old, the data may still be current enough to be useful to the cyber-criminal. From that perspective, revisit your policies that specify what to do with old systems — and ensure that any data they hold is suitably destroyed.

In August 2008, a server turned up on eBay. Some guy bought it — along with its network attached storage (NAS) box, which contained unencrypted backups of data CDs. Details on that server included names, addresses, bank-account numbers, telephone numbers, and customer signatures. Professional assessment: This machine was sold inappropriately on eBay. (We've even seen a story about a million people's bank details turning up on an auction site — at a price that figures out to 268 people per penny.)

Old computer equipment is considered almost worthless, so companies tend to get rid of it for free (or nearly so). Although disposal of that equipment is now governed by the WEEE directive, there's no provision for disposing of the *data* before the equipment meets its destiny. What's needed here is the creation and consistent enforcement of proper data-disposal policies and procedures.

Even if you have a policy that forbids storing data locally on endpoint machines, such storage often happens as a mistake. Many of us have saved work only to be unable to find it — because, through the magic of computers (*I didn't do anything different — honest*), it's been saved somewhere unexpected: the local hard drive.

How to destroy electronic data

This might seem like a simple task — just delete it, right? Wrong! It seems easy, but it's actually difficult to delete electronic data permanently — because, as with all things IT, there are decisions to be made.

What's it stored on?

There are a number of places that electronic data can be stored; each of these has to be considered separately:

- ✔ **CD-ROM and/or DVD:** Here the simplest (because crudest) method works best: shredding. Use a crosscut shredder for best results — or outsource the job to someone who can cut the pieces even smaller.

- ✔ **Tape:** Backup tapes should also be destroyed at the end of their useful lives, these are best to be shredded (or *fluffed,* as they say in the trade).

- ✔ **Hard drives:** There are a number of different strategies for destroying the data on a hard drive — it just depends on how complete you want to be!

- ✔ **Delete the data:** Don't forget to "empty the Recycle Bin" (or click the Trash icon, or whatever else confirms a deletion). Of course, there are tools to recover the information, so this simple measure doesn't do an adequate job if you're trying to get rid of sensitive data.

There are free applications that you can run on the endpoint (laptop or desktop) that securely delete the data by overwriting it.

- ✔ **Delete and overwrite:** This is the most common method. There are a number of standards that govern how many *times* the data should be overwritten — and specify various patterns of overwriting the data. The U.S. Department of Defense recommends one called (catchily) DoD 5220-22.M. It overwrites the data seven times, and is faster than the most secure (Gutman) method, which overwrites 35 times.

It is often difficult to tell where the data is. The OS and the users between them put all sorts of information all over a hard drive. You might think that the stuff all winds up in My Documents (in Windows) but it doesn't. If you delete and overwrite, it's best to do the whole disk, and then reformat it.

- ✔ **Shred:** *Shred a hard disk? You must be crazy.* (Hah. That's what they *want* you to believe . . .) There are companies out there that do shred hard disks — grinding them up to fragments of a particular size (for example, 7mm). Why? Simple: Although overwriting works, there is a possibility that the data can still be recovered. Okay, so that has to be done in a lab — with a scanning electron microscope — but if it *can* be done, you can bet that the *secret* agencies around the world can do it. Hence shredding.

✔ **Incinerate:** Seriously? You bet. Once, at a conference, we showed a small box full of shredded disk-drive fragments to make a point about destroying data properly. Afterward, someone came up (he was wearing a long trench coat and didn't give his name), pointed at the box, and said, "We can get the data back from that." It turns out that because storage densities are so great these days, some (obviously not all) interesting information is still recoverable from shredded drives. Of course, we had to ask how to destroy data so well that our friends in the trench coats couldn't read it. The reply: "Incinerate it — we can't recover data from smoke. At least not yet."

Not all information has to be destroyed, and not all information has to be destroyed in the same way. Non-confidential information that you don't care about can just be thrown away (in as *green* a way as possible).

Can't I just use a magnet?

You could try what a friend did a couple of years back (though we don't recommend it) and play with an astoundingly powerful magnet right next to a computer. Not far away, a nice 19-inch monitor sat patiently waiting to be permanently wrecked if the shadow mask were to get magnetized. Of all the things that people know you aren't meant to do, *ever*, our friend was probably doing it right then.

In theory, however, you can wave a grungy, hand-crushing neodymium-iron magnet close to a computing devices in perfect safety. Of course, magnetic field strength falls off roughly with the cube of the distance — means that fairly small magnets cause no ill effects to computers, and anything the size of a marble is okay if it doesn't get any closer than 30-odd centimeters away. But even though your hard drive is protected from these sorts of effects, a magnet the size of an iPod has to be roughly a meter from your PC or your monitor when in use, or the innards of the laptop will be permanently soup.

This also explains why the really small magnets in the closures of your laptop bag don't toast your laptop every night. It's worth pointing out that many magnetic fields won't do much at all to magnetic storage media, just as long as the magnetic field isn't really amazingly strong. So do magnets really mess up hard drives? Sort of, yes and no, and don't try it at home. Magnets can damage monitors and hard drives — but no, they don't instantly "zap" data.

Although magnets damage data stored on computer devices, it's often difficult to explain to your average Outlook user why that happens. To avoid confusion and keep it simple, we've been known to resort to abracadabra: "Don't put a magnet near your computer, or your head will suddenly go moldy and you'll see a lot of blue stuff."

Waving magnets around is simply not good enough to wipe data from a hard drive. There are organizations that specialize in getting data back from exactly those magnetized states. You could call one, perhaps, if you've just put a giant magnet on your laptop, but the big magnet is no good for wiping data beyond recovery. Sorry!

Disposing of old systems without losing data

You haven't *really* disposed of a system if you haven't destroyed the data on it. This means you probably need to revisit your system-disposal policy.

Systems should be classified by what information they hold (or might hold) before you can figure out the most cost-efficient disposal. For the vast majority, deleting and overwriting will be absolutely fine. If this is deemed not enough, then just taking out the hard drive for physical disposal will be adequate. From a recycling and reuse perspective, taking out the disk makes it difficult for the system to be used by someone else, so you might want to take that into consideration.

Strategies for system repair

When does a system leave your premises without being discarded? When it will be repaired. If data is going offsite, then it needs to be protected, no matter what the reason is. Assuming that it will be *okay* if you do nothing is a route to data loss.

Once more, there is a need to revisit the policies and procedures. This time it's about system-repair policies, and how to protect the data:

- ✔ **Onsite system repair:** In this instance, you can presume that the data will not be lost. However, the repair person *could* image a disk and steal the data that way.

- ✔ **Offsite system repair — disk OK:** If the hard drive is okay, then consider removing that disk before the system goes offsite for repair. That way the information remains under your control at all times.

- ✔ **Offsite system repair — disk fault:** This is probably the toughest one to deal with. In essence, you must trust that the third party will look after your data after carrying out the repair or recovery. Check with third-party folks assigned to do this work; make sure that their security (both physical and logical) is acceptable to you.

Often, when a system is repaired, the repairer requires access to the *root* or *administrator password* — and in some cases, the individual user's password as well. Often the passwords end up written on notes attached to the keyboard. (Ack!) Put one more step in place to secure those passwords — gauge it to which passwords are compromised in the repair process. For example, if the individual user needs to give his or her password to the repairers, that password should be changed right away *on the corporate network*, so that the system being repaired can't be used for unauthorized access.

The Unseen Sources of Information

When you start looking for data, you'll find more than you imagined — and in more places than you realized. The good news is that after you identify those places, you can counteract any risks they present. This section gives you some (ahem) *promising* places to look.

Local e-mail archives

E-mail is probably *the* business tool, and with it comes a number of risks. For example, people sending out the wrong information to the wrong people. This can, of course, be resolved, but there is another problem with e-mail: the local archive (or PST file, if you happen to use Microsoft Exchange).

E-mail has grown over the past few years (a bit of an understatement there!) — and the storage hasn't been able to grow at the same rate. Result: IT has had to introduce quotas to keep the mail server workable. Thus individual users have two choices:

- ✔ Delete old e-mail so e-mail quantity remains within the quota.
- ✔ Archive old e-mail locally (on laptops and desktops) so there is a record of all the e-mail that has sent or received.

The result is that most people use local archives to keep a complete set of records. This is good for the individual but bad for the company. If a laptop is lost, the information in all the e-mail that the individual has been involved with is also at risk. There is a solution here: Eliminate the local e-mail archive.

A number of archive solutions in the marketplace eliminate the local e-mail archive. Deploy one of these. This has a number of benefits:

✔ No local archive to lose!

✔ Better storage management:

- The individual's archive can be readily backed up and therefore restored if required. Control is with the IT department, not with the individual.

- Single-instance storage (SIS) can reduce the quantity of data that needs to be managed. Just one copy needs to be watched and cared for (the right number, from a data-loss perspective).

✔ Structured data retention. E-mail can be securely deleted after a pre-specified period of time.

✔ Archive solutions are transparent from the users' perspective. They won't even notice the change!

  If the solution replaces the local archive with another (*secured*) "local archive," then your road warriors can access their e-mail archives when they're disconnected from the network.

✔ Better governance and compliance. All copies of the e-mail will be available in the event of an e-discovery request.

SMS

With the advent of feature-packed cellphones (mobile phones) has come a flood of text messaging, often with all kinds of content attached. Even the text-message capability — also known as SMS (Short Message Service) — can be a source of potential data loss.

There are two things you can do here:

✔ Update the company policy on what can be sent by SMS (and what shouldn't be sent). This policy needs to include pictures and videos!

  Don't allow pictures of the workplace. The background can contain information useful to cyber-criminals. The classic awful example: passwords on sticky notes left on monitors!

✔ Deploy a solution to deal with SMS. As usual, there is more than one option:

- *Disable SMS messaging.*

  This is only an option if the mobile phone is a corporate asset.

- *Deploy a solution to capture SMS messages and archive them.*

  Be sure to tell the employees that this is the case!

The real deal on facsimiles (faxes)

Obviously the fax is a problem, even in this day and age of e-mail! Documents need signatures and people still want contracts and orders that they can hold onto.

Facsimiles (faxes) have changed over the years; nowadays organizations often employ an electronic fax solution — which means that the received fax is received *in electronic form, not on paper*. This is bad news from a data-loss perspective; it can be readily be e-mailed around to anyone, including who-knows-whom outside the company.

It is education and awareness that come to the rescue here, backed up with policy and technology. People must be made aware of the potential data-loss issues that are associated with faxes.

- ✔ If your fax distribution is paper based, be sure to enforce standard printed-document controls.

  Bottom line: Shred old faxes when they're no longer needed. In the meantime, store them securely.

- ✔ If your fax distribution is electronic, be sure to enforce controls on distributing faxes around.

In one company (a legal firm), faxes were electronically delivered and stored in a central shared directory. This was great from a management perspective, but there wasn't sufficient access control on the files created, so everyone could read all the faxes stored there! Yet another potential internal disaster.

As with e-mail, there are two sides to a fax: the sender *and* the recipient. It's worth discussing with recipients what they will do with the faxes that you send. What is their policy for dealing with both electronic and paper versions? In return you can publish your policy on dealing with faxes you receive.

Printers and photocopiers

Yes, the humble printer can be a source of data loss — and not just from the pages it prints out. Cyber-criminals can utilize a couple of unusual attack points if they decide to use the printer to steal data:

- ✔ **The printer's hard drive:** Most modern printers have hard drives in them. When a document is printed, it's initially scanned to the hard drive and then printed out. The drive's disk acts as a buffer; when it fills up, it then goes back to the start and overwrites the oldest documents.

So (and we're now in the hypothetical) a cyber-criminal who wants to steal information could steal the hard drive out of the printer. A familiar social-engineering gambit is to turn up dressed as a repair person for photocopiers or printers, hoping to be helpfully shown to all the photocopiers around the building — there to swap out the disks or copy them!

The newest printers and photocopiers have *encrypted* disks. If they're removed or copied, the data can't be compromised.

- **The network connection:** Usually printers are connected to the network. This network connection is often unprotected — and offers unfettered access to the corporate network. A cyber-criminal could use a laptop and attach to the network — gaining access to all the information he can see!

Deploy Network Access Control solutions so that *only* the printer can attach to its network port.

VoIP and answering machines

The age of electronic data interchange is creating issues that never used to exist; voice is no exception. Organizations are returning to the telephone for critical conversations rather than putting controversial or sensitive topics into e-mail.

Technology is available to deliver answering machine messages to the individuals' e-mail inboxes. When data is in an electronic format, it can be readily copied — and therefore lost. The rise of VoIP (Voice over Internet Protocol) has meant that it's possible for all phone calls to be readily recorded and stored. It's a gray area of documentation: Nobody's quite sure whether *normal* VoIP calls are, in fact, *electronic* records. If they are, then they have to be stored and controlled in the same way as all other electronic records (e-mail, for example). The general feeling, at present, is that they aren't electronic records — but that doesn't stop them from being useful to the cyber-criminal.

Policies must be developed that incorporate VoIP usage and identify best practices. Here are a couple of good starters:

- Conversations shouldn't be recorded without the other party knowing about it.
- Unless it's required for specific purposes, a VoIP call probably shouldn't be recorded at all.

If the data isn't stored, then it can't be lost or misused!

Digital cameras

The humble digital camera is a great way to copy information quickly. At least one of your authors always carries one, and has for years. It's the easiest way to make a copy of a whiteboard or flip chart without interrupting the flow of a meeting while someone copies the information by hand. However . . .

In some places, digital cameras are banned. Most of these are *secret* government establishments where all sorts of restrictions are in place. In at least one manufacturing company in China, the restrictions are nearly the same as those imposed by the government. They allow mobile phones, but cellphones *with cameras* are taboo. If you have a phone with a camera, you must check it at the door and pick it up when you come out.

Conference calls and Webcasts

Usually, Webcasts disseminate information to the public, so the data doesn't have to be protected. However, the same isn't always true for conference calls. They're often internal — and not for competitors to see, for that matter. Even so, there tends to be little authentication (other than a password) for the attendees.

Both conference calls and Webcasts are often recorded to enable playback at a later date — and those recordings are a potential risk until they're deleted.

Regularly changing password for conference calls is essential to prevent information from ending up in the wrong hands. A cyber-criminal is unlikely to have access to conference-call passwords, but insiders have access — and insiders leave!

Remote access

According to Verizon Business, one security hole is exploited four times as often as wireless: remote access. The problem with remote access is that it's often overlooked; if employees have had it for years, it isn't seen as a problem. The assumption is familiar: *If it works, leave it alone!* But just because it was okay in the past doesn't make it okay in today's world. Something needs to be done.

Remote-access policies benefit from periodic reassessment and revision in light of the risk of data breaches. Here are some essential questions to ask:

✔ **Who has remote access?** Hopefully it isn't everyone! In older systems, remote access was separate from the main login account, so even if the main account was disabled after the employees left, they could still get in by using their remote-access credentials.

✔ **Why do they have remote access?** Is access really necessary? If not, then remove it. The chances are that they don't use it and so they won't miss it!

✔ **How do they access the network?** With broadband at home, the most common (and fastest route) is through that. However, there may be some systems around that still have modems attached, and those can dial into the system directly.

Before ubiquitous broadband connection, some engineers used to dial directly into their machines so they could work from home. Several years later, it was found that not only could you still dial into those machines, but *they now had access to the entire production network.*

✔ **What security is put in place for remote access?** There are a number of secure routes for remote access, but the most common is VPN (Virtual Private Networks). For corporate systems, for example laptops, this can be tied into the user's main account and require another password to connect. Additionally, the VPN account can be tied to a specific system as well.

Miscellaneous attack vectors

It's always good to have a catchall bucket. This is it. You should be aware of any and all types of data transfer and consider putting in place practices or process around them to protect them. However these aren't usual attack vectors, so they're lumped together here:

✔ **Bluetooth:** It isn't just for phones, you know! Both computers and phones should have their Bluetooth capabilities configured to ensure that only paired devices can attach to the network. The network should *not* accept requests from anyone who cares to ask.

✔ **Infrared:** Once again, make sure that it's either controlled or switched off.

✔ **FireWire:** Data in, data out. It needs to be controlled, especially on laptops.

✔ **Serial and parallel ports:** More often used to connect printers, which is generally fine, but perhaps there is information that shouldn't be printed? Solutions exist that will control what can and can't be printed, according to content.

✔ **Modems:** These are sometimes insidious simply because they're set up by individuals who want to call in to their computers at work. Of course, if anyone *else* calls in, they get access too. So ban their use.

A connection through a Virtual Private Network (VPN) system is probably fine, as long as it has appropriate username and password access controls.

✔ **Wireless:** This is only mentioned here to make you look elsewhere in the book. (Kidding.) Just keep Wi-Fi in mind as a possible place to lose information, even if it's not exactly *unlikely*. Check out Chapter 12 for more about protecting the perimeter and keeping bad stuff out.

Dealing with the Printed Word

A study by the Ponemon Institute in February 2008 reported that 24 percent of data loss occurs through printed documents (Figure 19-1 shows an example). Nearly a quarter of all data loss is from print. This has been going on for years (make that centuries). Before the current vigilance over data took hold, one or two stories each year would trumpet some records being found on the street or in a dumpster; we used to think it was rather careless, and we thought no more about it. Of course, the world was simpler then. These days we *have to* care about data — especially if there's a chance that the information mentioned in the paper might be *ours*.

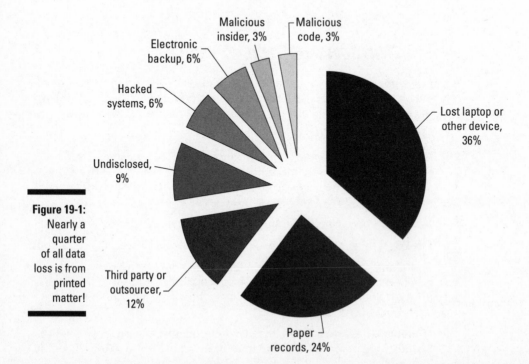

Figure 19-1:
Nearly a quarter of all data loss is from printed matter!

The good news is that the printed word is bulky. (Just try carrying a million customer records home with you on the bus after they've been printed out!) So we aren't necessarily looking at quantity, but quality.

Printed documents are useful; if they weren't useful then they wouldn't have been printed out. They also tend to aggregate in certain places — on desks, in meeting rooms, in trash bins, next to photocopiers and fax machines, as well as in the recycling bins that are no doubt dotted around the company.

Put up a sign

Start the process with education. During World War II, there were slogans such as *Careless talk costs lives*. The idea was that you didn't discuss secret stuff in public, just in case someone was listening a little too closely. The same is true when it comes to looking after printed matter; perhaps there should be a new slogan to highlight the issues of careless disposal of documents. Figure 19-2 shows what it might look like.

WARNING
Careless document disposal costs reputation

if in doubt – shred it

Figure 19-2: Getting serious about controlling printed information.

Look at how to change the culture when it comes to paperwork. Ever wonder why some companies have clean-desk policies? Sure, they keep the office from looking like a dump, but they *also* help ensure that sensitive papers aren't left lying around.

Cleaning up after meetings

Meeting rooms are chameleons. They can play host to the CEO and his reports, filling up with discussions of the next board meeting, followed by a bunch of engineers going through a patent application and then a customer with some consultants.

The one thing they will have in common is notes and documents that could be of interest to the next group (or to someone you don't want perusing them). You can implement some simple solutions:

> ✔ It doesn't take long to collect papers and shred them or take them out. Make it a policy to do so.
>
> Post a few notices, or install a shredder in the conference room.
>
> ✔ Ensure that whiteboards and flip charts, as shown in Figure 19-3, are cleared or removed (in case someone with a digital camera is walking past and decides to take a copy).

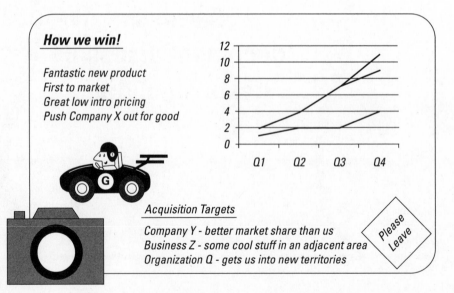

Figure 19-3:
The white-board can be so con-venient — as a way to steal data.

How we win!

Fantastic new product
First to market
Great low intro pricing
Push Company X out for good

Acquisition Targets

Company Y - better market share than us
Business Z - some cool stuff in an adjacent area
Organization Q - gets us into new territories

Please Leave

Conference rooms often have a projector attached to a dedicated computer. The computer will always be logged on and may be attached to the network. Ensure that data is properly deleted from this machine if it has been used for such a session, and make sure that the system doesn't have access to places on the network that you don't want people to see — unless they use an appropriate username and password!

Revisiting the document shredding policy

Most organizations have document shredding, either onsite or offsite. In light of a number of instances where offsite shredding hasn't happened and whole documents have been found that were previously *thought* to have been shredded, it may be time to revisit the shredding policy.

For most printed information, offsite shredding is adequate — but there may be some information that your organization can't afford to lose or have compromised. For this hypersensitive stuff, onsite shredding becomes the only option. Information that should be shredded onsite includes:

- Board reports
- Financial reports, especially predictions
- Intellectual-property paperwork (if it's disclosed outside a company, then the company can't file a patent on the idea)

The good news is that the information tends to come only from certain meetings and certain individuals. Installing a secured shredder for the CEO would probably remove most of the threat!

A temporary change in operational procedure often makes people do silly things, because they're trying to deal with the change and not thinking about the data or how to control it. In one case, for example, the system for entering credit-card information was broken. Instead of disappointing the customer, the credit-card information was written down so it could be entered later (when the system was working again). Unfortunately, no one thought about *what would happen to the paper* after the details were entered. They were just thrown away when they should have been shredded.

Pick a shredder, any shredder

Shredders are cheap and easy to buy. Although any shredder is better than no shredder, it's better to get a *crosscut* shredder instead of one that just creates strips. So, when selecting a shredder, ask yourself a few questions:

- ✓ **Crosscut or strip?** The former gives better security as the paper is cut into smaller pieces.

- ✓ **What else should I shred?** Old credit cards, CD-ROMs, and DVDs — they're almost as cheap to buy, so if you have other data sources that must be destroyed, then buy a shredder that does it all.

- ✓ **What capacity do I need?** In effect, how big a bin do I want — or, how often does it need to be emptied!

- ✓ **Where will I put it?** If you buy a shredder and you want people to use it, and then put it somewhere obvious! You could put it next to the printer — or next to the paper recycling bin if you have one.

- ✓ **Who will empty it?** Sounds like a stupid question, but who will do this? If it's part of the cleaners' job, make sure they know it. If it's the paper-recycling contractors' job, let them know. Don't let the bin fill up until it stops the machine and defeats the reason for getting it.

While you're thinking about shredders, go out and buy one for yourself at home. Shred anything and everything with sensitive information on it before it's thrown away:

- ✓ Bank statements
- ✓ Credit-card statements
- ✓ Old credit cards
- ✓ Unsolicited credit-card application forms (especially those with *pre-approved* on the front cover — you don't want someone applying in your name!)
- ✓ Utility bills and invoices

If it has your name and address on it, shred it!

Chapter 20

Revisiting Policies

- -

- -

*A*lthough the IT department would like to believe that the business revolves around technology, the truth is that people and processes are critical to running a business. IT is the enabler.

Unfortunately, the policies and procedures that employees use on a daily basis now must also evolve to match the changes in the world around us. That change is based on a simple premise: All data has a value to *someone*. Regrettably, that can be someone inside the company who abuses a position of trust and data access — or it can be an external hacker or cyber-criminal. Either way, if they get hold of your data, it doesn't look good for the business. All interactions with sensitive or confidential data now must be examined — and the policies and processes changed accordingly — with one goal in mind: Protect the data.

People are the greatest asset to any company. However, when it comes to security and data loss, they're also the weakest link.

The People Factor

Where would a company be without its people? It wouldn't exist. So when a necessary change comes over the horizon, all the people affected by it should be involved in responding to it — not just the managers.

Companies typically have dozens of policies for their employees, covering everything from acceptable dress codes to Internet usage. They also cover behaviors when purchasing and selling items. The good news is that there are policies; the bad news is that few people operate by them — and even fewer revisit them when they're updated. If there is a shortcut to doing something, then someone will find it. Before you know it, it will become a sort of *best practice* — best for the individual, though not necessarily for the company.

Taking this behavior in context with data loss, we begin to see some of the issues at hand. People don't go out of their way to lose laptops, but if somebody puts one on the back seat of a car because *I was only going to be away for two minutes and it didn't seem worth putting it in the trunk* — and the laptop gets stolen — then the real barriers start to emerge. Changing business culture is tough, especially the part of it driven by human nature.

What can a business do? For openers, understand the issues at hand — and then work through the changes needed to fix the problems, or at least improve them. Keep in mind that the new process must show a benefit to the individual as well as to the company; if it doesn't, it will be labeled as "red tape" and be "cut through" (that is, circumvented).

Identifying broken processes

Where to begin? Businesses are made up of processes. At the macro level, there aren't many of those — but at the micro level, there are far too many to even contemplate changing.

Working groups are a great way to discover processes. Top-level processes can be found out if you talk to managers, but to find out what really happens on the front lines, you need a working group of individuals involved in the process — from every department involved.

Stick to the topic at hand: Protect the data. We aren't trying to fix every broken process in the business. We're simply trying to identify processes that fail to keep information secure.

Tracing the information from its creation to its destruction is often the best way to discover what happens to it along the way. In the good old days, a common technique called *data-flow diagramming* was used in designing systems; it can come in handy here. Another handy and time-tested concept is the Use Case: The idea here is to look at what actually happens and use that to guide your understanding of the process. (Figure 20-1 combines a Use Case with a data-flow diagram in a twin blast from the past.) If you concentrate on a real-world scenario, everyone in the group can participate. The Use Case is also a versatile tool for explaining and checking the process to ensure that what's described is what actually happens. (What a concept!)

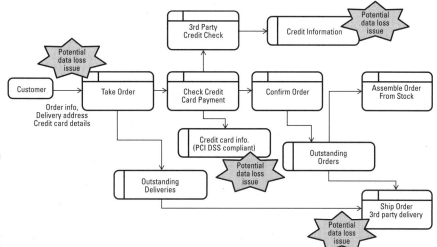

Figure 20-1:
A data-flow
diagram
around a
Use Case.

Using a whiteboard or an electronic board is a great way to collaborate when putting the process together. Whenever the information is *touched* by people or systems — or leaves the company — look closely at the security measures in force at that point. It may be that no one in the room knows what those measures are. For example, is the data encrypted? And who are all the people who can access the information? Finding out such details becomes a way of gathering leads to follow up later.

After the top level of information has been uncovered, individual interviews can be carried out to find out *what really happens*. Often, when you're interviewing individuals, other information comes to light, such as

- ✔ **Process changes:** Major stages, phases, or milestones in the process at the end of the month, quarter, or year.

- ✔ **Exceptions:** What happens when something goes wrong?

- ✔ **Shortcuts:** The process is one thing but the reality is something else. This is why it's important to talk to the people involved at the hands-on level — not just to the managers!

- ✔ **Other recipients:** Often the data is collected and processed for one reason, but other people happen to need it, or see it, or use it. This is particularly true of generated reports — often old and out of date (and so ignored), but still created week after week after week . . .

Beware of the law of diminishing returns. Working groups and interviews are great for what they are — a means to an end — but they don't actually *do* anything. (That comes afterward.) Attempting to find every little detail can waste a lot of time and effort. Set a short period of time (for example, an hour or a morning) for meetings — and then decide whether to hold further meetings as necessary. Don't set up a two-day session and think you'll find all the answers all at once. This will be a somewhat iterative process; you have to decide when enough is enough.

Interview techniques to identify data at risk

The goal here is to come out with a list with three main components:

- ✔ All pieces of data you must protect
- ✔ All processes that these pieces of data are involved with
- ✔ All parts of the business that are involved in those processes

Interviews are a key part of this process. First rule of interviews (and should also be for meetings), there needs to be someone who is taking notes — and that isn't the person asking the questions or running the meeting!

Notes are often the only record of an interview, so they have to be accurate and free from ambiguity. Replaying the content back to the interviewee ensures that there is understanding and it also helps to jog the memory on exceptions. Usually it's better to interview people separately; you pick up anomalies more readily. If a manager is in a room, often the more junior employee will try to answer the questions in a way that pleases the manager — but which may not be as truthful (accurate) as you need.

Decide what questions you want to ask and how you want the interview to flow. Open questions (that don't just require a simple *yes* or *no* answer) get the most information. It's also best to set expectations, explain why you're doing this, and help your subjects understand that you're asking their help, not looking to penalize them. Here are some typical questions:

- ✔ **Would you tell me what you do?** This is a great question to put people at ease.

- ✔ **What applications do you use? How often do you use them?** These questions often uncover the fact that people do more than it says on their job descriptions! You should also ask whether they use any particular applications while they're covering for people who are away.

✔ **What data can you access?** Getting people to understand what data is can be an issue. You can start by asking what forms they use, and then which options they use in their computer applications.

✔ **What processes are you involved in regarding this data?** Again, there can be an issue of understanding when talking about issues. An easier way to start can be to pick some of the processes you have discovered before. For example, what do you do when an order is received? Or how do you help customers when they call up for support?

✔ **What happens if the system is down?** This is important to ask as it often uncovers anomalies in procedure. Sometimes the answer can be *nothing*(!) — other times, they write things on paper. If they write down sensitive information, then you need a policy to cover how they dispose of it later.

✔ **Are there any special procedures for the end of the week and/or month and/or year**? Often data is transferred at the end of specific time periods, or more people get to see it.

✔ **Who do you send data to? Who do you receive data from?** As part of a double-check, ask who the data goes to — and who it comes from. Find this out for paper records as well as for electronic records (such as e-mail, files, and CD-ROMs). Account for it all.

✔ **Who else has access to the system?** While a strange question to ask, people share usernames and passwords for applications! Especially when helping to cover during vacations and sickness.

✔ **Who covers for you when you're on vacation (or out sick)?** Another lead in the Great Data Hunt.

✔ **We are also talking to X, Y, & Z; is there anyone else involved?** Another double-check to get complete coverage of a process involving sensitive information and other people.

✔ **How can we improve the process?** It's a great way to finish an interview — and to encourage buy-in. If processes change, then gathering input from the *real* people will help drive the adoption of new processes.

✔ **Anything else you would like to add?** You might have missed something obvious!

You can also use the interview to help the person get a handle on where to find the documents that spell out company policy — and to start thinking about some of the things they cover. Do this at the end of the interview rather than at the beginning; if you start with the policies and your interviewees admit to not having read them, they wind up on the defensive early on. No point making the process harder than it has to be.

Common Policies That Put Data at Risk

Many companies have policies and procedures that put data at risk all day, every day. These common practices are often overlooked because they're so common and so are forgotten. Take a look down the list, see how many apply to your organization, and then do something about the ones that do!

- ✔ **Sending sensitive data through the mail:** So much information is so readily available — and so many people are after it — that it's at risk even if it's traveling by "snail mail." If it's a large quantity of data, some folks may think the easiest way to transfer it is just to copy it onto a CD-ROM and send the disc through the mail. But if that data isn't encrypted, it's at risk. Then the process that puts the data on the disc — and the disc in the mail — needs to be fixed.

- ✔ **Sending sensitive data through e-mail:** Is e-mail safer? Yes and no. If the e-mail is internal (and the e-mail *system* is all internal) then yes, it is more secure. But do you allow people to send e-mail outside? If so, how do you keep data from escaping though that route?

- ✔ **Distribution lists:** E-mail features such as distribution lists and auto-completion of addresses are a real risk — especially if the distribution list also contains external people.

- ✔ **Taking sensitive information home:** Some of your interviewees will cite a need to take sensitive information along so they can to do their work. Yes — but do they really need it? If the information is out of corporate control, how is it protected? (In general, people take information on laptops or PDAs, so securing the device will also secure the data. One example of this approach is full-disk encryption.)

- ✔ **Traveling with e-mail archives:** E-mail is the language of business, but do people need to carry it all with them? Often they have their own e-mail archives because of storage limitations imposed by IT depart-ments. They may not notice that e-mail *also* contains a lot of sensitive information. It would reduce the risk if employees didn't have personal archives — which means IT will have to implement archiving and pre-vent employees from creating their own archives. The good news is that e-mail archiving also helps with corporate compliance and storage-management issues.

- ✔ **Poor document disposal:** Is it easy for people to shred confidential information they've printed out? If not, then make it so. This principle also extends to the disposal of other media, such as CD-ROMs and tapes.

- ✔ **Poor equipment disposal:** How do you get rid of old computers, mobile phones, and PDAs? Is all the data scrubbed from them first? It should be.

Developing policies and procedures to prevent data loss

Preventing data leaks by designing secure policies and procedures is based on a simple idea: Information first. Of course, practice is completely different because people think about functionality rather than information security. Changing the culture so it puts security first is tough.

 Designing a new policy or procedure usually means changing yourmind-set. In this case, think like a hacker or a cyber-criminal — not so much in a technical way, but definitely with a "devious" eye toward the information you have inside your organization. For example: What could you do with it if you were a cyber-criminal? It's also good to read about recent security breaches and how they occurred; it all helps when looking at designing a new policy. For example, look for these events when you see data-loss incidents publicized:

- **Mailing a CD-ROM:** The disc could be intercepted and the data stolen.
- **Using a laptop:** The machine could be lost or stolen.
- **Developing a Web application:** SQL injection attacks are a real issue.
- **E-mailing customer details:** The message could be sent to the wrong person.
- **Backup tapes going offsite:** Tapes could be lost.
- **Getting rid of old computers or sending them for repair:** What happens to the data on them?

The most important part is to involve the people involved in the current process — and get their input and buy-in for the new one.

 Processes, policies, and procedures need to be intuitive:

- If you must explain it and then explain it again, revisit it.
- If people must do things in a convoluted manner, revisit it.
- If it isn't obvious how the process protects the data, revisit it.

Correcting broken processes and policies

Writing a new policy to correct a problem is easy. Getting people to abide by it is a whole new ball game. That's where technology can help.

With any luck, you will have engaged with all the people who are involved with the broken policy — and they will have had input into how it can be fixed. If this has happened, then putting the new policy in place should be relatively simple.

You can answer a few straight-ahead questions to make the change easier:

- ✔ **Why are the current policies and/or processes broken?** This is normally obvious, so a simple explanation is in order.

- ✔ **What are the (potential) consequences if you don't fix it?** For data loss, this is usually simple: You end up on the front page of the newspaper with your reputation damaged and your customers walking away.

- ✔ **How will the update fix the problems?** Once more, this should be obvious: The data will be protected from the threat or risk and all will be well.

- ✔ **How will the new policy and/or procedure make people's lives easier?** This is tough. It's important to find a way the change improves people's life at work. Perhaps the answer is more automation, or an overall simplification of the process in question.

- ✔ **If there is new technology involved, when will training occur?** Skipping the training phase is a terrible habit we have; rarely is any training put in place for new applications. Think of the guy who's intimidated by technological learning curves but does fine after he's up to speed. He's probably not the only one.

- ✔ **What is the time frame? Will there be a period of overlap? Who can people go to if they're unsure?** Central points of contact and a published calendar of events are the simplest ways of approaching this question.

- ✔ **What will be the process to suggest further improvements?** As most business-improvement books show, the only way to manage change is to keep doing it. "Process remediation" (as it's called) is never a simple matter of putting a check mark in a box. Be sure you revisit what you've done — and make sure that it's what you expected.

The old process: CD-ROMs were being sent with unencrypted, sensitive customer data on them — at the end of every week — from one office to another. The new information policy said that *all* sensitive information had to be encrypted if it traveled offsite.

It was a junior employee who carried out the process of pressing Option 5 at the end of each week, inserting a new CD, waiting until it ejected, and then popping it in the mailbox. The employee didn't know whether the data was encrypted — but a visit to the IT department with a blank CD ascertained that nope, the data *wasn't* encrypted. A process change would be required.

The reason for changing: Risk of data loss. If the CD were lost, the company would have to make a disclosure to all its customers, which would be expensive and damaging to the company.

The new process was still to press Option 5 — but *then* to direct the data to local disk for storage (rather than to CD). Several options were then considered:

✔ **Send the data by e-mail.** Rejected, because the file was too big.

✔ **FTP and/or transfer the data electronically.** Rejected, because it required access to other systems, which was seen as a security risk.

✔ **Don't send the information.** Rejected — the information was still needed.

It's surprising how much data is transferred just because it always *has* been — when no one actually needs it anymore. Force of habit is a lousy way to run a business.

✔ **Encrypt the data onto the CD and send.** This was the option that was agreed on. The follow-through became a process unto itself:

- A small program (batch file) was written that the employee would run: It would create the file, use a predetermined key to encrypt the data, and then copy the encrypted data onto the CD. Then the disc could be sent normally.

- A change request was added for the application; the next version should encrypt the data as part of the standard export process (known to the employees as Option 5).

- The process at the other office also had to change: The data was unencrypted before it was read back into the system.

- Another step was also added that ensured that after the data had been read into the system and verified, the CD was destroyed.

   It turned out that old CDs containing unencrypted data had piled up around the office. Nobody was sure whether all the discs were still there. Nobody knew what was supposed to happen to them after they'd been used.

- A simple audit trail was also set up which monitored when the CD was sent and received.

   This was done with a small batch file that added a line to a log file and then e-mailed the employees and their managers to say that the task had been carried out. This enabled the person on the receiving end to expect a CD — and follow up if it didn't arrive.

More complex? Yes — but also a lot more secure. The biggest issue, from an IT perspective, was to ensure that the encryption was kept safe. In the end, the solution was very literal: They decided to keep the key written down and locked away in a fireproof safe in both offices. Though not ideal, it was a cost-effective solution to the problem!

Part V
More Preventative Measures

The 5th Wave
By Rich Tennant

"Somebody got through our dead end web links, past the firewalls, and around the phone prompt loops. Before you know it, the kid here picks up the phone and he's talking one-on-one to a customer."

In this part . . .

While it would be great if you could wave a magic wand and have technology solve all the problems — it won't happen. This part of the book looks at why technology is not a silver bullet and how people and processes need to be brought into the equation to create a solution.

It looks at some of the longer term actions that you should be considering, such as creating a Data Loss Crisis Team and an Information Protection Policy.

Finally it looks at the problems that suppliers and partners can cause you if they are careless with your data. They lose the data and you get the blame!

Chapter 21

Technology Is Not a Silver Bullet

*Y*ou've probably heard a lot of hopeful buzz about how information technology can be used to combat data leaks. It's exciting stuff, but (say it with us) *technology alone is not a silver bullet.* This chapter explains why, and lays out a more thorough and effective approach to fighting data leakage.

To ensure that you implement a complete solution to data loss, your organization's plan has to include three major elements, as shown in Figure 21-1:

✔ **People:** Human nature can make your people vulnerable to security attacks, and often they don't even know it.

✔ **Process:** You're ahead of the game if you've worked out a set of procedures for dealing with data leaks.

✔ **Product:** You must find and deploy the hardware and software that meets your organization's (and its information's) particular needs.

Okay, if you're already champing at the bit, the next chapter looks at some products and solutions to implement your data-loss solution. But before we get to that, here's a look at the other two components required: your people and your security processes.

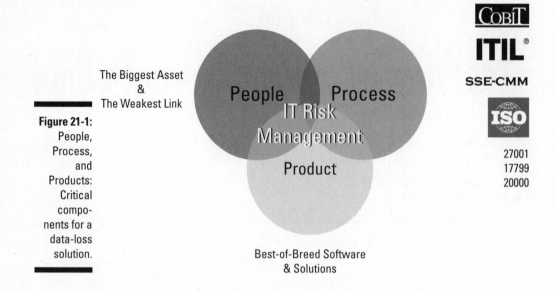

Figure 21-1:
People,
Process,
and
Products:
Critical
compo-
nents for a
data-loss
solution.

Social-Engineering Attacks

These days cyber-criminals are after data that will make them money. This data doesn't have to be bank-account details or credit-card information; it can be *any* information they can then use to construct an attack. For example, a phone number serves as a foot-in-the-door for a phishing attack on an individual.

With that in mind, the bad guys' goal is to get the individual to do something that will enable them to get access to information they can use. Although Chapter 3 looks at IT security threats that can be initiated through the Internet, that isn't the only way to get the goods. Another approach is *social-engineering attacks* that play on human nature in remarkably simple ways to get end-users to do what the cybercriminal wants them to do.

Figure 21-2 shows a mind map that summarizes social-engineering attacks. Each of the areas on the map warrants a closer look.

Piggybacking

Piggybacking (or *tailgating*) is the simple act of following someone through a security door to gain access to an area that would otherwise be prohibited.

A white coat and a pair of glasses do wonders for a trespasser's credibility. This trick, together with looking confident and acting confidently, can gain the criminal ready access to most parts of an organization.

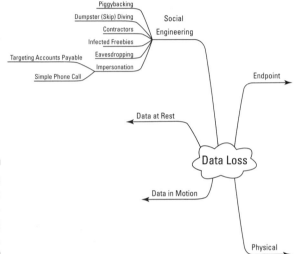

Figure 21-2:
A mind map of social-engineering attacks.

Dumpster diving

Dumpster diving (known as *skip diving* in the U.K.) is as unsavory as it sounds: Criminals look in the trash, rubbish, garbage, and other detritus that a company throws out. This isn't dissimilar to criminals looking through household waste to find information that enables them to steal an identity. It's the same process, just on a bigger scale.

Dumpsters or other industrial waste containers often contain paper records and (more frequently these days) electronic data storage as well. The hoards of data can be as simple as a CD-ROM, an old or broken computer, or a USB memory stick. Of course, not all information is useful to a criminal, but all that trashed information offers an opportunity to find *something* of value.

Contractors

When an employee is hired, there's an extensive selection process with technical interviews — and, if required, background checks. This makes a company relatively confident that it's hired a good person. When it comes to contractors, however, background checks get problematic. The reputation of the individual contractor is equated with the reputation of the contracting company, which isn't always a valid assumption. For some contractors (cleaners, for example), staff are relatively low-paid and short-term.

For one bank in London, the cleaners turned out to be a source of data loss. One of the cleaners had been bribed to put USB keys with *keylogger* software (which records every keystroke a user types) into any computers they saw. These would then be rotated once a week and the data harvested. The cleaners had access to all areas except the data center, and so had unprecedented access to computers. The software was silent, so there was no abnormal network traffic. The trouble with this type of attack *is* that it's silent. Even when it's discovered, you have a hard time telling how long the attack has been going on, or what specific data or information has been compromised.

Data is distributed across the organization; there are copies on laptops, servers, mobile phones, and in e-mail systems, as well as on USB drives and CD-ROMs. Cleaners could have access to these systems, but so could other contractors. Modern photocopiers have hard disks in them, and are often attached to the network as well. If a photocopier repair person turned up on the doorstep, would you let that person in? Would you then helpfully show the way to the photocopier? If so, then your data could be walking out the door when that person leaves. While a lot of the haul would no doubt be innocuous, other information could be useful to the criminal, including end-of-year financial reports, board papers, and details of sales deals.

Encourage a company culture in which employees challenge contractors to provide identification; arrange with companies under contract that their employees display their identification at all times.

Impersonation

Phoning someone in the organization and pretending to be someone "legitimate" is a simple, effective social-engineering attack. People seldom question whether the person on the other end of a phone call is who he or she claims to be, especially if that someone purports to be farther up the executive ladder.

A successful attack was carried out by phoning the IT support desk and impersonating the assistant of an executive who was out on a customer visit. The executive was out of the office and couldn't be reached; as the "assistant" feigned getting increasingly agitated, the password was reset, and the attacker was in. Fortunately, in this instance the executive was visiting a security company that had said they could get access to his e-mail system within 30 minutes . . . and that's how they did it.

By spending a little time preparing (in the trade, they call it *pretexting*), criminals can piece together enough information to be convincing — especially if the targeted person has never met them.

Phony invoices were sent to the accounts-payable department of a supermarket chain. The invoices were for genuine services but they didn't come from company invoicing. In this instance, the criminals nearly got away with $10 million (spread over many invoices) before being discovered and stopped.

If impersonation is discovered, it's essential to make that discovery known to others inside the company, ASAP.

Consider a range of different ways to authenticate users. Banks use more pieces of information, such as pieces of an address or a date of birth, to help authenticate the user at the end of a phone line; it's high time IT support did the same thing.

Controlling freebies

A *freebie* is something you find offered free of charge, and pick up because it looks good to you — or something of apparent value that comes to you "for free." (They're also known as *road apples* — with connotations of "windfall" — in some parts of the globe!) These days a freebie often takes the form of a USB memory stick, or a CD-ROM that offers interesting information or a prize. These crop up in conference rooms, at trade shows or exhibitions, and sometimes in the mailbox.

A penetration test was carried out and it was a simple attack: Putting a bowl of USB keys on the reception desk at the start of the day. People assumed these were legitimate, and so took them. Virtually all of them were plugged into corporate machines by lunchtime — and the devious little gizmos promptly e-mailed the data on those machines back to a central site.

In another case, it was the offer of a free vacation that made people put a CD-ROM into their computers, even though the CD-ROM was given out at a train station.

One organization printed 1,000 CDs with an offer for a free gift. All the disc really had on it was a piece of code that sent a message back to its originators. Some 750-odd people blithely put the CDs into their corporate computers.

Computers make it easy for data-storage devices (legitimate or not) to be plugged in and used. If the computer automatically runs anything put into it, it runs the programs on the device; therein lies the problem. This "automatic run" feature can be exploited by criminals, especially when coupled with the freebie effect: Someone picks up the free gadget, plugs it in, and *voilá* — an illicit program is running on your machine, infecting it with whatever the bad guys want to put in there — viruses, trojans, keyloggers, you name it.

Never plug free USB memory sticks or CD-ROMs into your computer if you can't *guarantee* that they're legitimate. In case you forget (everybody picks up freebies at conferences or exhibitions), make sure that your endpoint protection (see Chapter 8) is up to date; this simple precaution can prevent a malware infection.

Create and implement a policy to deal specifically with freebies. Educate your colleagues and staff about the dangers of USB sticks and CD-ROMs — and (specifically) about why they shouldn't plug them in at work or at home unless they know exactly where they came from and can trust the source.

Eavesdropping

Listening in to conversations is a classic way to finding out information. It's been used since time began. Often a company's employees have a favorite bar or restaurant. Given the appropriate circumstances, criminals find this out and drop by to listen in. It isn't commonplace to discuss confidential usernames and passwords in a casual social context, but it happens.

In a social-engineering experiment, commuters were stopped at random and offered $20 for their usernames and passwords. Nearly 20 percent of those asked *were happy to give out their usernames and passwords* in return for the cash! (Of course, whether they actually gave out *current* usernames and/or passwords wasn't checked — that would have been tantamount to hacking — not a good idea!)

If you ever think your password has been compromised, change it immediately. If you think your username has been compromised, ask whether it can be changed.

Use appropriate levels of password complexity that match the importance of the usage you have in mind. Using (say) the same username and password for a subscription-service account as you do for your bank account could be disastrous. (But you knew that.)

Understanding that these activities occur enables both individuals and companies to develop a security-awareness program. One big step in that direction is to revisit your organization's data-related processes and procedures to protect data from leaking.

Processes and Procedures

A recent survey by Symantec found that 82 percent of data loss was caused by insecure policy, or by theft or loss of something that contained the data. Figure 21-3 shows the percentages of data loss from various causes; note that only 13 percent of data loss occurred because of hacking. Of course, the particular cause can also suggest what may happen next:

✔ If data is maliciously removed, then chances are excellent that it will be used illegally.

✔ If a laptop computer is lost, then it may be genuinely lost, misplaced, or otherwise described as "never to be seen again."

✔ If a laptop or other handy data device is stolen, its disk might be reformatted and system resold *without* the data being compromised. But don't bet on it.

The nightmare that these three outcomes have in common: You don't know.

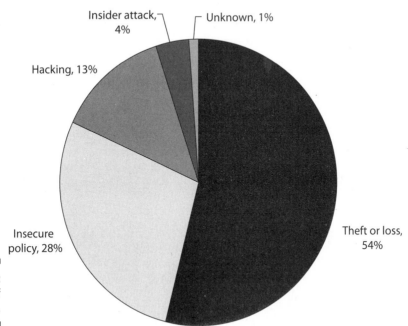

Figure 21-3:
Causes of
data loss.

Theft or loss is responsible for 54 percent of data loss, and can also be described as the result of an *insecure business process*. A number of standards or guidelines can be used to help an organization become more efficient and to develop best (in this case, more secure) practices.

The trouble with standards

In essence, a *standard* is a set of guidelines or procedures that are created and made available to an industry to encourage *best practices* for performing a particular task. The problem is that standards proliferate; many industries have too many to sort through. To the unwary, this welter can cause more confusion than good.

From the perspective of data loss, the four most popular industry standards established by professional standards organizations are

- ITIL
- COBIT
- ISO27001
- SSE-CMM

The biggest problem an organization has when it's looking for security standards is that there's all this *choice*. If only one standard existed, then the choice would be simple — you'd just pick "the standard approach" — but no such luck. Worse, several of the standards have specifications that overlap; others seem to contradict each other. If one standard doesn't do the job for an organization, it may try to stick together a patchwork of component parts from various standards, and end up increasing the amount of effort it takes to implement a data-loss policy that works. So it's worth taking a closer look at each one before you start dissecting them.

ITIL

The United Kingdom's Office of Government Commerce periodically updates its IT Infrastructure Library (ITIL) — version 3 was released in May 2007 — as a set of techniques for effectively managing IT infrastructure, development, and operations — specifically regarding *IT services*.

So what makes IT a service? Well, consider what IT does that you probably don't even think about (unless you happen to be in IT), such as system backup or provisioning of new servers or applications. When IT becomes a service, these are delivered like a more traditional utility (telephone, power, water) — so all the costs are known by everyone; you have a few standard-ized offerings instead of everything being bespoke (which is the way IT tradi-tionally works), and you pay for what you use. The new Software as a Service capability (see Chapter 18) is another example of IT delivered as a service — you pay for what you use, and it's standardized. Most companies, however — especially larger ones — have not adopted the SaaS model; instead, they're transforming their internal IT departments to run as service providers — and a lot of them use ITIL.

ITIL is a "library" in a literal sense; it consists of five hefty books, each one describing a different IT discipline. We aren't going to delve too deeply, but rather look at where these can help you mitigate against data loss. The five sections — that is, *the five disciplines* — are

- ✔ **Service strategy:** So you're going down the IT service route. Where are the rat holes and what is the best practice?

- ✔ **Service design:** This one describes how IT services can be designed. Taking an early look — at design time — into how data can be lost can help you avert disaster.

- ✔ **Service transition:** Transitions that move your organization from one IT service to another can often expose your data to loss. By thinking through the consequences before a transition occurs, guess what — disaster can be averted!

- ✔ **Service operation:** Of course, if you've designed an IT service you will want to use it. Hopefully your strategy and design will have ensured that there won't be any data loss — but you can never be too sure. Sometimes there are shortcuts from design to implementation, which can create problems. ("But *we* never do that!" Are you sure?)

- ✔ **Continual service improvement:** As with all services (IT or not), if you want to stay in business you better improve, continuously. Improvements (or *changes*, as we like to call them) can result in bad things happening to your data. This requirement keeps an eye open so you don't drop the ball.

Here the primary focus is on managing your IT department *as a service* — or, as they say in the biz, "delivering *IT service management* (ITSM)." The business and its processes are king here; IT *serves* it. Originally created by the U.K. government's Central Computer and Telecommunications Agency (CCTM), this standard is being adopted across the globe.

Each of the five disciplines has a well-defined process with individual steps that show inputs and outputs for each one. Figure 21-4 shows them in a bird's-eye view of ITIL.

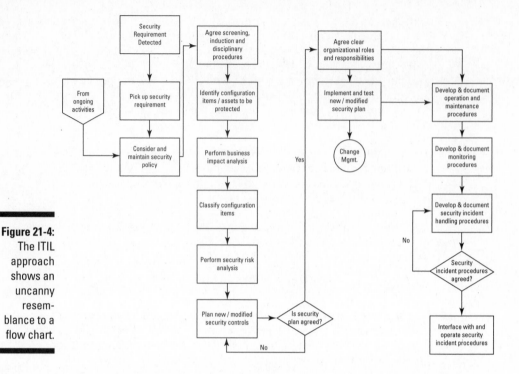

Figure 21-4:
The ITIL
approach
shows an
uncanny
resem-
blance to a
flow chart.

From a security perspective, the ITIL standard has some clear strengths:

✔ Its framework ensures that all decisions are made at the strategic, tactical and operational levels.

✔ It recognizes that processes are *iterative*. They go through modifications to meet changing requirements (with any luck, in a controlled manner).

✔ It encompasses policies, procedures, and processes. If your organization is good at those, it's a natural.

✔ Hardware and software vendors have already done considerable work on automating support for all five disciplines.

While no one vendor can help with all of ITIL, many vendors have mapped their products onto specific areas of the standard. For example, Symantec has products to help with Network Access Control; it's a key part of service operation. Symantec also has products to cover service operation. However, a different vendor would be needed to cover authentication and authorization access control.

Want to know a little more about delivering IT as a service? We just happen to have a book to suggest: *Delivering Utility Computing: Business-Driven IT Optimization* by Guy Bunker and Darren Thomson, published by John Wiley and Sons, Ltd.

COBIT

The standard known as Control Objectives for Information and related Technology (COBIT; not sure why they left the *R* uncapitalized) has been around for a while. Two organizations — the Information Systems Audit and Control Association (ISACA) and the IT Governance Institute (ITGI) — put it together; the latest version (4.1) defines 34 high-level processes and more than 200 control objectives in four domains:

- ✔ Planning and Organization
- ✔ Acquisition and Implementation
- ✔ Delivery and Support
- ✔ Monitoring

The standard's primary aim is to help organizations — in particular, their business managers and IT users (rather than IT staff per se) understand the IT systems they have and use. Management can improve IT support for business processes by setting up appropriate monitoring of IT processes and infrastructure.

In security and data-loss scenarios, COBIT can help identify the business processes that involve customer and confidential information — and then help you design, develop, and implement changes to those processes to protect the information.

For example, a company looking to implement a new application could turn to COBIT to help; they can use its best practices in each area:

- ✔ *Define the information architecture* (from Planning and Organization section)
- ✔ *Acquire and maintain the technology infrastructure* (from Acquisition and Implementation)
- ✔ *Ensure systems security* (from Delivery and Support)
- ✔ *Monitor the processes* (from Monitoring)

ISO/IEC 27002

Although COBIT was initially created for the IT community and has become an internationally accepted framework for IT governance, ISO/IEC 27002 (previously 17799) is a standard based on best practices for security management. Where COBIT is broad, the ISO standard is focused on practical security.

The International Organization for Standardization (ISO) and the International Electrotechnical Commission (IEC) publish a number of standards and are continuously updating them. The first incarnation was a copy from the British Standard 7799, which then became ISO 17799 before the latest release, which is ISO/IEC 27002.

This standard provides best-practice guidelines for people who are responsible for Information Management Security Management Systems (ISMS). Information security is defined in the context of confidentiality, integrity, and availability (abbreviated *CIA* and described in Chapter 5). CIA describes data in terms of

✔ **Confidentiality:** Who can see this data, and who can't.

✔ **Integrity:** Does it matter if the data changes? (Incredibly, in some cases it really doesn't!)

✔ **Availability:** Can we get to the data all the time? Some business functions need it to be there 24/7; others won't be disturbed if it takes a week to reach them.

The standard has 12 sections, including risk assessment, access control, business-continuity management, and compliance.

ISO/IEC27001 enables an organization to certify its security-management processes and procedures so they're consistent with the practices described in ISO/IEC27002.

Adhering to this standard is accepted globally as a state of excellence; matching your practices to it can give you a useful credential for doing international business.

SSE-CMM and/or CMMI

The Software Security Engineering Capability Maturity Model can also be used in defining — and (more important) understanding — an organization's processes. The Capability Maturity Model was originally developed to assess government contractors' processes to successfully complete a software project.

The CMM describes five levels of procedural maturity:

✔ **Initial:** Hey, you haven't really started yet. Let's get a stake in the ground.

✔ **Repeatable:** So now you're doing the same thing right, over and over, and you can get it to work roughly the same each time.

✔ **Defined:** You've probably written the process down so you don't forget anything.

✔ **Managed:** Not only is the process written down, other people can do it when they follow the instructions.

✔ **Optimized:** You've done the process enough to figure out how it can be improved for efficiency.

The goal of any organization is to move through the levels from Initial (chaotic) to Optimized (up, running, and well documented), which is an ongoing state that includes a process for continuous improvement. Specifying goals and measuring results will be essential to each level of this process. Assessments are made by authorized assessors; plans can then be drawn up to help an organization move up through the levels.

SSE-CMM has been known as the Capability Maturity Model Integration (CMMI) since 2000, but is still commonly called SSE-CMM. It's currently at version 1.2 and has 22 different process areas.

PCI DSS

The Payment Card Industry Data Security Standard was developed by the major credit-card companies as a way to help organizations who process credit-card transactions to prevent fraud. Although this standard isn't designed to be used specifically for the prevention of data loss, it's very useful when you're looking to safeguard credit- and debit-card information.

As with the ISO and CMMI standards, organizations can have audits done to certify that they're compliant with this standard. For PCI DSS, Qualified Security Assessors (QSAs) do the auditing; smaller companies can self-assess.

Because PCI DSS is targeted at a very specific area — credit-card information — it's one of the most comprehensive data-security standards to emerge recently, and is often applied to data loss.

Although PCI DSS is targeted at credit-card data, you can apply it usefully to other types of data in your organization.

Choosing a standard

Although there are almost too many standards to choose from, you still have to choose which one(s) to apply. So which one do you go for? Well, two general steps will help you find out:

- ✔ The easiest way to decide is to ask whether anyone in your organization has had experience with any of the standards. If someone has, then that person's experience can usefully influence your decision — regardless of whether the experience was good or bad.

- ✔ If no one in-house has experience of any of the standards, then take a look at where your organization is weakest — and adopt the standard(s) that will strengthen those areas. The ITIL guidelines are a great place to start, and they're very easy to customize to your needs.

Time to reevaluate

Processes and guidelines like those from ITIL and COBIT are very good are creating and improving processes but they don't necessarily answer a key question. Why?

Processes and procedures, even those considered best practices, grow and change over time. Often decisions made initially for good reasons aren't revisited unless there's an obvious problem. Here are a couple of examples:

- **The old way:** Imagine (even if you have to grit your teeth) customer data being held on a laptop. A current best practice is that data leaving the organization site should be encrypted, *especially* if it's on a laptop. However, it's worth revisiting the original decision.

  Rethinking: Ask (for instance) why someone has to have the data on there in the first place. The answer may be rooted in historical reasons — say, an old process specified that a copy of the data was taken locally so the individual could work on it out of the office. But is that still necessary? Network bandwidth has increased, and broadband, always-on connectivity may make a thin client a more secure way for a user to access the data while out of the office. That way the data remains in the data center. One possible way to set up such a thin client is as a virtual machine on the user's home computer.

- **The old way:** Imagine backup that's been carried out for decades, with the result that all that data is stored on tape. The current best practice for disaster recovery and business continuity is to ensure that more than one copy exists — and that one of the copies is held offsite.

  Rethinking: Before data loss became the issue it is today, all that data used to be stored *in the clear* — unencrypted — because that made it easier to manage. However, with data loss now a global problem, it's time to reevaluate that decision. If data will go offsite, then it should be encrypted — and this applies to backup tapes as well. Even if the data is going from one site to another, the data should probably be encrypted *before* it's in transit — just in case the vehicle it's traveling in is in an accident and the tapes get lost. There are other technological advances — such as disk-to-disk backup and data deduplication (see Chapter 14) — that could be in use to move data to another site; evaluate these too when you revisit the backup process.

Ask the question

Continuously ask the question: *Why?* Why do you need access to this data? Why do you need a copy on your laptop? Why do we transfer data unencrypted? Why, why, why? Along with why, make sure that you propose a solution — such as full-disk encryption for laptops, or perhaps a thin-client approach.

Asking questions and revisiting decisions in light of new technology and new threats means that you can update your organization's processes and procedures with two goals in mind:

- ✔ To prevent data loss that might have gone unnoticed previously
- ✔ To prevent potential data loss that has now become a risk because of recent changes

Treating Data Loss as a Disaster

Disasters used to be imagined almost entirely as obvious disruptions of everyday life — fire, flood, terrorism, or even simple power outages. Data loss is a new type of disaster, and should be treated as one. Its consequences can be just as great as those that come with any traditional scenario.

A plan for disaster recovery (DR) and/or business continuity (BC) looks at the organization as a whole — the people, the business processes, and the supporting infrastructure — and puts together a plan to deal with all disruptive eventualities. The plan has to be effectively communicated to the employees so they know what to do in the event of a disaster. These days the plan must include effective responses to the threat of data loss.

You need three basic components for dealing with a disaster:

- ✔ A help desk for employees and customers.

- ✔ Frequently asked questions (FAQs).

   After you create a list of FAQs, be sure to update it regularly.

- ✔ Modified support-call workflows to deal with the incident.

Customers will want answers that you may not have right away, so an open communication policy is essential.

When financial information is lost, customers will want to know:

✔ *Is my money safe?*

✔ *Is my credit rating protected?*

Rapidly putting credit-check mechanisms in place and offering simple ways to move accounts will help rebuild confidence.

The Importance of an Awareness Program

If you're going to get organized and consistent about preventing data loss, everyone in the organization must (a) understand data-loss threats, and then (b) alter their behavior to match (c) clear and effective processes for protecting the data and the organization. Here are some starting points . . .

Security training for everybody

Security is only as strong as its weakest link. An organization's security policy must treat everybody consistently. It's no good educating only the managers if the people they manage have daily contact with sensitive information. Similarly, there's no point in educating only the end-users if board members have critical information under their control — and don't appreciate how easy it is to leak or lose.

Security training is for everyone in the organization, from the board members to the cleaners — and beyond. It should include any suppliers and partners that have access to critical and sensitive information inside the business. While these people may not need to be trained in the same way as your employees, it's important that they understand the risks and consequences of losing the data they access.

Focus on *why* this is important. All too often, security and technology change an organization's procedures in ways that are seen as a hindrance to getting the job done. Gather feedback from people on how you might add more security in ways that improve, rather than diminish, efficiency.

A recent study by the Ponemon Institute calculated that 38 percent of all data loss occurs through a partner.

A retailer in the U.K. lost some information when a partner — a data processor — had a laptop stolen. The machine had 26,000 subjects' records on it. This laptop wasn't stolen from a car or an office. It wasn't even left in a taxi; it was taken during a break-in at the data processor's home. The data wasn't encrypted, so the incident was reported to the police and the U.K. Information Commissioner's Office. The following steps were taken:

- ✔ Notifications were sent to each of the data subjects.

- ✔ A Web site was set up with frequently asked questions (FAQs) and contact details as well as up-to-the-minute update information.

- ✔ A call center was created, so people could speak to people (not machines).

- ✔ Credit-reference checking was made available.

This occurred just after a high-profile case, so the authorities also issued an enforcement notice: Within 90 days, all company laptops that held information about the subjects whose data had been lost would have to be encrypted. Imagine the expense. Imagine the hassle. Imagine how the situation would have changed if the data had already been encrypted on the stolen laptop.

Data loss is a rapidly changing area of law enforcement; the interpretation of laws can change on a case-by-case basis. That makes security awareness even more important to provide to partners outside the organization.

An ongoing program

As technology and work practices change, threats to data are also continuously changing — and criminals are getting smarter in their attacks. Your organization's security-awareness program must reflect this reality.

Issue regular updates, coupled with announcements when a new threat is discovered. Be sure to make announcements in such a way that no one misses the information. Use the following media:

- ✔ E-mail.
- ✔ Your organization's intranet.
- ✔ Internal conference calls (for major alerts).
- ✔ Posters. There's nothing like seeing a security-alert poster when you get to work!

Keep the words short and to the point. You don't want to require a magnifying glass to read the small print!

Building a culture that protects data

Regular security training can reinforce the values required to protect data. Everyone has electronic data that's looked after by other individuals, both inside and outside the company. It's imperative that organizations understand the implication of holding personal data about their customers and employees. The data itself doesn't belong to them; it belongs to the individuals concerned.

For most companies, the bottom line is success in the marketplace — but data security is also good business. Every business should manage data to the most appropriate level for its unique operational, marketing, competitive, and financial situation. Finding the optimal level of data-management investment requires considerable effort, and taking the time to investigate and understand the interdependencies will certainly help to better quantify any potential data issue. But having made this investment it would seem naïve not to ensure that all that investment isn't wasted by simply not training employees on the dangers and implications of a data breach.

An organization was diligent about ensuring that all its security policies were up to date — and had a perfectly good policy to control the movement of data within the organization. Unfortunately, the security policy was "classified"; only executives and senior management could view it. That didn't seem problematic until a junior administrator was asked by his immediate superior to send some data to another part of the organization. He promptly downloaded a large mass of customer personal data, in complete breach of the policy — but only because he wasn't allowed to know what the policy was in the first place.

It's reasonable to request that employees protect sensitive data with the same respect, due care, and attention they expect from others who look after their data. But they need the tools to do so. Your data-loss prevention policy belongs in their arsenal.

By encouraging employees to pay closer attention to the various ways in which they interact with data — and using that awareness to help identify ways to protect the data in their care — you can create a strong foundation for an information-protection policy. To help that process along, you can create incentive programs that encourage data protection, whether the improvements involve changing the company databases and applications or modifying business processes. Incentive programs aren't always about money. Consider other types of reward, such as the presentation of plaques that acknowledge all that effort:

- ✓ Information Security Employee of the Month
- ✓ Best Customer Security Idea of the Quarter
- ✓ Customer Data Champion

Chapter 22

Long-Term Prevention

. . . .

. . . .

*U*nfortunately, data loss, data leaks, and data breaches are here to stay. Electronic information is how our businesses, and even our society, survives. Information has unarguable value — to those it belongs to, and to those it does *not* belong to. The consequences of data loss can be dire enough that short-term, knee-jerk reactions to data breaches are clearly a substandard way for a company to govern itself. The reputation of the company is at stake. What it needs is an effective, long-term view of data loss — and that means creating an information-protection policy.

Creating an Information-Protection Policy

An *information-protection policy* is an overarching set of agreed-upon practices for looking after information in your organization, regardless of whether it's paper-based or electronic (including e-mail, files on disk, structured databases, data on Web sites, you name it).

It's worth repeating: Security is only as strong as its weakest link. Don't let that weak link be protection of your data.

Policies tend to be written down and then ignored. For your information-protection policy to be effective, it has to be clearly understood, consistently applied, and followed by everyone — from the CEO to the cleaner and from suppliers and partners to customers. All have important parts to play.

As the importance of data becomes more widely understood, new roles are popping up. Consider creating a new position in your organization that addresses this new priority. The most common titles for such a position are *Chief Information Security Officer* (CISO) and *Chief Information Risk Officer* (CIRO). The goal (surprise, surprise) is to ensure that the organization's data is secure and subject to as little risk as possible.

This new position often reports to the CEO (Chief Executive Officer) rather than to the CIO (Chief Information Officer), which might seem counter-intuitive, but consider: If the CIO's job involves making information *more* available, the findings and actions of the CISO/CIRO could run counter to that priority by *restricting* information. If the CISO/CIRO's actions have an impact on how the company uses IT — and they will — don't be surprised if that bothers the CIO. So: Keeping the two roles separate without the conflict of interests is best for everyone, and *especially* best for the data.

CISOs differ from CSOs (Chief Security Officers) by being more specialized. Normally the CSO handles both physical *and* IT security. Having a CISO puts IT security in a new role that includes (a) general system security and (b) maintaining security in application development.

Long-term strategy to handle data loss

The first step toward getting data-loss issues under long-term control is to acknowledge that there is a problem — even if you aren't too sure what it is and what the real risks are. The next step is to set up a data-loss crisis team.

Creating a data-loss crisis team

With data leaks making the news every other day it pays to be ready, just in case. Having a data-loss crisis team in place makes you ready — and also helps drive a long-term strategy for data loss.

This team is similar to the one you probably have for Disaster Recovery or Business Continuity — they are prepared *just in case*. The team should include those who would be involved if a data-leak event occurs:

- ✔ **CEO:** At the end of the day the buck stops with the CEO and he or she will probably be the one who is on the news and making public comment.

- ✔ **CIO, CISO, CIRO:** The other primary executives who may be required as the external face or are needed to investigate the event internally.

- ✔ **Marketing and /PR:** Contrary to popular marketing opinion, there *is* such a thing as bad press — and a data-loss event is it. Marketing and/or PR will need to be involved in the short term — *and* in the longer term, to reassure customers that their data is safe with you.

✔ **IT:** While IT isn't the answer to everything, the IT department needs to be involved. IT folks can assess the loss as well as put technology in place to reduce the risk. For example, deploying full-disk encryption on laptops has wider implications: If the laptop is lost, the data is secure — and you won't have to disclose the loss.

✔ **Sales:** Front-page news usually pounces on customer data that's been compromised — and bad publicity affects sales, so the sales side of the business needs to be represented. Your salespeople can then work with marketing and the other areas of the business to put together an appropriate and timely response to present to your customers.

Tasks for a data-loss crisis team

An effective team needs to be focused and have deliverables which can be readily measured. In the event of a data leak, what is the process that is going to be followed and the timeline for it to happen?

✔ What was the information that was lost?

✔ How many customers are affected?

✔ Can you prove it?

✔ Who needs to be notified? How will they be notified? By when?

✔ Who else needs to be informed, for example shareholders? Credit-card companies?

✔ How are you going to track progress and ensure that anything else that turns up is not lost in the chaos surrounding the incident.

✔ Do you need to put new processes in place to prevent fraud?

✔ How will you keep your staff — as well as your customers — informed of your progress in responding to the incident?

The long-term goal is simple: Ensure that data is kept secure at all times and in all locations. (Oh, is *that* all?) The difficulty is knowing what you have and appreciating that it changes every day. This is why discovering data isn't a one-off event; it must be ongoing.

Discovery — an ongoing effort

No matter how many processes and procedures are put in place, people will always circumvent them. So it becomes an ongoing task to keep track of your data and discover where it's migrated to *now*. Additionally, remember that you're looking for sensitive and confidential information — so while a credit-card number may remain the same over time, other types of sensitive information can and do change. Here are a couple of examples:

✔ A simple document that describes corporate strategy might only become classified when it lists a set of acquisition targets.

✔ For many companies, acquisitions and mergers are a continuous process. When a new company is acquired, it has to be brought into the fold and put under the wing of the information-protection policy. Discovering where to find all the sensitive and confidential information that must be protected is an important part of this process.

The good news is that technology can help with the discovery process — across the entire IT department, as shown in Figure 22-1. Be sure, in particular, to watch out for these:

✔ Laptops, desktops, PDAs, and other mobile devices

✔ Network-attached storage units

✔ Servers of various types, including file servers

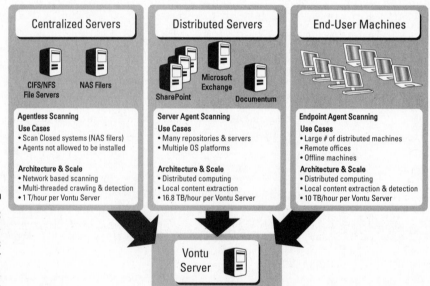

Figure 22-1:
Data discovery across the entire IT estate.

(Courtesy Symantec Corporation)

To build up a complete picture of the problem, you have to create, monitor, and periodically update a risk profile that includes all company information in motion (as shown in Figure 22-2).

While you're on this ongoing voyage of discovery, be sure it happens in a consistent manner; you want to prevent anomalies from occurring.

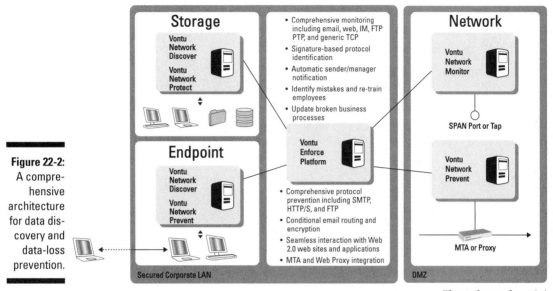

Figure 22-2:
A comprehensive architecture for data discovery and data-loss prevention.

(Courtesy Symantec Corporation)

The importance of consistency

If data discovery isn't done consistently, it can leave holes in your information-protection policy. For example, if data is efficiently stopped from leaving via e-mail but can readily be copied to a USB memory stick, you have a problem.

We use Symantec's Vontu Data Loss Prevention software to discover data across all aspects of the IT environment and to monitor data in motion. This single solution can update policies and deliver them to everyone who needs to see them. If the corporate information policies change, the technology can reflect the changes appropriately, quickly, and efficiently. But whatever means you use, these goals remain the same.

Moving on from discovery

After the sensitive data has been discovered, the next step is to implement policies to protect the information. This shouldn't be an overnight rush job, or it will create more problems than it solves. Hasty new requirements tend to impede productivity because they instantly stop how people currently work.

For one bank, protecting account details was critical. When monitoring for account details, they discovered them all over the place — in e-mails, on laptops, and liberally sprinkled around the organization.

Simple employee education was carried out to explain the risks and consequences and to tell them what was going to happen. Then they *turned on* their information-protection policy. Having initially monitored the situation, they started out with a policy looking for at-risk records (for example, those sent in e-mail messages) in groups of about a thousand at a time. This resulted in a relatively small number of policy violations. They trained the people involved to watch for the problem, and altered the process that had exposed the data to risk.

After these issues were resolved, the bank turned up the sensitivity of its policy to look for fewer records. When those issues were resolved, they repeated the process. This all took time, but over the course of 12 months, they reduced risk-exposure incidents (by 90 percent); they also reduced the severity of the risk and the number of at-risk records (which dropped from over 1,000 to 3).

Protecting information is, like so many things, a journey: Your expertise matures over time. Figure 22-3 shows how the policy can be refined over time to maximize protection.

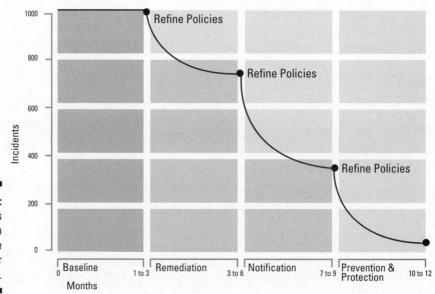

Figure 22-3: Data-loss prevention policies are refined over time.

Less data, less risk

The less data you have, the less you can lose — and so the risk is lower. Of course, the trick is to *get* less data — enough to do business effectively, and no more — in a world where data growth is nearly 100 percent from year to year.

"If you haven't got it, you can't lose it." — Susanna Sherrell

Reducing storage of data to a single instance

Single Instance Storage (SIS) is one way to reduce the amount of data you have. It can be deployed in several ways:

- ✔ **Backup:** With the advent of disk-based primary backup rather than tape, "smart" applications have become the norm. If the file already exists in backup storage, then the software doesn't bother to transfer the same file again, and stores only a pointer to the information. You end up with fewer data transfers over the wire (which is good for remote offices and remote workers), fewer redundant copies, and less data to manage — it's win-win all around.

- ✔ **Live data:** How many times do you need the same file on a file server? Solutions exist that ensure improved efficiency when they store live data: There is just one copy, saved to a file server; if someone else copies the same file, then only a pointer to the original content is stored. From the end-user's perspective, nothing has changed. From the IT administrator's perspective, there is now a whole heap less to manage — and there is more storage available for new stuff.

Archiving

The other way to reduce the data out there is to archive it. Multiple systems can be cleared of old information — which can be stored in one centrally managed archive. Single Instance Storage has a part to play here; the approach can even work on such notorious accumulators as e-mail.

Deleting the old stuff

So we all have lots of data that's well past its sell-by date — but do we delete it? No way. To keep from getting buried under the old stuff, you can put technology in place to archive it — and then, after a specified period of time (the *retention period*), delete it automatically.

Deleting old information *is* allowed — provided you abide by any legislation specific to the data you're handling. For example, health records are kept *for the life of the patient plus two years.* A lot of financial information is required for seven years. Articles of incorporation must be kept forever. Clearly, working out a retention policy is important, but when you have a good one in place, you can use automatic classification to pick out the data to be deleted. That saves you (or anyone else) from having to do it by hand.

Even if you might like to get rid of certain information, you may not be legally able to do so. For example, if the health authority doesn't know the person has died, then how do they know to delete the record? If there are any disputes around the data, then data is kept (this is called *legal hold*) until the dispute is resolved.

Auditing for governance

The biggest issue with auditors is that they want proof. From an auditor's perspective it's all about proof. Of course auditors are also associated with compliance and you want to be in control at all times. That's a sign of good governance.

Auditing is a tedious task (which is why it happens so infrequently), but there's proof that companies with a mature Governance Risk and Compliance (GRC) policy have a twin advantage:

✔ They suffer fewer security issues.

✔ They enjoy a reduction in the costs associated with GRC.

Figure 22-4 (adapted from the 2008 IT Policy Compliance Group Report) offers a glimpse of this happier state of affairs.

Many businesses have multiple compliance needs (from a legislative perspective); solutions exist that can collect and store all the information required. Then you can slice and dice the data in whatever way you need to meet your compliance requirements. We use Symantec Control Compliance Suite to manage various security feeds and keep the information appropriately available for compliance. Control Compliance Suite produces reports intended for auditors' use, and provides controls designed for good governance.

Work toward good governance. It helps you every day. In particular, on auditing day.

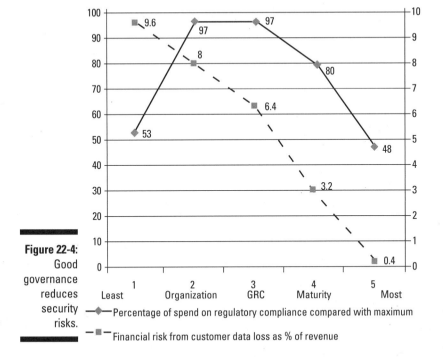

—◆— Percentage of spend on regulatory compliance compared with maximum

— ■ — Financial risk from customer data loss as % of revenue

Revisiting Decisions You've Made

So now you have a great process in place, and fantastic technology that watches for silly mistakes. You've got it wired, right? Why would you ever have to revisit the decisions you've made? The answer is that the world doesn't stop. It's changing around you, often at a pace that's tough to keep up with — which means there's no such thing as a "once and for all" solution.

Regulatory changes

Perhaps the most important changes you have to watch for are in the regulatory and legislative arena. Your organization's legal team should be riding herd on that issue; check with them on a regular basis and make sure your security procedures meet their current requirements.

Threat changes

While we would like to think we have a complete picture of the threats that can come from malicious insiders and cyber-criminals, the truth is that they're forever coming up with new ways to try beating the system.

The good news — so long as it doesn't happen to you — is that data losses and breaches are frequently in the media; you can keep up to date with what brought about the latest debacle. In addition, you can keep an eye on specialist security sites. For example, Symantec's ThreatCon and The Internet Storm Center tell you about emerging security issues, some of which could result in data loss.

Technology changes

Data-loss prevention technologies are relatively new, so they're being constantly improved. Couple this with the emerging changes in threats and you get a kind of arms race: There are new products being released to counter new threats. All the time.

Other technological changes actually create opportunities for cyber-criminals. For example, the advent of Wi-Fi — as a capability not only for laptops, but for cellular phones — makes it an attack vector for data thieves. In response, firewalls and intrusion detection have been introduced for mobile phones, just as they've been available for laptops. As more devices connect to the Internet, more cyber-criminals look at the adoption rate for each one — and then look for weaknesses in the technology. On the other side of the coin, security companies are doing the same thing, but with an eye toward protecting the devices.

Changes in legislation also mean that products change; new ones emerge in response to the new regulations. For example, new compliance reports and new data discovery become necessary in light of new capabilities. The information that now needs to be protected could reside on different devices or as different data types. Here are some examples:

- ✔ Data *in the cloud* (you know — that nebulous outline in the network diagram that means "the Internet," where everything is delivered as a service and you only pay for what you use).
- ✔ Data held by service providers or outsourcers.
- ✔ Data held by suppliers and partners.

✔ Data held on mobile phones and PDAs.

✔ Voice mail.

✔ Telephone conversations in general.

✔ Information held on wikis, blogs, and other chat boards.

The challenge is to keep your data current, legal, lean, and protected — all at the same time.

Chapter 23

Partners and Suppliers

. . . .

In This Chapter

▶ Assessing the risks of third-party suppliers and partners

▶ Setting up security audits for third parties

▶ Identifying data threats from providers of software as a service

▶ Weighing the risks of Service Oriented Architectures

▶ Asking your potential suppliers and partners about security issues

. . . .

*I*t's a scary thought, but more than 12 percent of data breaches occur through the efforts (or lack of effort) contributed by partners and suppliers. In effect, even if the breach isn't your fault directly, you could still end up as front-page news — only because your customers' data has been lost (or found) by a partner or supplier. People never remember the intermediary, but they always remember you!

A government department had outsourced its data processing to a third party on a different continent. Unfortunately the data was lost. No one even remembers the *name* of the third party. What they remember is that the government had, once more, lost information. Worse, this particular citizens' government had already outsourced its data processing *before* people started to ask why their data was being processed on a completely different continent. (Ouch!)

Preventing Data Loss by Third Parties

You have enough of a struggle to keep your own information under control — let alone trying to control some other organizations' stuff. But the need can't be ignored. Third parties are a major cause of data loss.

As with all service agreements, you have to *agree* on what the supplier will do to prevent data loss — and what that third party will do if a breach occurs. It isn't enough to trust that they're doing what they say they're doing; you have to check to make sure it's happening. That's your responsibility.

You won't have to scrutinize *every* supplier or partner you have. It's only a must-do for those that have sensitive or confidential information. The criterion to use: If this partner lost the information, would it cause embarrassment or financial consequences for your organization?

Information-security audits

As organizations began to realize the importance of planning for disaster recovery and business continuity, they also realized that they'd have to ensure that their partners' and suppliers' plans were also up to snuff. If one of your suppliers has a problem that they can't recover from, you don't want that problem forced down the line to you. The same is true for information security.

Internally your understanding of data security and the risks and consequences of data loss should be growing. (After all, you're reading this book.) You can start selectively applying what you've discovered to your suppliers and partners. The easiest way to do so is to carry out an audit and ask some questions:

- ✔ Do you have an information-security policy?

- ✔ Do you back up your data? The answer to this should be *yes,* and the next question must find out (a) whether the data is stored onsite or offsite and (b) whether it is encrypted.

  If it's offsite, then it *really* needs to be encrypted!

- ✔ Do you enforce access controls over our information?

- ✔ Do you share our information with your partners and and/or or suppliers? If so, then what do they do with it? (You might want to ask why they share it. Is there a way to do business *without* having to share sensitive information?)

- ✔ Do you have a data-loss crisis team? Or, what is the plan in the event of a data-loss incident?

As data loss is a relatively new problem, you can expect that the answer to some (or all) of these questions will be insufficient to meet your high standards. In that case, you may have to familiarize your partners with what you do and why you expect what you expect. There may even be ways that you can reduce the data you share with them so you don't have to worry about them losing it at all.

Sometimes the data-loss incident could have been completely avoided if *only the right data* had been shared. In one such instance, someone considered it "easier" to transfer all the data in a database rather than a subset. The result:

Sensitive information got lost. The reason: Money. It was seen as *expensive* to subset the data; of course, the cost of taking (and securing) a subset would have been a fraction of 1 percent of the total cost of the incident.

Outsiders inside your data center

These days, for reasons of efficiency, it's common to allow outsiders into the data center and give them direct access to the organization's data. It is, as always, important to understand the potential risks and consequences — as well as the benefits — of giving third parties access to corporate data.

An aircraft manufacturer we visited revealed that it now has more people accessing the data in their data center from outside the organization than from inside. These include

- ✔ **Partners:** Aircraft manufacture isn't something only one company does by itself. It needs many partners to work on designs and on building the actual airplane. Sometimes they're all over the globe.

- ✔ **Suppliers:** Just-in-time manufacture and delivery has been around for decades. The easiest way to make it happen smoothly is for the suppliers to *watch* what's happening in the process, and then deliver their piece of the project when you need it. (Projects always change from the original time scales!)

- ✔ **Consultants:** You employ them, but they aren't your employees!

- ✔ **Customers:** They want to keep track of how their particular orders are doing, and to respond to any questions on the fit-out that is occurring.

With any luck, the companies you deal with will be around for a relatively long time; the specific people in them may not. Consider giving high-level access to particular individuals rather than to whole companies. Also consider how you might cancel that access when those people leave. (Of course, this also means you need to know *when* they leave!)

Potential threats from Software as a Service (SaaS) providers

Software as a service (SaaS) offers some unique opportunities and challenges to business. The good news is that smaller organizations get access to applications and expertise that only larger companies used to be able to afford. The bad news is that many then put their information at risk.

The risk is that the service provider can be compromised — and then they do something they shouldn't with your data.

Most applications give the administrator complete control over the application and the data. This is actually a weakness. If the administrator can see the data, but isn't under your control — say, as an employee of the service provider — then consider whether they *should* have access to your data! Of course, the service provider could lose your information in the same way you can (lost backup tapes and network hacks come to mind). The solution to the problem: Don't provide the administrator with in-the-clear access to your data. The data should be encrypted before it goes anywhere — and only you (or your company) should have the key.

Some SaaS-enabled applications allow you to impose this restriction. Be sure that you impose it on backups in particular. You really don't want your backups wandering around without your knowledge.

Figure 23-1 shows some potential issues that crop up when you're using a Software as a Service provider. Remember: These aren't deal-breakers, but you should ask about them *before* you commit your cash.

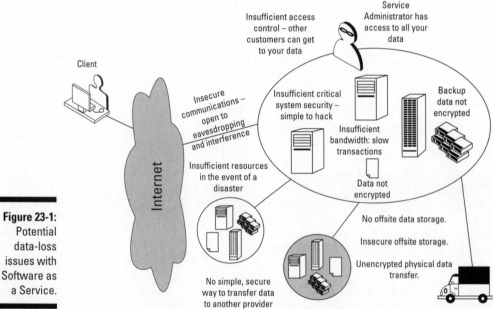

Figure 23-1: Potential data-loss issues with Software as a Service.

Ask your service provider about security — specifically about whether its administrators have access to your data, and whether the data is encrypted.

Of course, the downside of withholding complete control and access to your data is that if you lose your encryption key, you're on your own. The provider won't be able to recover your data; you'll only have yourself to blame.

Service Oriented Architectures and Data Loss

One step removed from Software as a Service (SaaS) is Service Oriented Architecture (SOA). It's a similar situation: A third party (who may be in-house or outside) handles and processes your data, but doesn't have all of it all the time.

As Figure 23-2 shows, SOA offers a couple of interesting possibilities when it comes to data loss:

✔ If the provider has access to your data and stores it on its own systems, it can be lost or compromised there.

✔ The service can disappear, and take your data with it!

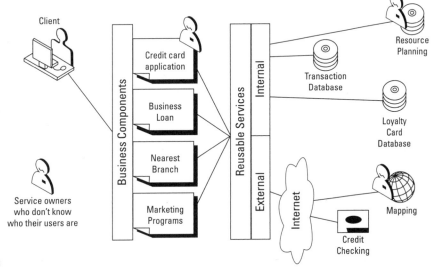

Figure 23-2:
Service
Oriented
Archi-
tectures
offer a
wealth of
possibilities,
some scary.

If your provider doesn't know that you're using its service — or doesn't know that it's actually you (not some anonymous IP address that connects on occasion), then it may have no qualms about changing the service or removing it completely. In fact, it's better for the provider to disappear than to change without you knowing about it. If the service is gone, then at least you know it's gone — whereas if it has changed, you may not notice for a while. If, for example, the service is providing maps for you, you don't want it to suddenly change its units of measurement when it's working with default distances — and fails to tell you. The maps will still work as maps, but the distances will appear in the wrong units. Subtle and unintentionally nasty.

If you're using a service, whether it's internal or external, you need to speak to its people about some basic issues:

✔ Make sure that they know you're using their service.

✔ Find out whether they have a list of *customers* — and whether there is an e-mail list you can join to get updates.

✔ Find out whether there's a mechanism for requesting updates or changes to the service (these are also known as *enhancement requests*).

✔ Find out whether there's another service you can use if this one either breaks or goes away.

✔ Find out what their information-protection policy is.

Of course, if they don't have any sensitive information and never keep any, this may not matter. Just make sure they don't start with yours.

Who can you trust?

Is there anyone you can trust? Absolutely. If you don't trust people with at least some of your information, then you can't use their services and you can't offer those services to your customers. So you have to trust "everyone" — and "no one" — selectively: Build trust with your partners and suppliers — and make sure they can trust you.

Information usage and security are critical for partnerships, and must happen between the right people. The CIOs don't have to be long-winded; they should (a) answer your initial questions and fears and (b) go into the right level of detail to keep you happy. Get the answers in writing; be sure to follow up on any additional questions that either of you have.

Fending off dangers in third-party data processing

If you're using a third party to supply or process data — and your business depends on that data — take a close look at what you can do to ensure the integrity of both the information and the service.

Because you aren't in control, you need more monitoring and checks built into the system — in particular, the right to do some checking:

✔ Is the service is up and running?

✔ Is the service is performing adequately? What does that mean? Well, if it usually takes (say) ten seconds to perform the operation and it's now taking two minutes, then the throughput could affect your ability to do business.

✔ Is the data that the service sends back correct (and in the correct units — for example if asking for distances should it be miles or kilometers)?

You'll need to have ready a dummy transaction with a well-known result, so you can test the service on a regular basis for accuracy.

✔ Are there are other alternative service providers? There should be; that keeps all your eggs from landing in the same basket. If there are other providers you can use, you must check them continuously for data integrity as well. What happens if the quality of their work falls off and they're no longer compatible with your requirements? You don't want to discover incompatibilities too late, or find your old provider gone just when you have to switch providers.

Don't believe that a Service Level Agreement (SLA) is the answer to all of your problems. While these offer some level of comfort, if the service goes away and your business depends on it (and you haven't any alternatives), then no matter how much money they offer, it won't bring your company back. You have a responsibility to check and reassure yourself that your partners, suppliers, and contractors are doing what they're supposed to be doing.

Questions to ask

Here are some questions to ask yourself — and your partners and suppliers — before entering into an agreement to work together. Even if the questions seem like overkill — you may have been working with them for years — asking will save you a lot of time and hassle in the long run.

These are the questions pertaining to information; you will probably have a whole heap more questions about other things such as data availability!

✔ **What is their information-protection policy?** (Assuming they have one, of course.) What does it cover? Is it confined to the messaging systems — and does that include Instant Messaging, Web-based e-mail, and corporate e-mail?

✔ **Would they be happy for you to come and audit their information-protection policy and procedures?** How often?

✔ **What size of organization are they?** This is really important for SaaS or other service providers. Remember: "On the Internet, no one knows if you're a dog." There are some fantastic small service providers doing some amazing things with Web 2.0, but are you happy to bet your business on them? Or do they have a more impressive bark than bite?

✔ **How many other customers do they have?** It's good to know that you aren't alone. On the other hand, if you *are* their biggest customer, they might be more responsive to your requests for enhancements.

✔ **What alternative providers are there?** Ideally you need more than one. That way, if one goes down, you can quickly switch to another.

✔ **If they're storing data for you, how easy is it to retrieve all the data and put it with another provider?** In other words, is it possible to migrate your data? Is there a heavy financial cost if you do?

✔ **Do they depend on other partners and suppliers to provide the service?** If so, then what are their data-protection and sharing policies?

✔ **Do they have procedures for a data breach?** How would you both work together in the case of an incident?

✔ **Do they have access to your data?** If so, then is there a possibility that one of their other customers who might be one of your competitors, get access to your information? If the data is encrypted, where does the access occur — hopefully before it gets sent over the Internet?

✔ **What other security do they have?** Are their applications and servers secure from hackers? Do they have good audit trails so they can see whether the service or access has changed?

✔ **Do they offer any data segregation?** You may not require it, but you might like to think about it.

Here's the scoop on *data segregation*: IT departments usually have some kind of underlying framework to support their applications. This framework can have component parts that handle a range of tasks — from maintaining database libraries to managing and routing messages. Most structured data stores need more complex mechanisms to access data storage (such as databases or data queues). If data can be segregated in a way that reflects organizational requirements, then users can be given access to specific information according to specific requisites. Basically, you're making sure that when users log in to your systems, they're seeing what they're supposed to see — rather than other people's stuff.

A marketing company was putting in a utility computing infrastructure for all its subsidiary companies to use. There would be greater efficiencies for all; customers would get a better level of service because they could all share the IT infrastructure. One of those customers (call it Company A) was a tobacco company — and those folks stipulated that none of their data should wind up on a system with any other customers' data — not on the servers, not on the disk storage, not even on the tape libraries and tapes. Everything had to be completely segregated.

The reason wasn't that this Company A's data would be subpoenaed (as it frequently was), but rather that some *other* customer's data would be subpoenaed — and the other guy might spot Company A's data in there and go looking at it "out of interest".

The requirement was feasible, so it didn't cause a problem — but this example highlights a couple more questions to ask prospective service providers:

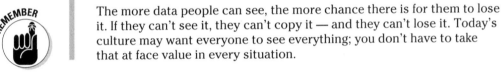

- ✔ What happens if they're shut down for legal reasons, or have their hardware — including the machine that holds your data — impounded?

- ✔ How do you ensure that nobody's looking at data that's none of their business?

The more data people can see, the more chance there is for them to lose it. If they can't see it, they can't copy it — and they can't lose it. Today's culture may want everyone to see everything; you don't have to take that at face value in every situation.

Part VI
Dealing with the Inevitable

The 5th Wave   By Rich Tennant

"Oh, Arthur is very careful about security on the Web. He never goes online in the same room on consecutive days."

In this part . . .

In this part we look at what happens when you do lose some data. Don't kid yourself, this is inevitable — not a question of *if*, but *when*. I mean, if banks and governments can't get it right (yet) what chance do you have? The answer is . . . well, you can at least be prepared — and that will minimize the damage.

It also looks at the rise of social networking and the data loss risks it brings.

Chapter 24

In the Event of Data Loss

"It won't happen to me."

Government official

"Are you kidding? It'll never happen to me."

CIO, Large Manufacturer, Inc.

"It's really unlikely. It sure won't happen to me."

CEO, Household Name Bank

"What just happened?"

Too many of us, when it happens anyway

So . . . you've secured your IT environment, or at least you thought you did, and then one morning you get a call . . .

Sometimes a data breach is pretty difficult to spot — especially where it involves the bad guys stealing data for subversive purposes. They don't want to be caught, so they hide the crime. (After all, you don't get your average cat burglar ripping off a house and then marching up to the nearest policeman to say, "Guess what I just did?") So sometimes it can be pretty tricky to spot that a breach has happened, and it can take considerable time to realize that it has happened at all.

Of course, some cases show up on the radar right away. Say your sales director has left his laptop in the back of his car and it's been stolen . . . so one morning you get a call . . . Yikes. According to the sales director, it wasn't his fault. He'd even left the laptop out of sight in the trunk, but the car was broken into, and the laptop went away. What will you do? In the immortal words of *The Hitchhiker's Guide to the Galaxy* . . .

Don't Panic

First, you aren't alone. You just have to pick up a paper and see that this is happening to other organizations, every day. Data loss is a potential disaster, not necessarily on the same scale as losing a building to a fire, but a disaster nonetheless. At least you can be ready — and you get ready by thinking through the problems that might arise upfront.

> *Forewarned is forearmed. Our familiar theme.*

There are three major requirements for damage limitation:

- ✔ **Create a plan:** At least, if you have a plan, you know whether things are happening according to it — and if they aren't, you can adjust accordingly.

- ✔ **Mobilize the troops:** Your people are your best asset; get them on the case.

- ✔ **Deal with the media:** The old adage of *any press is good press* doesn't hold true in this instance, so it's time to get your thinking cap on.

Creating a plan

The only way not to panic is to have a plan — and if you have a well-developed plan in place ahead of time, then so much the better. If you don't, then here is a great place to start!

Build a team

You are all in this together — the reputation of your company depends on how you act — so build a team with all the appropriate people in it. Open communication among the stakeholders is critically important.

- ✔ **The leader:** CEO, CIO, someone with gravitas, the ability to make decisions and to make things happen. At the end of the day, nothing should happen without the leader giving the okay.

- ✔ **Legal:** They will be involved; there could be lawsuits and all sorts. Get your legal eagles in the team.

- ✔ **IT department:** It might be a paper-based data loss, but more likely it will be electronic. The IT department needs to know what has happened — and work on a plan to mitigate it.

✔ **Sales and lines of business:** As often as not, it's their customers' data that's been lost. So keep them involved and get them working as part of the solution. Get them to call customers to inform them of what has happened — *before* it's all over the front page of the newspaper.

Don't do what one government agency did. It mislaid a pile of citizens personal details, and then spent about $5 million sending an irrelevant letter to all the affected taxpayers — *after* the news had hit the national papers and TV news.

✔ **PR and marketing:** Finding a positive side to a data-loss incident is certainly a challenge. The PR and marketing departments will draft responses, statements, press releases and so on.

Focus on the positive:

- *What you have done to mitigate impact on the customer?* If you've lost customer credit-card records (for example) and you've matched those records back to the credit-card companies and informed them of the issue, you're clearly doing the right thing — and the public needs to know about it.

- *How have you plugged the hole in your defenses?* Have you installed database-security software, or put your entire workforce through a mammoth training session? If so, publicize that this loss *can't* happen again because of specific measures you've taken.

If you know exactly what happened, it's probably worth telling. Covering up is never as effective as facing (and telling) the truth — and no matter how good you may be at concealment, people will know that data was lost.

Find out what happened

Often organizations don't know what actually happened in the course of a data-loss incident. You need to find the answers to some simple questions.

The response to the incident will depend on the answers.

✔ **What information is involved?** Is this names and addresses, or is it bank-account details or health records; what about Social Security Numbers?

✔ **How many customers are affected?** Is it a handful or millions?

If you don't know how many customers are affected, then you must assume it's *all* your customers. If you know how many but you can't prove it, then you must assume it's *all* your customers.

✔ **What was the exact chain of events that lead to the data loss?** Is this a lost laptop or someone hacking the customer database? Was an individual at fault, or is a business process in need of fixing?

✔ **Do you need to watch for potential fraud?** Is the information sufficient that someone can open a bank account or start using a credit card? If so, then you may need to put additional checks in place in case the information is used fraudulently.

Inform the appropriate people

Obviously the customers need to be informed, but you may also need to inform banks and credit-card agencies so that they can be on the lookout for fraudulent activity. You may also need to inform other specific authorities such as the Information Commissioner's Office in the U.K. or the state bodies in the U.S. The U.S. has rules and regulations based on each state, so you will need to find out in which state the breach occurred and then take appropriate notification action.

Create a project office

You should track all the activities and have a single point where people can go to get an update. Create objectives and timelines — and track them. Here's a quick list of basics to put in place:

✔ When will all the customers be informed by?

✔ When will other notifications have been sent?

✔ What is the plan for press briefings? What is the organization's stance on the situation — does everyone know what this is?

✔ Do you need extra capacity for support desks, Internet and intranet connectivity, and Web sites?

Monitor every task that members of the team are doing or will have to do.

While there is a core team who will act in resolving the issue, you must not forget about the rest of the employees. This is a time when bad press can lead to decreased morale; you should do something about it.

Mobilizing the troops

Companies are built on the strength of their people. How those people react in times of a disaster makes or breaks the company. Data loss is no exception.

First thing: It's done — the data loss or breach has happened. There is no point in pointing fingers or placing the blame; the reality is that it has happened and everyone needs to pull together to respond. (There will be plenty of time afterward to analyze what happened, think retrospectively about why it shouldn't have happened, and so on. In the meantime — move on. There are steps to be taken.)

A well-informed workforce will work better than one running on rumors. Get the word out. The CEO or CIO needs to send out an e-mail to the troops on what happened. Not all the facts may be known at this point, but the word needs to go out — detailing exactly what *is* known and when there will be more to know.

Hopefully you'll have a plan and can point employees to it. There may well be changes in role for some of them, so here are some questions for which you'll need to provide detailed answers:

✔ Who is heading up the response?

✔ Who should they go to if they have questions?

✔ Where can they find answers? On the company intranet?

It's important that the employees know what is happening, that management has a plan for dealing with just such an incident, and that they're a significant part of the solution — both now and going forward.

While it isn't necessary to print T-shirts with *I survived the great data-loss incident of 2009*, it might be worth doing something overt to thank the staff when it's all over. For example, you might distribute a coffee mug with a reminder on it of how important customers' confidential data is!

Dealing with the media

When the going is good, you can't get enough media attention; when the going is less good, you can't get rid of them. The media — as we all know — loves a story where the big business is at fault and the little guys (you and me) are the ones in trouble. Data loss is just such an event.

Data-loss events have been happening for decades; you'd think the media would have become bored with the story. (Who remembers the great string shortage of '54?) However, this isn't the case; every day, all across the globe, there are stories about data loss, data leakage, and data breaches. (Hmm. Maybe data is more important than string? Call it an inspired guess.)

Figure out who will be the main spokesperson

This has to be someone senior, with "Chief" in his or her title, who can make decisions. Ideally it should be the CEO, CIO, or — if you have them — CISO (Chief Information Security Officer) or CIRO (Chief Information Risk Officer). All press and media should be directed to this person.

Has your main spokesperson been a member of the press? Does he or she have media training? If not, then consider bankrolling a course for that person. It's a great skill for this particular spokesperson to have — and it can be used to benefit the company at all times!

The press can be tricky and fickle, moment by moment . . . not all of them, but sometimes they can take things out of context (by accident, of course). Your company must be specific and unambiguous about everything it says to them. Here's an example of why . . .

In January 2008, 38,000 sets of credit-card details were hacked from a retailer's Web site. The company warned that because it met "leading security standards" and still got hacked, other major retailers would be vulnerable to the same attack. The press pounced: What did they do *right?*

✔ The organization notified its customers within days of the breach happening.

✔ The stolen data was encrypted, and the organization publicized this handy fact (a great reason for the bad guys to give up in disgust).

✔ The organization flagged the breach with banks immediately, and closed the security hole within hours of the attack.

Have your facts straight

There is nothing worse than having conflicting stories in the press. Get all the facts together and present them in an orderly manner. Think through the sorts of questions that reporters will ask and have a printed sheet for them to take away. These are the same questions you'll put in your FAQs.

If you don't know something, admit it — and say you'll have the answer at the next briefing session.

Offer frequent updates

Remember that the media like to keep on top of a good story (until a better one comes along!) — so offer them regular updates. Schedule briefing sessions where they can find out the answers to outstanding questions and ask more.

This may seem a little over the top — you might be just a small company and believe that no media would ever be interested in a data-loss incident at your company. Don't count on it. Small towns have local news — and local news reporters are always after the story that will make their name and put them in the big leagues. The press could use your company as an example of a wider problem; even if it's simply a name-and-shame list, even that much negative publicity could have disastrous effects on your business.

The Ongoing Project

One of the many unfortunate things about losing data is that there isn't a quick fix. If you lost a laptop, and then that laptop reappears six months later, how do you know whether the data on it was used by cyber-criminals?

Even if it wasn't used, was it copied? Are they waiting to use it? If they did use it, how do you know they won't use it again?

The sad fact is that even if the data *is* used in the short term, it could easily be used again, and again, and again. So dealing with an incident will be an ongoing project — and if you lose data more than once (it happens), these steps could well be around for years — and even become part of the way you do business.

What happens when you lose data and the media finds out about it? Well, for openers, there will be a rush by your customers to find answers to some anxious questions:

- ✔ What has happened?
- ✔ Does it affect them?
- ✔ What will you do about it?
- ✔ What compensation will you give?

These first questions will then be followed up by further, deeper questions:

- ✔ Can you guarantee it won't happen again?
- ✔ What happens if their details are used at some future date?

The best way to deal with these questions is to establish a support desk.

Support desks and supporting your customers

Without customers, you don't have a business. So it pays to look after them — true, losing their data is no great way to inspire their confidence, but you can improve their estimation of you with a help desk.

Even if you already have a help desk, you'll need to beef it up:

- ✔ **More phone lines:** Don't keep your customers hanging on the phone longer than you need to. They will be angry before they start — don't make it worse.
- ✔ **More people:** You have more lines; you do the math — you need more people.
  - • Who will you use?
  - • Do they need to be trained?
  - • Can you train them ahead of time?

> • Can you train them on the specific details within two hours of a data loss?

✔ **More Internet bandwidth:** We live in an online society, where many people turn to the Web for answers instead of trying to get through on the telephone. However, as with the support desk, there will be an increase in requests; make sure that your Web site can cope.

A bank in the U.K. didn't lose any data, but it did have an event that caused customers to lose faith in it. Many customer accounts were online accounts, so when too many people rushed to the Web site to move their money, the Web site collapsed under the strain — and customers' faith nose-dived. It took several days to get the bandwidth and Web-site capacity needed to start rebuilding customer relations.

How quickly can you ramp up bandwidth and processing capacity to your Web site? While this is specifically about the external, customer-facing Web site, you might need to consider beefing up your internal site on the intranet to keep your employees in the picture as well.

✔ **Publish and maintain FAQs:** *Frequently Asked Questions* (FAQs) are an essential part of the arsenal when you're dealing with a data-loss incident. There are a number of FAQs you should produce:

> • External FAQs for customers
>
> • External FAQs for media
>
> • Internal FAQs for employees

Let it be known that there is information available — and where to get it. If it's on the Web, it can reduce calls to the support desk.

Remember to tell people when to expect updates. For example, *every day at 12:00 noon until further notice.*

Minimizing customer impact

A data-loss incident affects a company from a customer-impact perspective — in two ways:

✔ Lost sales when customers move their business elsewhere

✔ Lost business due to downtime as the organization grinds to a halt to deal with the incident

Both of these cases are bad, but you can't ignore either one. You must consider what you can do to minimize both kinds of damage.

Consider sales promotions, advertising, and other events to ensure that customers remember what you do best — your product —instead of dwelling on what has just happened. Although a data-loss incident will provide a lot of bad press, you can use it to build brand awareness — as long as people are visiting your Web site out of interest, make sure that they know exactly what you do, what you're doing about the data loss, how it will be prevented in the future, and what you can do to help them.

Supporting your existing customers with help desks, FAQs, and Web sites will go a long way toward keeping them happy, or at least happier. If they think you're doing all you can, and that you're taking steps to ensure that you won't make the same mistake again, then they may stick with you. At the end of the day, if you're selling something cheaper than someone else, then customers will buy from you — we all like a bargain. But that brings us to the next point . . .

Minimizing customer impact is all about your ability to satisfy the concerns of customers, partners, employees, and shareholders — and to show or prove that you are in control. Failure to do so will result in an exodus of existing customers, prospective customers not giving you their business, partners finding alternative collaborations, employees (usually your best ones) resigning and going to the competition, and shareholders withdrawing their financial support.

This won't be business as usual. This will be business as you've never seen it before. The IT department will be running around like headless chickens to shore up the infrastructure to make sure that what happened won't happen again, sales personnel will be either seconded to support — where they'll be proactively or reactively dealing with worried customers — and the executive team will be doing damage control. And this won't be for just the day of the loss; this will be for months — so you have to think about how to move the business forward anyway. Don't let it stall.

Part of the plan needs to be how you keep business as close to "usual" as possible, and how to keep attracting and maintaining customers.

Read the newspapers. There is a continuous stream of stories on data loss — figure out whether you're at risk in the same way. You'll need to ask hard questions of yourselves and the people around you. You may not like the answers you hear, but at least listen. You can then assess the risk and the potential consequences — and get some different perspectives on whether something needs to be done. Not all solutions have to be expensive!

Ensuring that it won't happen again

This is the million-dollar question: *Can you prevent something like this from* ever *happening again?* Well, no, you can't — nobody can — BUT you can minimize your risks and benefit from mistakes — both your own and those of others.

If you've had an incident — say, you lost a laptop — then you know what you went through to put it right. You can now look at other sections of this book to find out how to prevent that from happening again, what technology to deploy, and what processes to change. Of course, *there's no patch for mistakes*, so if your employees are still doing something foolish, then there will always be a risk.

In June 2008, a senior civil servant left intelligence documents marked "Top Secret" on a train. In spite of a ban on taking laptops outside the governmental department, this particular spook simply left the bright orange envelope on the seat when he got off the train.

In the process of finding the sources of information and data leakage, you might like to look at using a combination of workshops, interviews, and data analysis to uncover where the breaches occurred — and therefore how you might close them. This will give you an insight into how you can mitigate quickly (and most effectively) against further data breaches before they have a similar impact on your organization.

Take a look at the relationship between data-leak risks and key business functions:

- **Business operations:** Are any of your business processes less secure than they should be? Which ones?

- **IT operations:** Does IT have the resources and training it needs to handle the threats of data loss?

Then review the following aspects of each department:

- **Organization and culture:** What's the prevailing attitude toward data loss?

- **Policy and enforcement:** Has policy kept pace with the threat landscape? Are existing policies consistently enforced?

- **Discovery and protection:** In light of a data-loss incident, how should you improve these capabilities?

- **Monitoring and prevention:** What everyday measures can you put in place to improve data security?

Check these aspects of operation at every layer of the IT infrastructure: endpoints, networks, servers, and storage.

To properly address past and future risks, an organization should first conduct a review that identifies and categorizes any potential risks found, and creates appropriate priorities to deal with them. Only then can the organization define and adopt a risk-management framework that's truly adequate for its business.

Chapter 25

Preparing for the Future

*T*he trouble with data loss is that while the subject is as old as the hills, the consequences are only just being realized. It used not to be a crime to lose your laptop or to send an e-mail to the wrong person — but now it can put you on the front page of major newspapers around the globe — and not in a good way.

In the olden days of the Dark Ages — around 2006 — employees were trustworthy and honest (most of them); they had access to sensitive information and they were trusted to do the right thing with it. After all, what did they think they would do with it? Sell it? Ha!

Times, they are a-changin' — and now all information is valuable to someone. Corporate data, whether customer lists or company secrets, now commands a price on the black market if you know where to look. Malicious insiders are starting to make a name for themselves as threats. It's time to look at some of the futuristic technology — already here today — that can help combat the malicious insider. Here's why . . .

The Decline of Implicit Trust

One of the basic security strategies is authorization and authentication. Employees are granted access rights to applications and to data depending on their jobs or roles. Security is based on the employee doing the right thing with the information he or she has access to. This is *implicit trust.*

In too many cases, this is now an incorrect assumption. You can't trust automatically that your employees will do the right thing — not because they're bad people, necessarily (even though there may be some of those), but because the game has changed. One of the unfortunate changes: Employees are usually unaware of the dangers that come from failing to treat personal data or company intellectual property with some reverence. As usual, lapses on the part of a few folks cause problems for everyone else. However, with your company at stake, it pays to be cautious — even if it feels a bit like the Orwellian Big Brother.

An employee at DuPont (a world-class multinational chemical and healthcare company) was leaving for a new job with a competitor. Nothing strange there — employees frequently leave to go to new jobs in the same industry, often with competitors. However, this particular employee decided that it would be a nice "welcome gift" to bring some confidential information with him from his old company. He had access to the intellectual-property database, and decided to take copies of various files from it with him! He was caught and prosecuted — the fair market value of the data he had taken was estimated at $400 million.

Another employee was from a Formula 1 team who took designs from one company to the next. This employee didn't realize there was anything wrong with what he had done (allegedly). After all, the miniscule design detail was from a tiny piece of the F1 car that he had personally worked on — effectively he considered it to be his design piece. It didn't cross his mind that although he had designed it, it was the intellectual property of the company and did not belong to him — a fundamental (but really easy) mistake to make. He was found out — and in this case, *the new company* was penalized by the sport for "cheating." The fine was $100 million.

Unfortunately, these aren't isolated incidents. We live in an age when everyone demands access to everything — and companies have vast amounts of data to access. Often access is granted for a specific reason or a limited time period *but then forgotten about*; some folks continue to have access when they really don't need it. That's a data-loss incident just waiting to happen.

Although much of this book is about the unstructured data that resides in files, the database is king of corporate information. Customer records, orders, personnel records, and intellectual property all reside in databases or information warehouses. This data is the next to be targeted by cyber-criminals and malicious insiders. One major reason: Structured data is easiest to access, store, and move — because it's a fraction of the size of unstructured data. You can get 25 million records on two CDs — including name, address, date of birth, children (along with their names and dates of birth), and so on (but only about six classic Yes songs will fit).

Malicious insiders already know all they need to know:

> ✔ **Exactly where your critical data is:** For example, which applications hold the customer lists, which the intellectual property.

> ✔ **How to get at it:** It's part of their *day job* to use this information and the IT department has given them access.

> ✔ **(Possibly) who will pay good money to have access to it:** The buyers don't have to be sinister men in overcoats. How about your competitors?

The insider threat must be considered and protected against.

Analyzing application access

If applications and their underlying databases hold such a lot of confidential information, then surely it's possible to audit who is accessing what? The answer is yes! Most applications have log files and audit trails. In the case mentioned earlier, the DuPont employee was caught because someone *noticed* that he had accessed 15 times the amount of data accessed by the next highest user. Because he had handed in his termination notice, his activities were then looked into — and so he was subsequently caught. But the question remains: What would have happened if he *hadn't* handed in his notice, or people hadn't spotted his unusual application access?

One of the more worrisome phenomena of the "information age" is that we never seem to retire old applications and systems. Worse, these days it seems nothing ever gets turned off — and most IT operations have no complete or clear idea of what they're running at any given moment. So it isn't a bad idea to do an audit that compares these two numbers:

> ✔ How many applications your IT organization is running

> ✔ How many applications your users are accessing

Generally, these totals don't match — and that's a worry in itself. The tendency is that legacy systems are not as well protected as those you put in just yesterday. If no one is accessing an application, then talk to the business unit about retiring it. At the same time, look at the type of data the application created — and take appropriate steps to archive it or at least protect it.

When you're developing applications, be sure to include an audit log as a design feature. Ensure that individual users can be identified and their actions viewed. This can be as complicated or as simple as you deem necessary. Simple login times and durations are of use. Full audit trails provide much more information, but also create more — sometimes separating the forest from the trees is a tough task.

If all this information is stored, then there is technology that can help. It carries out the analysis automatically and looks for anomalies in user behavior.

Analyzing user behavior

What makes a good user? What makes a bad one? How do you know? The answer is that you probably don't. At the least, making that distinction is pretty difficult; unfortunately, you must tar everyone with the same brush — at least from a technological point of view. What's likely to happen is that you'll pick up some stray minnows while fishing for the pike — you might even pick up the odd pike that thinks it's a minnow (employee caught doing something wrong who didn't realize it was wrong).

Data is data is data. You might do something with it that seems perfectly reasonable to you — but turns out not to be. For example, it might seem that taking a design document from your previous employer that contains a concept you actually designed yourself is roughly in the same league as keeping stuff to support your résumé — but *no, it's not*. In the Formula 1 example, sure enough, the employee had created what he took — but that wasn't the issue. To the courts or the FIA, what was of most concern was the risk that someone could use that information to gain an unfair competitive advantage over another F1 team. If a user moves information, it isn't necessarily for subversive reasons; the problem is that after the data moves out of your control, someone else can access it more easily — and use it wrongly or inappropriately. At the end of the day, stuff you create for your company in company time or using company resources belongs to them, not you. If you take it away without their permission, that's theft!

According to a recent survey, an average 5 percent of employees are disgruntled at any given time. You'd be surprised at how few relatively contented ("gruntled?") employees there are. Of course, the difference between a disgruntled employee and one who will steal your information is pretty big. A lot of people might be unhappy at work, but it's a big step to walk out the door with confidential information, expecting to sell it or reuse it elsewhere. Also, let's be clear: This kind of activity isn't easy to spot. It isn't as brash as a hacker breaking into the network, or as tangible as someone stealing a laptop. If an employee who has legitimate access to the data takes a copy of it, you and your company may never notice it happening.

Applications do what applications do — and many of them do keep track, logging who does what and when. However, figuring out whether someone is doing something *differently* is the key to tracking down malicious insiders.

Bank tellers tend to only access one account at a time — usually when you're standing in front of them at the bank requesting something, as in Figure 25-1. Suppose a teller decides to access the top 1,000 accounts, or to run a report of the accounts with more than $100,000 in them. That would probably be out of the ordinary — and should probably be flagged.

The CEO of your company probably doesn't have access to your bank-account details — but the people in Human Resources and Payroll do. Curiously, the farther up the corporate ladder you are, the less access you have to personal (and customer) confidential information. Of course, the farther up the ladder you are, the more access you have to business plans and other confidential *corporate* information. So don't assume that only the boss has access; often that's not the case.

There is new technology available that will monitor access thresholds in order to spot when someone has downloaded more than they should. Basically, it works like this: After installation, it's left to monitor what "normal" is. At the end of a predetermined time, the system is switched from passive (watching) mode to active mode. Anomalous behavior now becomes an issue; warning bells are set off; see Figure 25-2.

The good news about this technology is that you can use it on Web-based applications too — and it can catch SQL injection attacks (where a cyber-criminal hijacks the application).

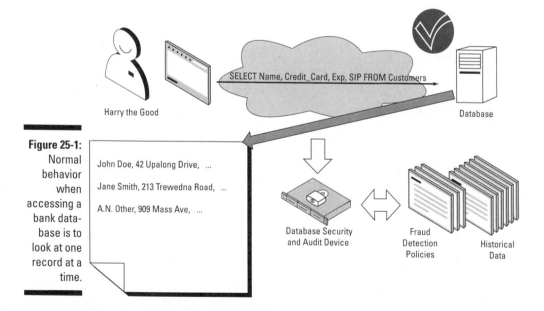

Figure 25-1: Normal behavior when accessing a bank database is to look at one record at a time.

SELECT Name, Credit_Card, Exp, SIP FROM Customers

Harry the Good

Database

John Doe, 42 Upalong Drive, ...

Jane Smith, 213 Trewedna Road, ...

A.N. Other, 909 Mass Ave, ...

Database Security and Audit Device

Fraud Detection Policies

Historical Data

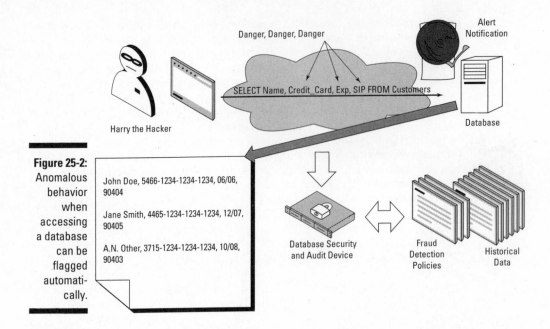

Figure 25-2:
Anomalous
behavior
when
accessing
a database
can be
flagged
automati-
cally.

If you want to deploy this technology, you need to have a good handle on which of your applications actually have confidential information. Without understanding this first, you could end up spending a lot of money to protect applications that don't need protecting!

Malicious data corruption

There is one other attack that has yet to be seen, or perhaps we should say *has yet to be publicized:* Data corruption.

If someone (or several someones) steal your data from a database, then it's arguable whether they *have* stolen it; after all, you still have it. They have taken a copy. You may not know it has been copied, and business may go on as it normally does. However, there is one thing worse than having your data stolen — having it altered.

This isn't usually something a malicious insider would do — but it *is* something a cybercriminal (or an ex-employee with a grudge) might do. Suppose your customer-records database suddenly changed a single digit in every phone number — you wouldn't be able to get to any of your customers. Of course, you have their names and addresses, so you can look them up, but the data has been corrupted. Now, suppose this change doesn't happen all at once, but over time — and rather than telephone numbers, it's credit-card details (or perhaps bank details for direct debits). Backups would continue but they would be backing up corrupt data. When that's discovered, recovering the information will be difficult; you'll have to recover and test multiple copies to find out when the corruption began. Then, when that's done, you have to restore the data and update it with *every transaction that has happened in the intervening time* — which (apart from being a nuisance) could well be impossible.

When designing applications, be sure to create an audit log of data that changes. Ensure that there is a mechanism for alerting the administrator if more than a specific number of records change in any given period. Customer information (for example) doesn't change too often — so to see updates happening *en masse* or too frequently should start alarm bells ringing.

Hiding Data You Don't Want Seen

Any organization always has at least some information it doesn't want everyone to see — and for legitimate reasons. This data must be protected — especially from prying eyes.

Various mechanisms are available:

- ✔ **Keep the data on restricted partitions.** Users must have specific access rights to read the information.

- ✔ **Encrypt the data.** Users must have access to the encryption key in order to decrypt the information and read it.

- ✔ **Restrict access to fields in databases.** Authentication and authorization features in applications ensure that only specified users can see the information.

- ✔ **Use redaction technology.** This process hides specific pieces of information in real time.

Before throwing technology at the problem, however, develop a set of policies first — regarding the sensitivity of the information and who should have access. It's good practice to have these restrictions set out so everyone can see the policy and can categorize their information accordingly.

For individuals worried about protecting specific files, Windows offers various tools for locking up documents, files, videos, music, folders, and so on. Generally speaking, the tools can be found in the features that set Properties or Security, or in the Protect Document options for your files — and here's how to use them:

✔ **To restrict access to a document for anyone on your (local) computer:** Right-click the document and then click the Security tab.

✔ **To lock up a Microsoft Word document, Excel spreadsheet, PowerPoint presentation, and such in Microsoft Office 2007:** Click the Review tab, and then restrict access by using the Protect Document tab at the far right.

✔ **Note that Information Rights Management (IRM) is a plug-in:** IRM can help to protect documents and e-mail messages from being forwarded, edited, or copied by people you don't want forwarding, copying, or editing your stuff. To do that, however, you have to install the Windows Rights Management Client (which you can download from the Web). After you're prompted to install the program, just follow the Install Wizard and you're done.

Information sensitivity and access

For preventing data loss, the fewer the number of people who have access, the more secure it is. If you don't have access to something, you can't lose it, misplace it, or use it for the wrong purposes!

Governments have always been good at categorizing information with respect to secrecy. How many secret agents have you seen go straight for the files marked *Confidential* or *For Your Eyes Only*? The other good thing about government is that it's role-based. If you have Security Clearance Level 2, then that's the level of documents that you're allowed to see. You need to develop the same approach within your company.

To reduce the complexity of the system, you need to minimize the number of levels of information sensitivity and the number of roles that can have access.

It doesn't follow that the farther up the tree you are, the more access you have. This is true for some types of information but not all. For example, employee personal details (which often include bank records) usually can't be seen by the CEO! In fact, employee managers don't usually have access to bank records — only the payroll staff does.

Governments typically have five levels of classification. If they can sort everything into five levels, then so should you:

✔ **Top Secret:** This is top category, reserved for information that would cause *exceptionally grave damage* to national security.

✔ **Secret:** This information would cause *serious damage* if it were to leak out.

✔ **Confidential:** This would create *damage* if it became publicly available.

✔ **Restricted:** This is the lowest of the classifications. This data, if leaked, would cause *undesirable effects*.

✔ **Unclassified:** This is the default bucket. If it doesn't fit into any of the previous categories, then it's unclassified!

You could probably get away without having a Top Secret category, although we imagine the company board would get a kick out of having papers stamped Top Secret! (Apparently NATO has a Cosmic Top Secret designation — who knows what information *those* documents might contain!)

If you don't like the government classifications, you can just have simple levels. After you've decided which data is sensitive and assigned it a level, you can deploy the appropriate technology to protect it. Here's an example:

✔ **Level 5 (Top Secret):** This information should be encrypted! It probably shouldn't be printed out. ("Oh [censored], no!" say all the secret agents out there!) If it's printed, then it should be shredded after use (or be eaten if you're a secret agent, or self-destruct if you're into special effects).

✔ **Level 4 (Secret):** Once again, this information should probably be encrypted. Perhaps this designation allows a slightly wider audience to have access to the key that decrypts the data.

✔ **Level 3 (Confidential):** Much information is confidential within an organization; you may consider encrypting it, but more probably a restricted file-system share is adequate. Access to the share could then be granted by role. Copying might be restricted, especially from going onto removable media such as CD-ROMs or USB sticks.

✔ **Level 2 (Restricted):** Probably this stuff should be kept on a restricted file-system share.

✔ **Level 1 (Unclassified):** Nobody cares about securing data at this level; it can be on a public shared-file system, copied onto USB sticks, whatever people want.

The other side to the coin is access: Decide who has the appropriate role or roles to access the information. With technology such as Active Directory, granting individuals or groups specific access rights is relatively simple.

Real-time redaction

Sometimes there's a need for some, but not all, information to be shared. In a letter, for example, you might want to hide the address (or perhaps the bank-account details) of the person involved. Well, you can *redact* what you don't want seen, as in Figure 25-3.

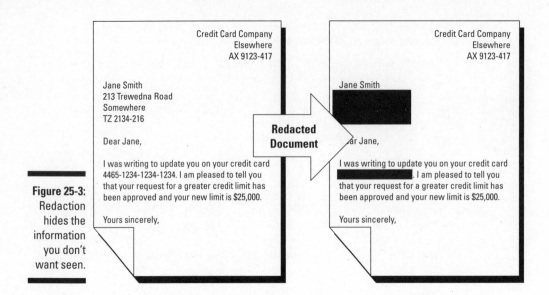

Figure 25-3:
Redaction
hides the
information
you don't
want seen.

This technique is akin to taking a black marker to the documents and blacking out only the text you don't want seen. It's most often used in legal cases where documents are shared, but not all the information is pertinent to the case, or there are privacy issues.

There are technologies that can do this automatically and nearly in real time. If your business has a lot of potentially sensitive information in documents that individuals see, though they shouldn't see the sensitive stuff (as, for example, in claims processing), then redaction is the technology for you!

Social Networking and the Dangers of Data Loss

Social-networking sites have become a way of life for many individuals. There are continuous stories in the press about how much time is wasted through employees using social-networking sites, or how you (as a company) can exploit social-network technology to improve sales, or teamwork, or whatever. The truth is that social networks are a source of data loss.

The Israeli military recently changed its policy regarding social-networking Web sites and posting of pictures. This happened after they realized that there was secret information about military bases available in the *background* of the "people pictures!"

You need a policy (or perhaps just some education) that sensitizes your colleagues to the risks of posting pictures from work on social-networking sites. You don't necessarily have to prevent it, but just ensure that the wrong information isn't posted by accident.

The information posted on social-networking sites isn't just pictures. There is often a lot of other information that can be used in phishing scams. Develop a policy that defines the do's and don'ts of putting personal information on social-networking sites — especially anything related to work. Here's a starter list of examples:

- **Pictures:** Don't post pictures that show *interesting* things in the background such as passwords on yellow sticky notes, security systems, control panels, experimental death rays . . . you know . . . *interesting*.

  If you can create and post pictures that show what a great place this is to work — *without* showing the wrong stuff — do it! If in doubt, don't.

- **Contact details:** Don't put your work-contact details on social-networking sites. These include your telephone number and work e-mail address! You can give the company's public-access information — but not your job title, and don't specify the names or titles of colleagues.

You can also add other guidelines that may not be directly related to work but can help keep individual users (and what they do for your organization) safe online, such as

- **Date of birth:** If you want to get a birthday e-mail from your social-networking site and are happy to have total strangers know your birthday, then post it. Otherwise . . . don't. Date of birth is a key component in identity theft; posting it on a social-networking site makes it easier for someone to steal your identity.

- **Holidays and vacations:** Don't put the dates that you're away on a Web site. If a thief comes across it (and you helpfully gave your address), then they'll know when you're away! (From a company perspective, if a cyber criminal knows that an individual is away, then they could call up to get a password reset. If they succeed, you may not know about it until the employee returns.)

Keep the policy simple — make sure that what is (and isn't) allowed is clear and easily understood.

There is one area where it's tough to have an appropriate policy — *business* social-networking sites. Visiting one of these and doing a search by company yields a wealth of information. You can often find large swaths of upper management listed — including when they joined, when they were promoted, and all sorts of other information. Most of the details are *hidden* unless you're a *friend* of the individual, which is good. A simple reminder to those people who use business social-networking sites to be careful about whom they add as a *friend* is usually enough. (The same advice holds true for other social sites.)

LinkedIn is a pretty diligent site as business social-networking sites go. It keeps asking me for *more* information that I don't want to give. The same applies to applications like Plaxo. Irritatingly, Plaxo now informs me of all my friends and colleagues birthdays, almost on a daily basis — all of which I know are incorrect. Plaxo asks for a date of birth when you register, and anyone who's savvy about the risks that go with this kind of stuff lies about their date of birth. In effect, it makes a farce of data capture if everyone is busily protecting their identities by lying about age, gender, residence, marital status, sexual orientation, religion, or . . . what . . . name? (By the way, if you ever get an Out of Office notice from one of us and feel it's a trifle terse, this is why!)

Corporate phishing through private individuals

We think of phishing as being done typically by cybercriminals against individuals. The doctored message and fake information are sent out to millions of people in the hope that a few will respond and register their bank-account details. Corporate phishing is much more sophisticated.

Social-networking sites can provide cybercriminals with a wealth of information. For openers, they can see what position is held in the company, perhaps snag an address, phone number, and e-mail address? Those friendly sites can also hold information on colleagues (*John X works with me, visit his home page here . . .*) — including when they're going on vacation or when the boss is away for the holidays. (*Having great fun this week as John, my boss, is away for a week.*)

Armed with this sort of information, the phisher can craft an appropriate e-mail and use it to attack your company.

A supermarket chain was attacked by targeting an individual in Accounts Payable. The scam was similar to an old fax scam: Send in a fake invoice and then demand payment. This time it was done through e-mail. Finding out whom to target is half the battle. In this case, invoices were for services rendered to the organization; it was hard to tell whether services had (or, in this case, had *not*) been carried out. The criminals were caught in the nick of time — but they nearly got away with $9 million!

Educate. Educate. Educate. When you hear about new and novel attacks, send out an e-mail to employees to bring them up to speed:

✔ **Outline the attack.** What happened and when and (if appropriate) to whom.

✔ **Outline the method of attack.** Was this phishing, visiting an infected Web site, a virus in an e-mail — what? The more detail you can give, the better armed the rest of your staff will be against the next attempt.

✔ **Explain the risk and the consequences.** If this was opening an attachment to an e-mail or visiting a dodgy Web site, explain the risks of doing this particular wrong thing — along with the consequences: You've had a data breach and the damage, at this time, is probably unknown!

✔ **Explain what could (or should) have been done to prevent it.** Reinforce safety measures such as

- Don't open attachments from people you don't know.

- Don't download stuff from Web sites you don't know are secure.

If you're dealing with a heavier-duty threat than that, you need to change a business process. And that will mean more education.

✔ **Explain any changes in process that will now occur to prevent the event from happening in your organization.** Perhaps it has to do with getting employees to ask authentication questions (say, to determine who's on the other end of the phone conversation), or encrypting data before it goes onto a disc and into the mail.

✔ **Give a contact name if people have questions.** In a crisis, it's natural for people to worry. Give them a name they can contact for a chat. Often this can help bring other potential issues to light as well.

User education is an ongoing process — often it needs several attempts before people start to get the message. You don't want to flood people's inboxes with stories of corporate phishing and new attacks every day, but providing a heads-up once or twice a month will get the message home.

Data loss in cyberspace

As ever, the online world is moving rapidly to the next big thing; the next generation of applications, often called Web 2.0, is giving us a richer and richer experience online. Result: More and more information is being put online — where it's available to be lost, stolen, or hijacked. Heck, if you thought we had data-loss problems in the real world, take a look at what's waiting in cyberspace!

Virtual worlds are at the forefront of new technologies. They're growing fast enough that a lot of organizations are setting up shop in these virtual worlds and offering goods for sale. As with a *normal* organization, the data held within the virtual world also needs to be protected or it will start to go away. Thieves have already been prosecuted for theft in cyberspace — here are just a couple of general categories of the loot they make off with:

✔ **Real-money transactions in virtual worlds:** Money can be stolen here just as it can in the real world.

✔ **Stolen virtual things that people can then sell:** Here the booty includes everything from houses to cybersex toys to clothes (skins) to textures. If you create it, someone may be able to copy it and then sell it! After all, it's only code . . . a few cut-and-paste moves are all it takes to copy something!

It's only a matter of time before customer lists and other cyber-artifacts are snatched — and affect *real* sales and reputations. Before becoming a presence in a virtual world, think about the consequences and create a plan:

✔ **Do you need to be there?** Is this just a fad or will it really result in increased sales?

✔ **Is it really worth it?** Does the investment justify the returns? What would happen if your corporate identity was stolen and compromised and you didn't notice for a day, or a week, or a month?

✔ **Is the virtual world secure?** As the owners what security they have — both inside the world and also on the servers in the real world.

✔ **If you offer stuff, can it be stolen?** The answer is that it probably can; however, if what you offer is *free,* then this reduces the likelihood that it will be stolen — after all what would be in it for the thief if they couldn't make money from it?

✔ **Is there any backlash or remediation if something is stolen from you?** Or can the thief run wild with your logo, customer list, or intellectual property — damaging your reputation with little concern that you will come after them?

✔ **What is the minimum you need to do to have a presence but maintain the security of your and your customers' information?** Is it just a storefront that directs people to your product in the real world?

Real or virtual, it's still a world full of human motives — some legitimate, some not.

Part VII
The Part of Tens

The 5th Wave   By Rich Tennant

"I started running 'what if' scenarios on my spreadsheet, like, 'What if I were sick of this dirtwad job and funneled some of the company's money into an off-shore account?'"

In this part . . .

*H*ere are a few lists for you, some quick hints and tips that you can act on today to prevent data leaks from happening. It also looks at some of the popular fallacies that lead to data loss incidents becoming big problems — and gives you some ammunition to prevent them from happening in the first place.

Chapter 26

Ten Tips to Prevent Data Loss Today

. . . .

*W*e figure that if you're reading this chapter first, it's because you're in trouble — or at least you think you might be. Hey, we've all been there, so here are some steps you can take *today*.

Identify what information you have that needs to be protected

Remember: We aren't looking for *all* information, just the sensitive and confidential information — the stuff that will make you (horrible) front-page news if it wanders off! Start with the obvious — customer details and product designs — and work from there.

Now you know what you're looking for!

Identify where sensitive information resides

This sounds simple, but is it? Computer systems hold the information — servers, desktops, laptops, and external hard drives. For starters. Then you have mobile devices, mobile phones, PDAs. After this come other gadgets such as digital cameras and perhaps USB storage devices. Finally, you have to list all the people with whom you share the information — partners, suppliers, and even customers.

Now you know where it is!

Identify who has access to sensitive and confidential information

The quick answer is *only those who should*. The actual answer is *more than you thought*. This is all about figuring out who has access — and who *needs* access. Chances are that 90 percent of the people who have access don't need it. Check it out, remove access where it makes no sense, and reduce the risk.

Identify processes involving sensitive information

How is the information used and why? Information is the lifeblood of an organization, but a small leak is like a shaving cut. It goes everywhere! By finding the processes that involve the sensitive information, you can work to protect them first. Manual process steps are fine as a first step to a more comprehensive solution.

Identify when and where data goes offsite

If data is sent offsite — whether as a backup tape, portable drive (in or out of a laptop), or CD-ROM — it should be encrypted. Although guarding sensitive data should be your number-one priority, it's good practice to protect *all* data that's going out for a stroll. Develop an encryption policy for sensitive and confidential information — and a process to go with it. You should track the items sent: Sign out, sign in, report. That way you know if something goes missing, but you won't have to worry — after all, *it's encrypted*.

Protect the endpoint

What do people lose? Laptops, mobile phones, PDAs. These mobile endpoints must be protected. Laptop encryption and anti-malware should be at the top of the list.

Protect information in motion

After protecting systems from physical theft, which is one of the easiest ways to leak data, you also have to look closely at protecting the data in motion. E-mail is the number-one culprit here. Look out for distribution lists that contain e-mail addresses that aren't within your company and consider putting a data-loss prevention application on the e-mail gateway to prevent your data from getting into the wrong hands. Then look at other ways information might escape, such as instant messaging and Web-based e-mail.

Revisit how reports and printouts are destroyed

Nearly a quarter of all data-loss incidents are from printed matter. Sensitive information has to be *suitably* destroyed, and its destruction checked. Put document shredders near photocopiers and outside meeting rooms. If you're using a third-party shredder, ask: Do they shred onsite? If not, then *should* they — at least for some of the information?

Revisit system disposal

How are old laptops, mobile devices, and servers disposed of? Is the data on them adequately erased? Create a policy and a process to ensure that disposal is done correctly every time — even if that involves cremating the information — and that you have a report to prove it. If you haven't done a good job with the destruction and the server turns up on an auction site, the results can be a tad embarrassing. (Classic understatement there.)

Start an education-and-awareness program

Send out an e-mail outlining one of the threats your organization has faced or expects to face, and the implications of data loss. Send out another one next week, and another the week after. Spoof an attack of some sort; make it one that can identify the people who fall for it — that really brings home the dangers. As with fire drills, this isn't something that happens just once and then rests on the assumption that everyone knows what to do. The message and the process have to be repeated regularly. The big difference between fire drills and data-loss education is that data threats are changing all the time. (At least all that novelty makes for a more interesting drill than standing outside in the parking lot in the rain.)

Chapter 27

Ten Common Mistakes

. . . .

*T*here are a number of traps that people fall into when they try to look objectively at the potential for data loss. Let's get some of those out in the open. Then you can do something about 'em.

"It won't happen to me"

Data loss isn't a matter of *if* — it's a question of *when*. In fact, it's probably happened already — you just don't know it. But even if it hasn't happened, assuming that it *won't* happen to you isn't an option. Be prepared.

Secrecy about data-loss threats

Data leaks are in the news every day — some might be really close to home! Far from being secretive about it, you should tell your staff about the threats that are out there — and get them to discuss what they can do to keep it from happening to your organization. It's the employees who handle the data; they're the best people to offer opinions on how to improve processes and procedures. Use the examples in the media to drive discussion.

Mistaking ignorance for bliss

You have the opportunity to turn each of your employees and co-workers into information-protection heroes by providing them with the needed awareness and training. Don't think this is something just for directors and VPs to worry about. Education has to be ongoing in the organization, from top to bottom. The mistake some organizations make is to go to all the trouble of creating and publishing a policy — and then forgetting to show it to the troops doing all the work!

Trusting your partners blindly

Trust is essential in any relationship, but partners and suppliers are notorious for causing data leaks. "Trust but verify." You must be in control of your data, wherever it is. Don't assume that third parties will be as careful as you are. Ask specifically about what they do to protect your information.

Delaying finding out where your data was — especially after a breach

One common mistake is to assume that you know where your data is. If you have a vague notion that *all finance information is on this server* . . . well . . . it probably isn't! You need to understand where your information is today, tomorrow, and the day after. If you don't know where it is, how can you protect it? If you lost a laptop (especially one that wasn't encrypted), would you know whether it contained customer details? If the answer is "I don't know," you would *still* have to disclose that fact to your customers — and suffer the cost and damage to your reputation. Find your data and track it!

Assuming that it will be business as usual after an event

A data loss, leak, or breach *will* change your business. You will have to introduce new policies, processes, procedures, and (probably) technology and auditing. Customers must be looked after for months (or even years) to come. Bottom line: *It won't be business as usual.* In fact, a contingency plan is a good idea, even if you think you've covered all the bases.

Assuming all data is equal

No, it's not. The data's value depends on the content. All data is *created* equal, unfortunately — but some data bytes are "more equal than others." You can overcome this problem by using data-classification processes and technology. Understanding that all data *isn't* equal will help you put suitable solutions in place. Underprotecting critical information will put your organization at risk; overprotecting noncritical data will be costly.

Giving data the same protection at all times

Timing and location make a huge difference. Solutions must reflect that the value of data changes over time. Some sophisticated technologies can help achieve this goal by providing dynamic storage, assigning data to a system of tiers that store it appropriately (according to its classification).

Assuming that people will do the right thing with the data

Unfortunately, implicit trust is no longer a valid automatic assumption. Just because you give people access to information as part of their jobs doesn't mean you can assume they'll take care of it as they should. Policies, procedures, and technology should be used to ensure that they follow through. And if employees behave ways that violate policy, point that out — and take steps to control and/or correct the fault.

Assuming that your current processes won't result in data loss

It never used to be a problem if you lost a laptop or a CD-ROM in the mail — but it is now. Processes that were fine even 12 months ago could well be inadequate now. For that matter, there's no reason to assume that the world — or, for that matter, your business — will be the exactly same in several years as it is now. A thorough, periodic assessment of your business processes — always with an eye toward discovering sensitive data and preventing its loss — is a survival need.

Chapter 28

Ten Tips to Protect Data at Home

· ·

*T*his book is all about how you protect data at work. Of course, we all have data at home as well — and it's just as much in need of protection. Here are a few tips to help you keep your information at home as safe as what you have at work.

Shred personal information

Cyber-criminals are after your information. Yes, *your* information. They'll use any means possible — and this means looking through your trash, rubbish, garbage — anything you've thrown out. Shred anything that could be useful to them: bank-account details, credit-card details, loyalty cards, utility bills, unneeded medical documents (such as old prescriptions), and any special offers — *especially* pre-approved credit-card application forms! (They used to send those with actual cards; if you see one of those, get some BIG scissors.)

All paper information can be recycled . . . even composted — but reduce it to *shredded* paper first!

Understand what personal data you have on your laptop

Although companies usually don't know exactly what information they hold (and this is bad), individuals are no less in the dark. What information *do* you have — and where is it? It could be on your laptop, a family computer, other computers, mobile storage devices, even the list of names and numbers on your cell phone. If you know where it is, then you can protect it.

Minimize the number of different machines from which you access the Internet. Okay, so you may not have to do this for absolutely everything on the Internet, just for critical information (such as that related to Internet banking and shopping). Restricting those transactions to just one computer will minimize the number of copies of information you have — which (in turn) reduces your chances of having it stolen.

When signing up for a service, consider which data is requested

All too often, Web sites want you to sign in — and along the way, put in information about yourself, sometimes too much for comfort. Take a look at what they're requesting, and then decide whether they really need it.

 Never use your Internet-banking password on other sites. Imagine what would happen if those other sites were compromised and your password was stolen. Cyber-criminals could then access your bank account!

Check the Web browser's address bar

When you're visiting Web sites, look in the address bar. If it shows numbers (an IP address, for example, `123.123.123.123`) instead of a name (`www.mybank.com`), then chances are good that the Web site is probably fraudulent. Don't do any business there!

There is no such thing as a free lunch. If a deal looks too good to be true, it probably is. If it's from a reputable site, then that's fine — but a lot of offers out there are designed to lure you to a site where you may be tricked into giving out your credit-card details — or end up with a virus, Trojan, or other malware infecting your machine.

Lock down your home network

In essence, this means your *wireless* network — but if you have a wired network, lock that one down too! If you have a wireless network, turn on the security features to prevent other people from using it. Unfortunately, some people also use other people's networks for bad purposes — and if they use yours, any damage they do with it will trace back to you!

Keep your anti-virus and anti-malware software up to date

Okay, so we work for a company that's famous for anti-virus software. No apologies there — the stuff works. But only if it's kept up to date! Viruses, Trojans, keyloggers, rootkits, and other threats are changing on a daily basis, so you always need the latest detection updates. Most anti-malware software will update itself automatically whenever you're online. Make sure yours does!

Install a pop-up blocker and Web-site checker

Pop-up ads are often a nuisance, but they can *also* be a danger to security. Most Internet browsers have pop-up blockers, so switch on that feature.

Again, most Internet browsers and anti-malware software packages have an anti-phishing and/or Web-site-check functionality. Turn it on. It might slow the machine's response a little, but at least you'll get some assurance that the Web site you're visiting is safe to visit. Don't assume, however, that just because you have this tool you can ignore other security measures. Unfortunately, you need them all. A layered approach to IT security in the home is the only way to manage the risk of information loss or security breach.

Educate your family

If more than one person uses the PC — especially if it's used by minors — make sure that all users know what is (or may be) a threat, especially on social-networking sites. Tell them not to download and install things without checking with you first; too many intriguing downloads or online freebies could put your data — or even your family — at risk. Encourage the kids to talk about their online experiences; you may find out a thing or two in the process!

Run anti-spyware and anti-adware programs

Running regular security checks on your computer(s) to check for spyware and adware is a good idea. Not only will it improve security, but it can also improve performance of the system — especially if you've been infected with spyware and the application can get rid of it.

Check browser plug-ins

So many attacks come through the Internet browser these days that you have to keep a careful eye on everything that's been installed. Educate everyone who uses the computer about the dangers of downloading and installing packages through the browser.

Visiting Web sites, especially social-networking sites, often results in a request that the user download and install a plug-in to do something — say, listen to some music, view photos, or watch a movie. Just say no! If you really want to install that piece of software, go to the Web site of the plug-in's provider (for example, Microsoft or Adobe); don't just follow the link.

Through the Internet browser's options, you can see what is and isn't installed — and delete anything suspicious. It's always best to go to the actual vendor site if you need legitimate browser plug-ins, instead of picking them up from other sites. That way you always get the latest versions with the newest security fixes.

Index

• F •

• *N* •

• *Q* •

Notes